Back From Beyond

A True Story About Dying to Learn the Meaning of Life

By: Lance Rennka, Ed.D.

© 2005
55–A North San Marcos Road Santa Barbara, CA 93111
(805) 450-1204
www.Lance-Rennka.com

Note for Librarians: A cataloguing record for this book is available from Library and Archives
Canada at www.collectionscanada.ca/amicus/index-e.html
ISBN 1-4120-7014-7

*Printed in Victoria, BC, Canada. Printed on paper with minimum 30% recycled fibre. Trafford's print shop
runs on "green energy" from solar, wind and other environmentally-friendly power sources.*

TRAFFORD
PUBLISHING™
Offices in Canada, USA, Ireland and UK

This book was published *on-demand* in cooperation with Trafford Publishing. On-demand
publishing is a unique process and service of making a book available for retail sale to the
public taking advantage of on-demand manufacturing and Internet marketing. On-demand
publishing includes promotions, retail sales, manufacturing, order fulfilment, accounting and
collecting royalties on behalf of the author.

Book sales for North America and international:
Trafford Publishing, 6E–2333 Government St.,
Victoria, BC v8t 4p4 CANADA
phone 250 383 6864 (toll-free 1 888 232 4444)
fax 250 383 6804; email to orders@trafford.com
Book sales in Europe:
Trafford Publishing (uk) Limited, 9 Park End Street, 2nd Floor
Oxford, UK ox1 1hh UNITED KINGDOM
phone 44 (0)1865 722 113 (local rate 0845 230 9601)
facsimile 44 (0)1865 722 868; info.uk@trafford.com
Order online at:
trafford.com/05-1925

10 9 8 7 6 5 4 3 2

Table of Contents

Acknowledgements

I wish to thank the people who have influenced me as I bounced through my life like a ball in a pin-ball machine.

The immediate family: my Mother – Lenora Bailey-Milhoan, my Father – Walter Milhoan, and my Brother – John Milhoan for agreeing to play major roles in my life's movie.

The ex-wife Judy Smith-Milhoan and sons Thane, Kirk and Brad who went through this dramatic learning experience with me, and continue through today to provide examples.

The current wife Shellie Gainer, who has been through other life times with me on our search together for opportunities to modify our behaviors.

The extended family: grandparents, aunts, uncles, cousins and in-laws, who have and will provide invaluable data through their life experiences.

It was Marine Resources Development Foundation (www.MRDF.org), Ian Koblick, and the employees who played parts in this exciting, life-altering "Grand Adventure." I hope they changed as a result.

Mother Nature, the Great Spirit, The Force, God, Allah, Universal Intelligence or whatever it was, which created the Playground Earth and infuses it with life and constant change, thus providing the spirits a stage and backdrops upon which to run sit-coms and soap operas. Life's a stage and we're all actors?

The I Am that I am a part of, which worked with me to design this life, and is providing the experiences and "bit players" to learn who I want to be through my previous lives, the present one and however many future lives are necessary to get *IT* right.

The other bit players in my life's movie, who played their parts so well. The friends, co-workers, teachers, companions, and those who I thought were enemies. Some had major parts, some only walk-ons, but all contributed in mirroring who I was and in so doing provided a view of me so the change process could begin.

The media who put on screen, play, and TV the good/bad, right/wrong, black/white and all of the other yin/yang factors from which I am learning.

The writers, who took the time to document both the fiction and real life experiences from which I'm able to glean data.

The religious organizations and alternate belief systems on this insignificant marble in space, who have settled into one campsite or another to provide crowd control, conflict, prejudice, and wars for us all to experience.

The leaders of this world who have put their yin/yang right in front of us, especially the President of the US who taught us the real meaning of sex. I just had to put that in here.

Cork Milner, my non-fiction writing instructor, and author of **Write From the Start** who provided me the learning and behavioral change necessary to write so the works are readable and enjoyable and who provided the one word I needed to be able to write – faction.

And to those who read this book, welcome to the quest, the adventure of survival, and the constant search for whom you are and want to be.

Enjoy!

Thank you all.

Introduction

Objective: This is an entertaining book, meant to open up "Possibility Thinking" on the part of the reader. Possibility Thinking requires you get outside-the-box of your perspectives, perceptions and emotions. Possibility Thinking is responsible for every advancement mankind has made and of course all the mistakes as well.

In a Universe with infinite possibilities and abundance, what kind of lifestyle would you create? Have you loosed your creativity on yourself? What kind of *YOU* do you want to create, or are you perfect just the way you are? What is holding you back?

If, in the real stories this book contains (by the way, reality is a figment of our imagination), someone gleans some life changing epiphany, sees a purpose in their life other than survival, or is in some way changed, blame not the author, take some responsibility. If it simply makes you laugh, grunt, think or cry that's after all its purpose. Above all, don't feel sorry for anyone, certainly not me, and least of all yourself. Avoid at all cost making a religion/cult out of this data.

This, like most of my other books, is an "oxymoron." With my education in education, it must have some educational value. But with my view of life, it must be fun to read (I'm a humorist). From what we learned in the compulsory schooling system, fun and education don't go together (oxymoron). However, learning is extremely enjoyable (we'll get into this later). I hope you're not taking life serious, it's not. Life is an illusion, and we're just acting out situational comedies (sitcoms) and soap operas. With a different perspective on why we're on this planet, maybe we can all lighten up a bit and have more fun.

The Chapter Format

I admit writing this book was entertaining for me. The challenge was to organize the experiences and what I learned in a manner which would be readable and enjoyable. After much writing, I decided to establish a standard format for each chapter, and divide the book into sections which made some sense. Therefore, the book will not follow the "timeline" of experiences, and thereby all of the critical elements will be much less confusing – at least to me.

I'll present Anecdotes – stories about my or someone else's experience(s) and relate my Personal Revelations – what I learned from the experiences and subsequent data input. Then include a Summary to insure you got the intended message.

This not a Ph.D. research paper with all the references, but in some instances, you'll be directed to additional viewing or reading.

Seeking truth, accumulating knowledge and experiences, and synthesizing data to problem solve has been a way of life for me. Facing fear and moving through it has allowed risky adventures to provide learning data. The adventures have resulted in many "dings" and a lot of pain, but pain is a fast and impacting means of learning.

Intense spiritual events starting when I was young generated a lot of questions not able to be answered by educators or religious leaders.

As the writing phase of my life began, the phenomenon of channeling was novel, required a willingness to be moldable talent and a certain amount of humility (against my ego based nature) to allow the flow of thoughts – not my own – to "occur" on the computer screen.

It took yin/yang life experiences to demonstrate the behavioral changes necessary to become who I want to be. Over time (40+ years), my Life Mission (ego/vanity control) became clear. My Life Purpose is to help people expand brain usage so they're better able to make wise decisions. My Passion, is public speaking.

My life path seemed to be a matter of choosing between multiple options. Looking back, the journey is a straight road. Every directional, life decision I made lead directly to here and now. Who I am is a result of the choices I've made, the life events I experienced and the behavioral changes I made.

This book is a brief look at a portion of the journey which helped create me in my own image (imagination).

The inference in this, you're doing exactly the same thing – differently.

I'm not trying to make a point, prove a point, or change your mind. I'll simply provide you some of my life experiences and what I learned from them.

You'll do with this information what you will.

Chapter 1
The Life Changing Event

At The Pearly Gates for the fourth time, I was nervous as the reservations book was checked for my name. The gatekeeper again said, "Your name's not in here yet. You're early again and too much entertainment, go back to Planet Ocean."

Starting my trip back down the Gossamer Path, shoulders slumped, disappointment in my heart, I heard the gatekeeper say again to the attending souls, "Find some more shit, and shovel more on, he hasn't learned his lesson yet."

"That's it!" I said, spinning around to face the gatekeeper, straitening up and squaring my shoulders, "I've been doing my best to do my duty to God, my country, my family, and my employers, and all you do is shovel on more shit. This time down, I'm taking care of myself!" Doing an about-face, I started marching back to Planet Ocean.

In the background I heard the gatekeeper say, "Hold up on the shit, let's see if he really has learned his lesson."

The lesson – Fix **me**, the way **I** want **me** to be – it's all about **me**.

Helen Keller summarized my life. ***"Life is a Grand Adventure, or nothing."***

This Grand Adventure began at the highlight of my Marine Diving Technician career. As Dive Director of the Puerto Rico International Undersea Laboratory, La Chalupa, the largest and most sophisticated under water habitat in the world, I was in charge of operations. It was December 31st, 1972, the four marine scientists and one technician had just completed a two week scientific mission in 75 feet of water, outside the barrier reef, seven miles off the west coast of Puerto Rico, south of Mayaguez.

The 600', heavy-nylon towline had been laid out on the 50 foot long, 20 foot wide deck, so the barge/habitat could be maneuvered from just outside the harbor entrance, down the narrow channel between the breakwater and coral reef, then into the harbor. Once tied to the dock, the five aquanauts would finish their 24 hour decompression.

After placing two wraps of the line around a bollard, I yelled to the crew, "Let's go."

La Chalupa began to move. By alternately slacking and holding the line tight, I lined-up the barge in the center of the channel. With the barge just off the end of the breakwater, the line hung-up on deck, couldn't be slack any more and had to be stopped off. I yelled for the deck technician, "Bud, line's tangled, clear it."

Bud raced around the cluttered deck following the line. As momentum propelled the 270,000 pound barge forward, the line began to slip around the bollard. "Hurry up Bud, I can't hold it."

Just before my left hand was about to be pulled into the wraps on the bollard, Bud yelled, "Got it."

I yelled back, "Get clear!" and released the line.

"Krraaaack."

The sound, like a rifle going off near my face, caused an eye reflex.

The recoil of the line under tension made the two wraps around the bollard jump up. The wraps caught my left hand, and launched me into the air.

Opening my eyes, I saw the forearm with two bones sticking out and the hand dangling from some skin and tendons. 15 feet above the water and over 20 feet out from La Chalupa, I gathered up the hand and forearm, pointed my toes and made a perfect dive.

I was now on a journey of discovery which continues. Why I was here on earth, all my beliefs and relationships with family, friends and strangers were about to under go radical changes.

Eight days after the accident, as a result of a medical mis-adventure (the first medical malpractice); a mid-upper arm amputation was performed.

In the between drug induced unconsciousness and full awareness, the hand moved, *That's weird, I wonder if they removed the cast in the operating room?* Darkness.

Pain, like hitting the crazy-bone, jolted me and the whole elbow and hand tingled. I tried to open my eyes, but a stabbing pain in the upper arm closed them tighter. Through the anesthetic fog, I could smell hospital antiseptic and the retched gas gangrene. Then darkness again.

Whoa, the hand's moving towards the wall, now under the bed, what's going on? I forced my eyes open, the arm was missing. *How can it be gone and still be moving?* In the dim light from the bathroom, my eyes followed the hand's room-wide path of discovery, but the hand wasn't visible. My brain was trying to process the amputation and hand movement when it felt like a hot knife sliced through the flesh of the upper arm, I gasped.

Judy, my wife, in the chair next to the bed, woke and asked, "Are you OK?"

"Well, I guess that's all relative. From a broken forearm to an upper-arm amputation in eight days doesn't make sense. "

"Do you need a pain shot? The doctor left orders to give you a shot, but only if you asked for it, as you demanded."

"I could use some, now! This is a little more than I can shut off with my brain."

"OK, just push the nurse call button by your shoulder."

The door to my room opened almost before I got my thumb off the button. The voice from the doorway asked, "Senor, listo para injection?"

"Si." I answered.

She hurried from the room.

The room light turned on and a petite, young, nurse approached the bed, hypodermic syringe in her right hand and an alcohol swab in her left. Her black eyes widened as they darted from the IV in my right hand to the IV bottle guarding my right shoulder to the swollen stump. I smiled and pointed to my right thigh, and kicked the sheet back too far, exposing my self. She stopped mid step, gasped and blushed.

"Pardon, Chica." I said, reaching down and tucking the sheet between my legs.

Before she had finished emptying the syringe, a warm wave of pain relief began to spread out from the thigh to infuse the whole body. *No wonder addicts get hooked on this stuff.* I thought.

As she stood by the bed watching my body relax, I read the name Lupe, taped to a name tag on her starched, white uniform. I thought, *Name tag, young, embarrassed, gorgeous, night shift - she's brand new.*

"Como Esta, Senor?"

"Muy bein, Muy bein, gracias Lupe."

"De nada." She said

"Es possible comeda?"

"Si, si, una momento." Lupe replaced the sheet, careful not to peek, and went for food.

While Judy cranked the bed up, I asked, "Well, how's it feel to be married to an amputee?"

"OK . . ., at least you're still alive."

"Yea, but doing push-ups is out. You'll have to get on top . . ., but not yet."

"That's OK, I don't mind being on top." She smiled. "Welcome back. The doctor said you only had three hours to live if he didn't remove the arm."

"I know. It had rotted to above the elbow, just forget it."

The three AM meal came cold, half a small baked chicken, mixed vegetables with rice and beans. For desert, flan with caramel sauce, white cake with chocolate frosting, and lime Jell-O with mixed fruit. For fluids I had, two milks and two cans of guanabana juice.

When I could slow down eating, I asked Judy, "How long since I last ate?"

"It's been about 18 hours."

"No wonder I was hungry. That was the best tasting meal I've had in the last eight days, maybe for a long time and that's no reflection on your cooking. It's like all my smell and taste senses are cranked-up."

"Go back to sleep now, the crew will be here in a few hours for your next chamber run before they go to work."

"Wake-up!" Judy's voice echoed in my head, "You have visitors."

My eyes opened much easier this time, and I said, "Bring'm on, and see if you can get me some coffee con leche y asucar."

Judy left and a parade of masked, green-clad people filed into the semi-dark room. I thought, *Oh, no, not more prodding of my sore spots.* Then someone hit a light switch and I recognized my crew from the habitat.

"Hey, guys, I really like your new uniforms. What's that all about?"

"They wouldn't let us in without them," Ian said, "You're in isolation because the gas gangrene is still contagious."

"How you guys doing, and what's going on with the lab." I asked.

"We're fine and the lab'll be ready for the next mission," Joe said, "the question is how are you do'n?"

"Had my shot, a great meal and I'm ready for the chamber, after I get a cup of coffee."

"We're really sorry about the amputation," Bud said, "None of us had any idea that was coming."

"Don't worry, I must have intuitively known, because it's no big deal for me; I just can't wait to get out of the hospital and back to work. I feel a lot better now. As one of the doctors told me, 'Sometimes you have to trim the branch to save the tree."

Mike stepped forward and held up a Playboy, "Got something for you."

"Oh, you wait till I'm missing an arm to give me one-handed reading material. How cruel is that? At least you didn't bring in flowers."

We all laughed. Mike turned to a cartoon. The cartoon showed a "floozy" looking woman lying in bed with a "pirate" looking man. The floozy was lying on the pirate's arm. The pirate's hook was around the woman's boob. At the bottom of the bed was a chest designated "Captain Hook." The caption at the bottom said, "You should see all the attachments it came with!"

I laughed hard enough to hurt my broken collarbone and ribs. When I could talk again, I said, "I've got to learn to sing 'Just a Gigolo.' I can carry all the tools in my brief case. There'll be no complaints, they pay their money, pick out their preferred dildo, it doesn't get tired or soft, and has adjustable stroke and rhythm. I can't wait."

We all laughed and again I had to control myself because of the pain. "Take that with you. If I get a hard-on after all the blood I lost, I'll pass-out."

Judy brought me the coffee, and we went through the normal, "I'm sorry," "How you feeling?" "Do you need anything?" comments.

"You need to get well quick," Ian said, "you're the only one who knows how to operate the lab."

"I'm working on that." I said. "Hey, where's my brother?"

"He took the amputation real hard." Joe said, "Last time I saw him he had a fifth of Don Q rum in his hand."

"Damn, he's getting drunk over **ME** losing an arm and I can't have a drink until I'm through with the antibiotics."

The medical technicians arrived with a gurney and the second trip to the hyperbaric chamber, used to treat the gas gangrene, began.

While being jostled onto the cot in the hyperbaric chamber, I felt a sudden warm sensation along my left side and just before my vision closed down, I exclaimed, "OH, NO!" and darkness. The suture had come off the main artery and I bled down. (The second medical malpractice.).

Dying

Leaning against the wall in the operating room and watching doctors and nurses busy working on a body, I felt strange, detached. The medicos were tying up an artery on a stump, and, because the veins had collapsed, they were doing a cut-in at the right ankle to get an IV started.

Just as they started milking blood into the body, the breathing stopped, then the heart monitor stopped ticking, flat-lined and a buzzer sounded. The medical personal began shouting and rushing about.

Curious, about what was happening; I floated up and looked down from above the operating table. I was startled to recognize it was my body they were working on, then a thought, *Let it go, its better over here.*

Right then, they jump started the body and whoosh, I slammed back into me.

I woke up some time later, in my room, with a doctor milking the fifth bag of blood into my leg. As the cool fluid flowed up my thigh, my blood pressure increased and I became more and more awake. He took my blood pressure and told the nurse, "Get another pint of blood."

Death was now added to my "life experiences." I had a chance to meet "God" or whatever you call the "overseeing spirit." The death thing was a real blow. All my life I felt bullet proof, and never thought about my mortality. There was no concept I could be killed. The soul was surprised when it found out the vehicle it was operating, the body, could be destroyed.

A death/out-of-body experience (OBE) will tend to change you. Maybe not right away, but with time to process the event, you look at "Life, Liberty, and the Happiness of Pursuit" from a different perspective.

You say I got part of the saying backwards? I don't think so. I got it right, because if you pursue happiness and get happy, then what? Drugs? Suicide? If you're always pursuing something, and **pursuit** is your happiness then you're always happy – much better.

You may want to go sit in a corner for awhile and think about that – it's a very important life lesson.

A real good exercise is to ask, "What would I do if money was not a consideration and I knew I was only going to live for one more year?"

What would you change?

Talk to people who've had close calls, heart attacks, or strokes and you'll find facing up to your own mortality is a real life changing experience.

Actually dying and getting/having to come back is even more intense, especially if repeated multiple times.

NOTE: 25+% of the population will **admit** to having out-of-body experiences (OBEs) before they leave this plane. It's OK to be out of your body and it's also OK to be out of your head (brain).

OBEs will change how you view life and death. If your body is dead and you have an OBE, you know your Soul's going to live beyond the body. When OBEs are repeated while the body is unconscious (under anesthesia) and while the body is actively functioning (during conversations and sex) the concept of Body/Brain and Soul/Mind will develop. This changes every belief you hold about who and what you are. An OBE begs the question, "Who's in charge of this life and what's it all about?"

Epiphanies, out-of-body trips, visions, past-life-regression, spiritual awareness, addressing new problems, controlling emotions, dealing with ego, taking responsibility, and learning to pay attention to life have made this one incident invaluable in helping me to become a better person. The belief I'm a better person is, of course, my opinion.

I wouldn't trade the experiences losing an arm and dying provided me for anything. I wouldn't care to do it again, but it's been a wonderful journey through life. The life lessons learned have provided me with the answer to the question we all have, "Why me, here, now?" Which was going to be the title of this book, but it was way too serious for a humorist.

Life-altering situations happen to everyone. They may be the result of an interpersonal relationship, natural disaster, accident, personal injury or illness, death of someone or something, heart attack, stroke, giving birth, unconsciousness, drugs or any number of other life events.

The interplay of my family members after the amputation, my reaction to the amputation and the process of rebuilding my ego all fed into the life-altering, learning opportunities I'm privileged to experience.

Summary

This is not a book about a traumatic accident, physiological and psychological problems or parapsychology. It's a story book with a lot of insights gleaned from some interesting life experiences.

I was a sailor, so some of the words have "flavor" (and maybe smell – like shit!) I tried other Politically Correct words, but they didn't "sound" right – not like I talk.

I don't believe in "accidents" so it's no accident you're reading this, it's meant to be – enjoy.

This book is about US, because we're all connected. We're all having similar but different situations and circumstances during our lives. We have questions unanswered. We're supposed to be learning from each other, because life's too short to go through everything ourselves. That's why the printing press, movies and TV were invented.

Remember **The lesson** – Fix **you**, the way **you** want **you** to be – it's all about **you**.

Out of Body Experience
(OBE)

Of all the things I've talked to people about, Out of Body Experiences have elicited the most responses. When analyzing why people were interested in OBEs, there were several common threads in the responses:

- Disbelief OBEs could happen due to a lack of any data
- Disbelief in the spiritual aspects of life – duality of Body/Soul
- Disbelief due to educational background – not scientific
- Belief in OBEs due to personally having had the experience
- Belief because OBEs prove the Body-Soul connection
- Belief because OBEs prove life after death

Anyone who wants to have an OBE experience can do so. You simply have to believe it's possible, gather knowledge and seek help if needed to guide you through the experience. In fact, everyone has OBEs during sleep and unconsciousness.

OBEs prove to those who experience them the duality of their nature and that the Soul will live beyond the body. They also prove the fact of reincarnation. After an OBE, the soul reincarnates into the same body in the same stream of time.

OBEs are Spiritual events. They provide opportunities for counseling and travel outside the body to gather data and solve problems. OBE counseling comes in the form of objective "third party" evaluation of an event. Multiple events can be reviewed during a given OBE. The review comes in the form of "awareness" of the lessons to be learned and the behavioral changes to be made. An OBE session may contain answers to questions or solutions to problems. Some OBE sessions may show the reactions resulting from a given action and how the "ripple effect" travels through the people involved, the environment and the universe.

Dreams are OBE "movies" being "played" as additional data and awareness of changes to be made. Dream meanings can be reviewed during OBEs.

OBEs may also provide you with "Intuition" and set you up for déjà vu opportunities.

During OBEs, you may find yourself visiting other dimensions, planets, or traveling to locations around the Planet Ocean. During these traveling sessions, it is possible, to gather specific information. Is this where the Sci Fi, which predicts our future, comes from?

So, are OBEs important life events?

Chapter 2
The Rules

First let's set some ground rules, guidelines, so there are no misunderstandings. I don't take anything serious anymore, so you can't take any of this serious either. In my death/near-death experiences I came to know God (or whatever you call the "I Am") as the Cosmic Joker, she's Whoopy Goldberg (my hero).

God certainly is not what my religious training had taught me to believe.

I'm about to lax philosophical so hang on a little bit. When able to step back, and accept I was going to live beyond the body, a major change occurred. Survival, which is the strongest of our basic programming drives, took on new meaning. It dawned on me – for real – birth is a death sentence. I knew for certain the body was going to get recycled back into the "Big Circle of Life" and my soul was going to continue on. Then hair, clothes, body shape, possessions, activities, knowledge, and skills became much less important.

Understanding how transient everything is, how could I possibly take any of it serious? When experiencing déjà vu, I knew time was not what I'd been told. Well that didn't leave me anything to hang on to. It messed with God, basic survival, and time - which doesn't leave a lot more, or does it? How about the Meaning of Life a Life Mission and the individual Purpose for Living? Wouldn't you like to know what those are for you if they can help you relax and enjoy life more?

You don't really expect me to tell you in the second chapter, do you? If I did, wouldn't that let you stop reading and just live your life, and then you wouldn't get to find out how I found out about my purpose in living, then this book would have written in vain or is that in vanity? So nice try.

Three Things

In a contemplative mood, I asked. "In general, what's the human/soul purpose on this plane?"

"Beyond the sitcoms and soap operas?" my Counselor asked.

"Yes." I answered. "There has to be more to this existence than just the entertainment value for the spiritual observers."

"Once you know this, there's no going back to being just the ball in the pin-ball game of life," the Counselor said, "Are you sure you're ready?"

"I believe it's time." I answered "I've ricocheted and been paddled enough to get my attention. I'd much rather be proactive than reactive."

"Ask and ye shall receive." The Counselor responded. "Each humanoid life is about three things: The Meaning of Life, individual Life Mission and individual Life Purpose. From these three different but connected things, the three dimensional grid of life is woven. These three things are the framework you used to write your life script.

"Each individual creates their own reality on the Planet Ocean plane in cooperation with the other souls incarnate. When the souls take on a body, they tend to forget their overall purpose. When presented with events they choose to act or react. The results of their choices are personality and character development – how they behave."

"OK, I understand the implications of making choices," I said, "and I get the yin/yang options, but where is the thermometer for all the different options? It seems mankind has demonstrated the worst and best of each different situation encountered."

"What would be the purpose of the will you were given, your creativity, if there was only one option? As for the thermometer, it's your conscience." The Counselor continued. "In each instance, situation, circumstance, or event in your life, you must make choices. As you have come to understand, every choice you make provides additional information from which you can learn and change your behavior – or not."

"So to not make a choice is to make a choice?"

"Of course, you chose not to make a choice. Deciding not to learn, not to change, not to advance is a choice and the application of your will."

"I did that a lot. Didn't I?"

"Yes, and you paddled yourself a lot didn't you?" The Counselor replied.

"The review of my life certainly showed me how I created situations to get dinged when I quit paying attention." I said. "But what about the bad things man has done to man down through history and up to now, like: wars, genocide, slavery, torture, rape, murder, suicide bombers and more in the name of greed or religion?"

"You've reviewed your past-lives. What did they reveal? Was there a purpose in you having been on both sides of those things you just named?"

"I'm getting that those were just lessons of the extremes so I had choices?"

"Yes."

"Oh!" I said. "The extremes in both directions are the thermometer and our ultimate choice is where on the thermometer we chose to function?"

"That's right." The counselor said. "Without the yin, there's no yang and no choice."

"But we all make bad choices."

"There are no good or bad choices, just lessons to be learned and behaviors to be changed." The Counselor said. "Remember the Buddhist saying 'I'll meet you on the other side of right and wrong'?"

"Yes." I said. "Make sure I summarize this correctly, I'm tired of dings and paddlings.

"Life provides opportunities to make choices. We're to use our conscience, previous life lessons and knowledge gained to make decisions. If we're willing to pay attention to other examples, i.e. movies, media, books, other people's experiences, etc. we can learn our lessons faster and advance quicker. Learning our life lessons is demonstrated in our behavioral changes."

"That's a good summary." The counselor said. "Humans are constantly being given opportunities, guidance, and counseling sessions, but few are willing to pay attention."

"I agree." I said. "I've been head-down, charging most of my life. It took multiple situations, circumstances, dings and emotional upheavals to get me to start paying attention, to start asking questions about what was going on and why?"

"Yes, you've been putting on quite a show. Think about the breadth of life experiences you've crammed into this one life. You've been on a quest for knowledge and life experiences few have accomplished." The Counselor said. "As an experienced, old-soul, you were refining your behavior in preparation for what is your chosen Life Purpose. Without your experiences, you wouldn't be where you are now. You had to become moldable talent."

"I'll accept that." I said. "You know gaining some control over my ego has been a process I fought and resisted with façade after façade. Looking back, it's obvious now, but during the process, it was a battle resulting in many wounds and scars."

"Yes, you were/are entertaining in your ego struggles. Remember, ego is an integral part of all human programming, and a battle being fought by most. You were/are not alone in that lesson." The Counselor said, "It's important you gain control, but not destroy your ego. Your ego is important in that it fuels your drive to your goals."

"Thank you for the lesson and I ask that you guide me as I define the three human/soul purposes."

"I am at your wish."

Meaning of Life

Participate in your life, pay attention, take responsibility, gather knowledge and use your imagination to multiply the knowledge. Learn your lessons, change your behavior to become who you want to be and leave behind a legacy of behavioral change. You're a creator! Create you in the image you wish to be. This is your greatest creation. Paint a masterpiece on the canvas of life.

The Meaning of Life is to gather knowledge and skill, learn your lessons, and change your behavior.

Life Mission

Create you in your own imagination. What you see in others you like, make it a part of you. What you see in others you don't like, fix it – you couldn't see it if it didn't exist in you. Love yourself so you may love others – learn and change your behavior.

Your Life Mission is all about you. It may involve several specific lessons and involves a common thread of changes you have scripted.

Life Purpose

Do unto others as you would have others do unto you. Be kind, considerate and share with others. Build others up by accentuating their positive aspects. Provide an example of how you wish others to treat you, through how you behave. Give of your positive energy, life experiences and the lessons you have learned. Take responsibility for your life and enjoy the process. Each individual's Life Purpose has something to do with helping others. While you're learning from others, others are learning from you – be a good example/teacher.

Your Life Purpose is all about others, and requires you to love yourself first so you can share with and love others.

What defines who I am?

Is who I am: skin color, birth place, living location, religious belief, family name, looks, education, occupation, possessions, relationship with nature and God, lifestyle, what is done for others, IQ, something known, emotional state, leaving a legacy for posterity . . . or is it something else?

I'm a unique individual, but what makes me different? Different from what? What makes me the same? The same as what?

It was obvious I needed to change my personality, but I had been told personality couldn't be changed. So I asked myself, *Who said I couldn't change? Where does personality come from? If I could change my personality, what would I change?*

Have you ever asked yourself these or similar questions? If yes, good for you. If not, why not? What if I told you life is just a series of questions needing answers. What if, in the answering of questions you find out who you really are, would that pique your interest? And if in answering the life questions you would simply generate more questions, would you still be interested in finding answers and discovering more questions? If you answered yes to the last question, congratulations!

Where I Came From

By the nature of my birth, I was born a white, Anglo-Saxon, Protestant, male in Denver, Colorado, USA. I was named Frank Ivan Milhoan. In the beginning I didn't think I had chosen this, but I know better now.

My Dad's dream for my younger brother and me was college degrees. Dad had to go back to high school to get a diploma, and lamented his whole life in the working class about not getting to go to college (it was offered by his company, but he "chose" not to go). My brother is a Doctor of Chiropractic Medicine and I have a Doctorate in Education – we fulfilled our Dad's dream.

My mother and her family thought I was going to be a preacher and save the world. I went to Evangelistic Training, but ended up with more questions than answers. I'm not sure if I'll ever fulfill my Mom's dreams. Given what I now believe, I don't think the world needs saving. It's doing exactly what we souls make happen and the overseeing spirit is allowing. I do, however, have a lot of "religious" questions – as you'll read.

My wife wanted me to support our family including three sons. I did that being a carpenter, plumber, electrician, mechanic, welder, machinist, electronics technician, instrumentation technician, oceanographic and marine biological technician, writer and publisher, video producer, commercial diver, SCUBA instructor, and commercial pilot.

I know exactly what your thinking, "Jack of all trades, master of none."

Well not quite, I made my living doing all of those things, so "Jack of all trades, didn't find any I couldn't master." How did I do all that in one lifetime? I very seldom did only one thing at a time and I got bored easily. I've always pushed the envelope trying to learn how to do new things.

If asked, "What are you?"

I answer, "A flexible and adaptable realist." I've used my diversified background to think outside the box. Outside the box is where change and the advancement of mankind occur.

One day at an airport bar, while waiting for my plane, I met a balding, Chinese gentleman. After a short conversation about the weather, current affairs, politics and religion he asked, "What's your birth date."

I told him, "August 31, 1940."

He pondered for a short time then said, "You were born in the year of the Dragon . . ., under the water sign. You have something to do with water."

I laughed and said, "So would being a Marine Diving Technician qualify? All I've ever wanted to do was play around and with water."

Looking at me and with a wise smile, he said, "You had no choice, you were going to do something with water."

"Thank you for the validation." I said.

The 50% Rule

Just to set the records straight, everything you have read, seen, heard, or were taught is at least 50 percent untrue, including anything in this book. This is The 50% Rule (I'll refer to it many times). That cuts me an awful lot of slack and puts the load on you to find out for yourself what is true. "Truth" has to do with perception and perspective. So "Truth" for you is not necessarily "The Truth" or "Truth" for anyone else.

Perception is what we know, primarily what we've been taught. For example, think about what we had been taught about carbon-based, oxygen-dependant life and the conditions under which it existed on this planet. Then the submarines found "Black Smokers" in the ocean depths. There are all kinds of creatures living from chemicals not oxygen-produced carbon-based food sources, as we believed/were taught. We had to completely rethink life (the 50% Rule). If after all these thousands of years of study and we didn't even have life on this planet figured out, what else do we have wrong?

A lot!

By the way, the single most important factor in our survival and the thing all of the Olympic games are about is gravity. No one has yet figured out how it works (or we could walk on water, levitate, and move heavy objects with ease), so just how much do we know?

Perspective is your viewpoint. For example four blind men describing an elephant, it just depends on where they're standing. Or the fence between properties, one side is white the other side is green. You can argue with your neighbor forever over the color of the fence, each from your own perspective, but until you see the fence from the other side, how can you know the "Truth."

So Truth to you is what you've learned/been taught (perception) plus your viewpoint (perspective), and that's not all truth or all of the truth.

Sorry to start off like this, but how else am I going to take you outside-the-box of your references. And if you don't get outside-the-box, there's nothing new and therefore nothing to learn. And, since learning is behavior modification, you will not change, and that's what life is about.

Oops, I almost let it out of the bag/book.

Body, Mind, Spirit

How many books and religions present information about Body, Mind and Spirit? Churches have split over interpretation of these three concepts. Wars have been fought over their interpretation. So if I give you my idea about these, please, don't start a new church or go to war, unless you're going to share the revenues/booty with me.

Body – The body is just a chassis which provides a vehicle to travel this planet. It is a data sensory system to collect input and store memory. The body needs fuel (air, food and water) and maintenance (clothing, shelter and repair) to provide the services required of it. When it gets old, diseased or damaged enough, it's disposed of and gets recycled back into the "Big Circle of Life" as cosmic dust and vapor – dirt. The Body is just an animal, albeit the most sophisticated.

Brain – The brain is the computer that receives the data the body collects, analyses it and presents solutions to problems. Its base program is survival. Survival includes: food, clothing, shelter and procreation. All of the data collected by the brain is stored in the body cells (not Brain) and is available to the "master computer in the sky" where the information is archived (kept on the master hard drive) for review.

Spirit – The Soul is an incarnated Spirit using the body and the brain to have experiences, which help it to define who it is and provide examples to other Souls. The Soul "dons" the Body, which becomes the Soul's "Virtual Reality Machine." The Body/Soul experiences are available for review by all the other souls currently incarnated and those in the "unseen" spirit world.

Mind – The Soul uses its mind to provide "intuition" to the Brain and assist with suggestions and directions to create the experiential events necessary to help the Soul develop Personality and Character. The soul is a part of God and, through the Mind, is "tapped" into Universal Intelligence – all the information from the beginning to the end. What do you know, you don't know you know? What can you do, you don't know you can do? Do you listen to your "Wee Small Voice?"

What You Are

First, you must understand what you – Body – are. You're a preprogrammed, programmable, reproducible android, a computerized machine/body, being operated by a soul. I know that's profound. I also know you don't want to think about your body as a machine, but humor me for awhile. Remember, I visited the source more than once.

A computer doesn't make mistakes unless it's given bad information (garbage in – garbage out). So the only way your computer brain could make a mistake, a bad decision, is if you had incorrect or incomplete information. I already told you about the 50+% rule of incorrect information. And if you don't have the data, how can you hold yourself liable for incomplete information? You're simply wandering through life gathering more data on which to base wiser decisions.

The problem, your computer weighs **emotional** data along with the rational data to make a decision. If your emotions cause you to override a rationale decision, what are you afraid of? You're afraid of something or you wouldn't make irrational decisions. That means a negative emotion in the form of fear is running your life. Fear is <u>F</u>uture <u>E</u>xpectations <u>A</u>ppearing <u>R</u>eal. Emotional fears are based on what might or might not happen in the future.

I heard you say, "That's not me, those are emotions."

"Well, they're your emotions."

I heard you say, "Oh, no, not my own responsibility."

Yes, and because it's your own responsibility, you can do something about it. If your emotions override a rationale decision, ask yourself, "What negative emotion is running my life?" And don't give up until you get an answer. Be prepared, it may surprise or hurt you a little – oh well.

Guilt Trips

As soon as you accept responsibility for everything happening to you as the result of your decisions, you can change your future. You can be proactive not reactive. If what you've done in the past was the result of a 100% correct decision, you can't backup and change it, you learned from it, you're changing your behavior "I'll never do that again!" You're willing to admit it happened. Then where's the guilt? If you can't accept this, someone will control you.

As I was trying to sort out life and religion (we'll get into politics later) I discovered all organized religions are just "crowd control." The control comes through the setting up of rules, which you violate or just think about violating and you're held guilty for – **sin**. If you've sinned, you must do something to atone for your sin, confess and pay money – if you want to go to heaven and avoid hell.

The control comes through guilt and you're played like a puppet through your life via guilt. Oh, the freedom when I gave up guilt.

Wait a minute, did I hear you say, "I thought I was free, but I do guilt."

You aren't free if you do guilt, trust me.

The simplest way to be really free is to give up guilt. Be prepared, it may cost you a relationship or two. But if you're ready, let's get after this lesson right now. Let's jump right in the middle of one of the biggest problems and misunderstandings running amuck today – guilt.

Where does Guilt come from?

You don't feel guilty about something which may or may not happen in the future. You can't feel guilty about the here and now, you haven't done anything yet. You can only feel guilty about the past. Can you back up one second and change the past? NO!

Well here's a gift from me to you. This alone is worth the cost of this book many times over. You never have or never will make a wrong decision. You **must** believe your computer brain is incapable of making a mistake.

"AH," I heard you say, "but I remember when I did _ _ _ _ _ _, I knew I shouldn't do it, and that was a mistake."

No, you made a 100% correct decision based on data-in, which may have been incorrect, incomplete and/or fear based emotions.

So you've been feeling guilty about that event ever since. Your fear-based emotions biased your rationale mind into making a 100% correct decision that provided you with more data.

Your choice is to review the incident/data; correct and gather new data; identify the fear, deal with the fear and alter your emotional base; decide to never make that kind of a decision again; and get on with your life.

OK, now give up guilt and be free! Freedom is avoiding guilt!

Your welcome, just live it.

Box of Reference

Everyone has their own "box of reference." On this, our journey together, my goal is to take you outside your "box-of-reference." Your "box-of-reference" restricts your view of the world, information and events. Try looking through a toilet tissue tube and you'll understand the concept – no peripheral view of life – up, down or sideways.

This box of yours also has filters installed. Now take your toilet tissue tube and install layer after layer of screen filters to get this concept. These filters limit what you're able to see through the box and they skew (modify) the incoming data. These filters were installed in your box-of-reference through your genetic memory, family, education, local and national culture, religious teachings, work experience, peer group, and all of your life experiences. These screens will not allow you to even "see" some things, other things the filters obscure to the point of being unrecognizable.

For everyone, their screens and box prevent them from even seeing or hearing some "Truths." Therefore, an individual's "Truth" is only true for them. If anything turns up in their experience which doesn't fit inside their box of reference, this new experience may be disregarded or is filtered (changed).

Every time you have an "automatic" negative reaction to new data or information, it's your filter-laden box of reference (programming) at work.

If you catch yourself saying, "I hear what your saying, but - - - ." you're expressing your box or filter. The "but" word means you're automatically rejecting something. Pay attention to "buts!" (Ladies, I was careful how I spelled that just for you, I know how you are about men's backsides.)

You need to kick some holes in your box and let some light and truth in. Step back out of life and look around with new eyes. Your "box of reference" is important, but most of what you "believe" was taught to you by someone else. Who taught you what, and how much of what you were taught was myth, perspective biased data, and just plain not true?

"If you aren't the lead dog, the view never changes." In other words, how many *original* thoughts have you had?

Change

There is only one thing you can depend on in life, and that's change. Change is threatening and risky, but it's all there is. Change in every aspect of your life is occurring second by second. Deal with it, or get left behind making buggy whips.

OK, the stage is set. We're about to jump right into the middle of my stuff. I'm going to share with you the life lessons I've learned, most of which congealed like "egg yoke left on a dinner plate to dry" after I lost my arm (After Arm Lose – AAL).

Well I didn't really loose the arm; I got rid of it to see what life would be like trying to do everything I'd been doing, with only one arm. Apparently my life was not challenging enough, so I came up with a way to create a problem.

You do know, if you don't have enough problems, you'll create some to solve.

That's lesson number one, always have problems to solve and choose them carefully. There's nothing a human likes more than problem solving. Look around, every manmade thing we have today is the result of a problem solved. Problem solving creates change.

Summary

You always make 100% correct decisions. Your decisions are based on data (what you've been taught and experienced) and emotions.

The data may be incorrect, incomplete or emotionally biased but the decision is still correct. The result of your decision provides you additional data with which to correct the bad or incomplete data and gain control of your emotions – pay attention to mistakes.

Everything you call a mistake is something which has already happened and which you can do nothing about, so accept it happened, analyze it and learn from it. Go and don't make that same mistake again (Go, and sin no more?). If you catch yourself looping, repeating mistakes, take yourself out to the woodshed and kick some butt, yours. And since the "mistake" is the result of a correct decision based on faulty information or fear-based emotion, correct the information (gain knowledge), learn (demonstrated by changing your behavior), then face your fear and move through it. Negative emotions can override rationale decisions. There are only two base emotions – Love and Fear. From these two base emotions all other emotions are generated. Emotions are the fuel used to "drive" you to your goals, but to avoid an "explosion" the fuel (emotions) must be under control. Find out what fear is controlling your life and deal with it.

Refuse to do guilt. You're free!

Ego is an integral part of human programming. Ego is the drive that gets things done. Ego is developed from: what you think about yourself, what other people think about you and, most important, what you think other people think about you (which usually isn't true.). From all this "thinking" comes your ego. Think positively about yourself, change as necessary and never assume (make an out of you and me – ass-u-me).

To learn, change and find the real truth, you must get outside of the "box-of-reference" your life has built. Although this is your total "belief system," it is not the "whole truth." Embrace Change! Open up and let the light shine in.

Body/Brain – Soul/Mind
The Duality of Our Being

Embracing the duality of our being explains all of the internal conflicts we experience. It provides a base to gather the data necessary to make rational decisions about how we want to live and what we want to become. With the basic dichotomy of "birth is a death sentence for the body" and "the soul has eternal life" the two entities, with different agendas are by their very nature in conflict.

So one question is, "Which one is the protagonist (good guy) and which one the antagonist (bad guy)?"

Another question is, "Which one is in charge, when?"

So if "human nature" (the flesh) comes into conflict with the "Soul's agenda" which one will win?

Should one be in conflict with the other?

Is the conflict between the two entities the basis of the problems we experience, or are the problems we experience the reason for being?

If the body is just trying to exist, live well, reproduce, minimize pain and expand pleasure, is the soul the perpetrator of all the problems?

If the Body's over two million year old basic program is Survival, and it has to die and be recycled, how can it not be in conflict with existence itself?

If the soul is a God, a creator, the writer of the life-script, then the soul has to be the perpetrator and the body human the victim. Does that change how you view the duality of life?

Can the Soul deny the flesh it inhabits and if it does, won't that alone cause conflict? Why would the Soul put on a virtual reality machine and then fight it by denying it exists? If the Soul's objective is to develop Personality and Character – which entity is developing the Personality and Character?

Is it possible for the Soul and Body to cooperate in fulfilling the Soul's Life Mission and Life Purpose?

After those questions, the corner may be a necessary place to be for awhile. After pondering those questions, you may want to review your beliefs and your actions for better understanding.

Chapter 3
Ask and Ye Shall Receive!

Between asleep and awake, in one of my questioning moods, I asked, *I wonder how my life experiences came to be. There must be some schedule of events and overall plan or what's the purpose? What am I not getting? What is life all about? Why are all of these bad things happening to me?*

Instantly, I was looking back at Planet Ocean from the moon.

"Quit taking life so serious!" My counselor said, "Can you see from here, you and the other humans are just putting on sit-coms and soap-operas. Find the lessons in your experiences and present them so others will enjoy reading about them. Some humans will actually learn and change their behavior as a result of reading your books. Then they won't have to go through the trauma you have endured to learn their lessons – unless they want to."

"The All-Seeing Perspective, Universal Intelligence (UI – read it as You and I) has created this playground for you. You use the body to gain experiences so you can have choices about how you wish to behave. If UI dictated how you were to be, where would the fun be?"

"Does that mean I'm in charge of my own life experiences?" I asked.

"Yes."

"Then I'm responsible for everything which happens to me?"

"Yes, you wrote the script."

"What about natural disasters, hurricanes, tornados, flood, earthquakes, ice storms, etc.?" I asked.

"You chose to put yourself where you could have those experiences, and agreed with other souls to let them happen. Mother Nature is at your collective will."

"That's an awful lot of responsibility to accept." I said.

"Well, you can either take responsibility or . . . play the ball in a pinball machine and react to everything like you've been doing."

"Wait a minute, you just inferred I can take charge of my life and run it the way I want it to run. That certainly hasn't been my experience or the way I was taught to believe. Can I really be in charge of my own life?" I asked.

"You have been from before birth. Observe."

The Casino in the Sky

The lights were flashing a million colors, reflecting off alabaster walls and sparkling through the crystal chandeliers. The lively background music was heavenly, and made standing still and concentrating difficult. The intermittent jingling of coins dropping, sirens whining, and shouts announced winners. Soothing liquid in crystal goblets never needed refilling. A positively charged atmosphere, entertainers, shows and dancing enhanced the experience. The changing colors of the Souls indicated those anticipating winning the Grand Prize.

It was my turn to throw the dice again. All I needed was an eight, and I would have enough winnings to get the Grand Prize. I shook the dice, blew on them, made my wish, and threw them down the long table. Squeezing the edge of the table to control my excitement, I focused as the dice rebounded at the end, and rolled until the five and three were up.

"Yes!" I shouted, "Its back to the blue marble for another experiential session."

Other souls at the table cheered, clapped and congratulated me. I danced to the music, and wished everyone, "Good luck!"

Anticipating what was coming next, I noticed how dramatically my vibration/frequency was increasing and the light I was changing.

A New Soul asked, "What's next for you?"

"I've got a lot of options and a lot of choices to make to plan out this next life," I answered, "and I promise it will be very entertaining for all of the Spirits and Souls. I can hardly wait!"

Another New Soul asked, "What kind of options?"

I paused for a look-around before answering, enjoying the vibrations of this heavenly entertainment center. "I have to choose my race, location, belief system and the objective of this incarnation. The choices have to be coordinated with other Souls who will be on my team." I said, as I watched my Spirit Escort materialize.

"What team?" asked another New Soul.

"There are several steps before you get recruited onto a Team. " My Spirit Escort said. "You have to decide what kind of 'Life Game' to play, decide which 'Position' you want to play, learn the 'Play Book,' then try-out and qualify for the team, Once you make the team, it's, let the games begin!"

"So I can't just jump on-in a body and start playing," I explained.

"That's right," the Spirit Escort said, "A lot of planning has to be done first."

"OK," I said, "Let's get started!"

I cashed in my winnings, received a receipt for the Grand Prize, a human body, then we drifted out of the Casino with other winners and their Escorts.

The first stop was the "Multi-media Room" where I was ushered to a private booth. Making myself comfortable, I pushed the ON button, and a Hologram surrounded me complete with sensory and emotional input. In super high speed, a review of my previous lives, starting with caveman times to present.

First up the Life Mission and Life Purpose for each incarnation was clearly presented, with multiple opportunities to play opposing roles and gender options.

The Hunter-Gather life times were survival and procreation trials with: injuries, fights to establish dominance, fire-starting, the smell of cooking meat, hunger during winter and seasonal migration with developing courage to overcome fear, the beginnings of competition for what appeared to be scarce resources and an awareness of Mother Nature's role in survival while being both subservient and dominating.

The Slavery lifetimes included: defeat, capture, rebellion, escapes, rapes, neutering, whippings, and starvation with feelings of helplessness and depression.

The City Planner in Egypt incarnation included: idol worship, slaves of my own, multiple wives, concubines, opulence and power with intrigue and a sad death.

My Maharaja's wife incarnation showed the cast system with discrimination, Hindu religion, exotic sex with OBEs, the resignation of my fate and smell of my flesh when burned alive with my dead husband.

I had some excitement with Genghis Kan in China and learning about empathy.

A Chumash Indian Shaman near Gaviota Pass traveling across the San Joaquin Valley and on to Wyoming: an educator, hunter, adventurer and traveler in concert with Nature.

A Moslem Sheik at war with the crusaders: horses, swords, multiple wives, defending my Moslem beliefs and lands from the infidels, proud and courageous.

A Pirate incarnation complete with storms at sea, roar of cannons, smell of gunpowder, sword fights, wounds, blood, rape, torture, treasure and feelings of regret.

As a Mountain-man in the Western US trapping, hunting, trading with and killing Indians, guiding settlers and realizing the injustices.

A female on a South Pacific Island living a comfortable and enjoyable life of luaus, raising many children, a pleasant time and dying of old age.

Many more incarnations, to numerous to list, were included in the review. To say the least, I'd been busy, and at times an adventurous and violent player from both sides.

Each review included my original script, the choices I made during that lifetime, and how these "Will Power" applied choices affected the lifetime along with the Karmic results.

The "Butterfly Effect" was evident in how my actions always brought reactions and sent ripples throughout the Spirit world and the Universe. What I did during my varied and different life experiences, and the decisions I made, had made a difference.

While reviewing the many incarnations, I began to gain an understanding of the importance of each lifetime and how every event and every choice affected my ability to fulfill my chosen Life Purpose.

After the Incarnation review, my first choice was which one of the "Nine Games" I would choose to play this time: 1. Individuality, 2. Diplomacy, 3.Artistic expression, 4. Technical detail, 5. Analytical research, 6. Responsibility, 7. Philosophical depth of thought, 8. Organization, or 9. Universal Love and Understanding. From this choice came my birth date. With the birth date (from Numerology – mine is #8 – 3 + 5 remember the dice game?) came my deep down inside feelings – the need to "organize" everything I would choose to be involved with.

From the Chinese calendar, I was born in the year of the Dragon under a Water Sign. The **venue** I would play in would have something to do with water. I think Swimming Instructor, Sailing Instructor, SCUBA Instructor Trainer, Marine Biological and Oceanographic Diving Technician, Commercial Diver, Dive Director of an Under Water Habitat project, Operations Director · of an underwater Treasure salvage operation, Aquatic Sports Director at a resort hotel, college Instructor teaching Oceanographic Equipment and Instrumentation, Commercial Fisherman, owner of a Mariculture Company, partner in a fish company and Director of the Scott Carpenter Man In The Sea Program fulfilled that design influence quite well.

With August as my birth month, my **astrological sign** is Virgo, but receiving a new sign with each death/near death experience left me fairly confused (or balanced) now.

Issued the "Play Book" appropriate to the Game of Organization, I studied the **play options** (parents, sibling, relatives, spouse(s), offspring, etc.). This led to choosing my Name, which would determine my **position** on the team (For information on how your name and birth date influence your life check out the Kabalarian Philosophy @ kabalarians.com, I changed my name/team position in 1983).

Another critical choice was my Attitudes, which determined **how** I would play the game.

The "Planning Room" was next and the walls were labeled with the choices needing to be made based on the Game, the Play Book and my position on the Team.

The first wall was labeled **Life Mission** with a question under it, "What aspect of your personality do you want to work on which will be a common thread throughout this lifetime?" The check list included at least one major personal "Trial." This would be an intense learning experience. It would take an extended period of time and be a common thread throughout the life events. This one choice blended the life together and provided the general set-up, early in life, of the opposite of the planned, end-objective. Without the Yin, there could be no Yang.

Given the lessons of my previous lives, and my willingness to learn and change my behavior, the obvious choice for this incarnation was Ego (Vanity, vanity, all is vanity). That meant I had to start off with extreme low self esteem, create an Ego Maniac, destroy the Ego and then rebuild it into an under-control power house (The meek shall inherit the earth). After 37 years "In The Desert" I am now writing **Body/Brain – Soul/Mind – Two Entities, With Different Agendas, Equals War** about reprogramming your mind to create the lifestyle you want including sections about Enemy #1 – Ego/Vanity vs. Friend #1 – Will Power.

The second wall was labeled **Life Purpose** with the question under it being; "What will you do to assist Nature, Humans, the Planet, the Universe, provide a good show for the rest of the Souls and Spirits, and collect data to be included in the Data Base in the Sky?"

As an "Old Soul" with much experience, and reminded that "My people perish from a lack of knowledge," my choice was helping humans expand their brain capability to increase the speed, memory and retrieval of information so they can gain wisdom to produce wiser decisions.

The venues chosen were writing, teaching and motivational speaking.

The third wall was labeled **Spiritual Aspects of Life Human** which offered choices in the demonstration of the power of the Spiritual realm through the "The 9 Gifts of the Holy Spirit." Tongues, interpretation of tongues, dreams, visions, healing, discernment and casting out of demons, the word of knowledge, the word of wisdom, and miracles. The "Holy Spirit" is just the "communications box" with Universal Intelligence (God) and the "pipeline" through which the "Force/Power" flows. Through the Gifts of the Spirit all things are possible. I chose them all.

NOTE: This is about Spirit not Religion.

The next wall was labeled **Gender**. Noting my questioning look, the attendant said, "Ah, yes, you forgot about this choice." Then asked, "Do you want an inny or an outy?"

Still confused, I asked, "What if I chose an inny?"

The booming voice replied, "If you chose an inny, you'll get brains but have to put up with periods and having kids."

"What if I chose an outy?"

"You'll get a handy thing to take along on a pick nick, but just enough brains to fill the head when it's soft and it will run your life."

NOTE: Depending on the "Gender" choice, you get a number of differing "Programs." There really is a difference between men and women. Brains or very little brains, which did you chose?

The next wall was labeled **Race** with a graduated scale of skin color to choose from. I remembered I had sampled a variety of incarnations in varying shades of skin color from shinny black to almost translucent white. I mused, *The shade of skin color did seem to have an effect on how I was treated in different places and some of the events that occurred during a given Life.*

The next wall was labeled **Family, Friends, Mentors, Acquaintances, Chance Encounters and Enemies**. Each person would have something to teach me and I would have something for them.

How the life lessons played out and when the interfaces occurred were up to the Spirit Coordinators (the Casting Directors) and depended on Will Power choices during the incarnation. Cooperative planning sessions during the incarnation would occur, during the body's sleep, at Starbucks in the Sky. The planning involved all of the Souls on a Team and would require constant review due to the dynamics of the ongoing choices of each willful soul. Basically, would the Souls learn and change their behavior or loop, repeating their learning experiences. In many instances, those who insist on looping are left behind (divorced in one way or another?).

In addition to the Soul's input (lessons and experiences from previous lives), with the family choice came Genetic/DNA programming. Of course programs could be modified and changed during the life by education, situations, circumstances and the willingness to learn and change (what this book is really about). Events would be scheduled to keep the overall process entertaining, i.e. personal relationships, work environments, experiences with nature, physical traumas and accidents, threat to survival situations and many more learning opportunities.

With the major choices made, the "Planning" session was completed and I moved on to the final stage – "Script Writing." Allowing plenty of "Wiggle Room," I wrote out and scheduled the major life events which would help me fulfill my Life Mission, Life Purpose and the original objectives of this lifetime. My Script and all of the other Team Player's Scripts had to be reviewed and integrated prior to the Team being "authorized to incarnate."

With script and winnings receipt in hand, I hurried into the hallowed chamber to collect my winnings (a body) from God. Delivering my Life Script, I waited nervously as it was reviewed.

"Your body awaits," the voice from the light boomed, "we're all depending on you to perform your Life Mission and Life Purpose. From your Script, it appears you'll be putting on some very entertaining sitcoms and soap operas again. Go forth and act – we'll all be watching. Oh, and have some fun this trip down."

The Factors to Consider

You did realize this story isn't just about me?

So why did *you* script your parents, siblings, spouse(s), children, friends, enemies, bosses, and co-workers to play bit parts in your movie? Why did you pick this time frame of man's advancement to live this life? How does the location you chose to live, fit into your plan? And what are you supposed to learn from your Life Experiences?

You wrote the script, you know what behavioral changes you need to make, and you're playing your bit part in the lives of others so they can learn. The other people are object lessons for you and you're providing object lessons for them. This life is your life – live it to the fullest. Quit blaming anything outside yourself for what happens. Take responsibility for your life – you wrote the script. Re-script your life as necessary, but realize the lessons not learned – behaviors not changed – will be much more intense next time, you'll see to that.

Determine the Life Purpose you wrote into your Script and make it your objective. It's interesting how, when you do that, serendipity jumps in to smooth the way. It's amazing just how hard and difficult life can be if you're not actively working on your purpose for being here, not willing to take risks, not willing to face up to fear and move through, not willing to move out in faith, not willing to learn and change. Remember, you "signed" a contract with yourself and others and you will be held to it – by you. You are responsible for your "whole" life – enjoy. And keep in mind that we're all watching – that makes it even more fun.

NOTE: Think about how the Souls duplicated and improved on the Casino in the Sky when they designed and built Las Vegas. The Souls use their God given creativity and the Genius they are to modify the planets they occupy and make the situations and circumstances of Life entertaining for all of us. Thank you.

You Choose Your Life

I lead a serendipitous, entertaining, adventure filled life. Complete strangers reinforce choices I've made and provide insight into the workings of the universe and the reason for my life adventures. Think about that real hard. You chose when to be born, and based on that choice, a general plan, a template for your life is laid out. Any questions about this, checkout numerology.

I've had multiple out-of-body experiences starting early in my life. It is very interesting to step back out of your body and watch your behavior from a different perspective. This "observer" viewpoint has enabled me to gain understanding about who I want to be. I realize, whatever is going on at the time is being observed from at least three different perspectives; my body's perspective, the observer's perspective, and the person's perspective with whom I'm interfacing – all are different. The observer's perspective is the best because it has much less emotional involvement, is more objective and it is usually much more entertaining.

From the perspective of the observer, I became aware that the soul, which is over 99% of who I am, is the operator and has made all of the decisions, except basic survival, and written the script of my movie.

Let's take a trip to the spirit world. As a soul, you can review any tape (life recording) in the "library" (Akashic Record) to review how any person in history played their role. If you wish to watch current events, you can observe first hand the life players mucking about on the playing field earth (or other planets). You simply take a seat/cloud, order your hot dog, beer, and peanuts then enjoy the game. If and when you get enthused enough, you can opt to join the players on the field.

But to do that, you must first be selected. The first challenge is the "casino in the sky" where you join the other hopefuls to throw dice, cut cards, or play roulette to determine who gets the next body. How else do you think man was able to come up with a place like Las Vegas? I'm kidding, of course - or not.

Once you've been successful and won a body, next you have to write your life script and have it reviewed for integration into the overall program going on in the playing field of life on earth. Drafting sessions go on with the coaches of the different leagues, and this is where your race is chosen. Then there will be a location selection – country, state, city and finally family. The souls get together and you all choose when to take on a body, who your parents, siblings, friends, enemies, bosses, co-workers, and friends are going to be, and what major roles (positions) you will each play so you can all have "behavioral changing" experiences.

This is a dynamic process, and involves a master director to keep everything moving and flexible enough to allow for individual wills to make mis-takes and have do-overs. Picture the souls putting the bodies to sleep every night and lifting off to meet around the water dispenser or Starbucks in the Sky to plan out the next day's agenda. If you take charge of your life, you get to help select what happens, if not, other souls decide for you. If you refuse to learn your lessons, then the souls – yours included – will plan out the next event that will give you another chance to modify your behavior – it will be more intense than the last time.

Will

In my religious training, I was taught man was given his own will as a test. To exercise your will, you must make decisions and do something with those decisions.

Then I was introduced to predestination. If an event was able to be prophesized it was predestined. If something was "predestined to happen," where was my will involved in making any choices? Could it be I selected the event to happen as a part of writing my life's script?

Think about prophesy – foretelling the future. There are many stories throughout the bible and elsewhere when prophets told what was going to happen in the future. Weren't they just reading the scripts that had been written? Aren't you able to predict the future? No. What about déjà vu?

Just when I thought I had everything figured out, along came the Karma thing. This was meant to explain why "bad things happen to good people" and "good things happen to bad people." So the Karmic debt/reward thing has to do with paying for screw-ups/good behavior in a previous life. That meant to accept Karma, you had to believe in reincarnation.

So if you lived in a previous life, and you exited the life before you got through all the lessons, you get to come back and work on becoming better. The belief in reincarnation will give you infinite patience.

During a Review Session, I asked, "It would seem my religious teachings and the Bible are in conflict with predestination, will, past lives and Karma, would you please explain these?"

My counselor answered, "If you've already laid out your life experiences to learn your lessons, isn't that exercising your Will. If you wrote your own script, then you predestined yourself to have certain experiences to learn your life lessons. If the script is written down somewhere, then it can be prophesized by a prophet. And if you think you deserved a reward or a hard lesson from a previous life, then you wrote Karma into your script.

"I hate to apply simple logic to the spiritual aspects of life," the Counselor continued, "but this is the only explanation that fits all of the religious beliefs, and since they're all partly right, they all have something in common – script writing. So you really can write.

"Now if you want to have some fun, go against your Zodiac sign and anything else that smacks of preplanning, predestination, and Karma. Exercise your will, change your script, and create a new experience. Then ask yourself if you changed your script now, or you wrote in changing your script when you originally wrote it. That should keep you in the corner for a while."

Summary

Your job is to take care of yourself, pay attention and learn. The proof of you learning your lessons is your behavioral changes. Trying to change others is just your attempt at controlling them and will definitely have adverse effects.

Determine what your Life Purpose and Life Mission are and try to get *IT* (you) right this time around.

Before you took on a body, *YOU* wrote your life's script, down to the minutest detail. This accounts for déjà vu, prophesy, Karma and reincarnation. Since you wrote the script, take responsibility, enjoy the journey and learn your lessons.

Chapter 4
How Did You Lose Your Arm?

I know I piqued your curiosity. I heard you say, "So Lance, how did you loose your arm?"

When asked that question, I answer, "Do you want the truth, or some really good stories? The truth's not a lot of fun."

Some Stories

As a SCUBA instructor, I have lots of stories, "Nothing between me and jaws but my knife, saber toothed abalone (a large snail), man eating kelp (an ocean plant that only eats men), eel attack, killer crabs, etc."

When playing in nature, its, "Lions and tigers and bears, oh my!"

Depending on how I feel, I answer, "Tried to be in two places at the same time and never got it all back together." "I lent someone a hand and they didn't give it back." "Never get into a fight with a Puerto Rican who has a knife!" "Oh no, forgot it again. If my ass wasn't on so tight, I'd have no-ass-at-all."

When finances are involved, "They told me it was going to cost me an arm and a leg, I got away cheap."

When someone puts their arm between closing elevators doors, I yell, "Don't do that! Look what happened to me." Then I hold up my stump.

The story I like the best is "One Night Stand."

You never heard that one? Well let's get this book started off right. There I was in a bar in Mayaguez, Puerto Rico drinking rum, dancing and having a great time when the bartender yelled, "Last call!"

I said, "I'll have two," and quickly looked around. There was only one woman left, so I made my move, and I can move good (well).

I woke up the next morning with my head beating like a base drum and needing to piss like a mad racehorse.

When am I ever going to learn, I said to myself, *I've got to stop drinking so much.* I pried open one eye, trying to see through the sand, and realized, *Oh no, it's worse than I thought. This isn't my room, I don't even know where the head is, and if I don't find it soon, I'll piss myself.*

I started to roll out of bed and realized there was something holding down my left arm. I looked over and she was so ugly I thought about one paper bag (for her head), then I thought about two bags (one for her head and one for my head in case her bag fell off). I decided not to wake her up, but I was caught just like a coyote in a trap and the only solution was to chew my arm off and get out of there.

I don't drink that much any more, I don't want to loose the other arm.

Now if that joke offends you, maybe you should just send the book back right now for a full refund before you go any further. I've told that story many times in many places – I wish it were true, it's a good explanation and it's funny, especially if you're missing an arm which could have been chewed off.

The Truth? (You asked for it.)

The truth is also entertaining, but doesn't bode well for doctors.

Once upon a time, in a land far away, I was Dive Director for the largest, most sophisticated Underwater Habitat in the world – La Chalupa –located 7 to 10 miles off the West Coast of Puerto Rico, outside of the barrier reef.

(That sounds like a story, and it started off right.)

Senator Pollack, from Alaska had come to visit his friend, Ian Koblick, the President of Marine Resources Development Foundation (MRDF) and dive down to the habitat. MRDF was the "umbrella" which operated the Puerto Rico International Undersea Laboratory (PRINUL) – La Chalupa.

While climbing back in the boat, after his visit to the habitat, Pollack twisted the hook on the prosthesis, which replaced the hand he lost to a grenade in WWII.

The prosthesis was brought to me to be straightened out. While working on it, my brain asked, *I wonder what it would be like to have only one-hand.*

Seven days later, while bringing La Chalupa back into the harbor, the towline under tension snapped, and the first thought, as I flew through the air gathering the hand and arm together was, *Shit, I'm going to have a hook just like Pollock.*

Although the doctors did attend me, they did everything doctors and hospitals can do wrong to get sued for and loose a medical malpractice lawsuit, including abandonment (at that time, it was cheaper to bury their mistakes than to treat them).

In retrospect, I'm not sure the best care in the world could have saved the arm. I programmed it's lose with the one questioning thought. (Be careful what you think!)

Oh yea, the reason I'm a mid-upper arm amputee and not just above the wrist like Pollock is because I was an egotistical maniac and had to do the "one-upsmanship" thing – better, harder, worse than – (its not just a guy thing either).

That's how I lost my arm, satisfied? I told you the truth was not a lot of fun.

One thing for sure about this experience and subsequent medical "mis-adventures" – I don't trust the people in white coats. Is there a reason they call what they do a "Practice?"

Why Did You Get Rid Of Your Arm?

Married, with three sons, doing the ultimate dream of a Marine Diving Technician, utilizing all of my skills, working twelve to sixteen hours per day, seven days a week. Solving problems no one had even dreamed about. Keeping people alive in a hostile environment using highly sophisticated life support equipment, pushing frontiers back, on the cutting edge of technology in my field, can't wait to go to work, don't want to go home and having the time of my life.

I was the only one in the world who was Director of a moveable Under Water Habitat – that's fairly exclusive. So why in the world get rid of an arm? What was I going to do for an encore? Was there a purpose beyond the immediate trauma? Was there a reason, a lesson to learn?

The answer to these questions is what this book is about. In my life experience, I found there was always a reason for whatever happened to me. It may not be immediately evident, but a delay, a car breakdown, a sickness, an injury, death – all were in the "plan." Getting angry because something happened which was not what I thought I had planned only hurt me it didn't alter the journey.

Accepting there is always a reason for whatever happens to me has made life a lot easier to deal with. If I didn't learn it elsewhere, I learned to "go with the flow" as a SCUBA diver, because if I tried to fight the current or surge, Mother Nature would kick my ass.

Stumped

After Arm Loss (AAL), I had the opportunity to experience being "Stumped" (pun intended). I disliked the feeling of being frustrated when I ran up against a "two-handed job." I found I could switch being "Stumped" to being "Challenged" – a slight inconvenience.

For someone who was "short handed," I would take-on impossible tasks with laser focus on the end objective then apply my genius and life experiences to figure out how to make a "two-handed job" into a "one-handed job." Sometimes it would take two weeks to build something so I could do a five-minute job, but the job got done.

With a shift of attitude from frustration to challenge I proceeded to solve "one-handed" problems with anticipation.

I'm now using "Stumped" regularly in conversations. "I'm stumped, could you lend me a hand? I promise I'll give your hand back, not like what happened to me when the last person I lent it to kept it." This works quite well when needing help with something. Plus it usually elicits a laugh.

Stumped was a word used often when I was young. I really had never connected it with me being short-handed until Mimi said the word in my writing class. After that, there was no choice but to adopt it for my condition.

I also thought about where the word "stumped" came from. Having cut down trees, I had the answer quickly. Cutting the tree down was easy, compared to removing the stump. When my forefathers cleared the land so they could build their homes and produce crops, they had to remove the stumps. If you left the stump or roots in the ground, you could lose a lot of crop producing land and destroy your plow.

Stump removal involved digging a big hole around and under the stump so they could chop off the roots and eventually remove the stump and roots with man-power or draft animals. They couldn't wait for the stump to be "recycled," which takes five or more years. So depending on what kind of tree it was (i.e. soft wood or hardwood), where it was, and what type of ground it was growing in (soft dirt vs. rocks), you could get "Stumped," bad.

I know you've stumped your toe. That's an easy one to figure out. Imagine a recently cleared area with the stumps cut off close to the ground, and then the leaves fall from the trees. You go for a walk, and kick a recently covered stump – not fun, you just got stumped.

There is a vital lesson in this. Whenever you're "Stumped;" take it as a challenge to your ingenuity, define the objective, get outside-your-box, focus and enjoy the problem solving process. Stumped is getting slowed down, not being stopped. Just remember, to do a proper job of removing the stump, you have to get a good portion of the roots too – be patient, persistent and plan on some hard work.

And you thought getting "Stumped" on a test question was rough.

If you're "Stumped" on a test question, cheat! Proven fact – you remember what you miss and cheat on – not what you get right (oops, more of that edumacation stuff). Remember, humans are designed to learn from mistakes. Wisdom comes from screwing up, learning, and changing behavior. Schooling "punishes" you for making mistakes – DA!

Is it any wonder why common sense (wisdom) is not common? If you're not "Wise" you didn't make enough mistakes – or was it remove enough stumps?

As a college instructor, I gave "You Can't Cheat On It" tests. Those tests really messed up the students. The tests took all of the advantages of cheating away from them. The students had to learn to "cooperate" (real-world of work) not "compete" (unreal-world of schooling with 12+ years of programming) with their fellow students.

I thought about changing the title of this book to Stumped, but decided Short Handed would work as well and finally settled on Back From Beyond. Besides, I didn't want people, who understood where stumped came from, avoiding the book by thinking it was about trees and hard work.

In the six years following the accident, I proceeded to do every occupation and sport I had ever done, over again. I found I could do almost anything with one arm. It took me longer to do certain things with one arm, but they got done. The lessons, the learning, the behavior modification (that's what learning is) were like an avalanche, with me in the middle along for the ride. I didn't get cut an awful lot of slack by my wife, my employer or my co-workers.

The best compliment was, "I forgot you only had one arm."

Until I lost my arm, the only way to do something was my way. I learned there are a gazillion ways to meet an objective. Not being able to do as much with one arm, required letting other people do things themselves.

The only problem was to define the objective properly, support others with tools, parts and assistance, and let them do it – their way. Some of their ways were faster some were slower. Some ways cost more money, some less. Some got done better, some not as good. But in the end the objective was met, and the people who did the jobs owned them, were responsible, and they had solved the problems themselves – much better.

If you're ever trying to do something consider time, cost, and quality – choose two.

Before Arm Lose (BAL) there was nothing I couldn't do. One of the hardest and most devastating lessons to my ego was learning to ask for help. For an egotistical, independent, smart ass like me, that lesson hurt like hell.

I was caught in a dilemma. I needed to find out what I could and couldn't do in a timely fashion. Whatever needed doing, meant figuring out how and doing it myself, first. Knowing when to just ask for help to get the job done on time became quite a balancing act.

The result was interesting. The transformation created an expert job, operation, and procedure writer. By just watching a job performed, I'm able to determine the sequence of events necessary to complete it.

Figuring out there aren't a lot of two-handed jobs in this world, meant sequencing the one-handed jobs correctly was all that was required. If something required two hands or speed, I got help.

Now, I'll even stop and ask for direction – boy has that saved a lot of time and gas.

Summary

Just accepting there's a reason for everything which has and will happen to you is a step towards enlightenment. Believing this lets you relax and be proactive whenever an event or delay changes what you thought should happen.

Sooner or later, you'll have to face up to your mortality. Accepting the body is going to die but the soul is going to live is actually quit a freeing act on your part.

In spite of what you think is possible, there are limitations to what you personally can accomplish. You can, however, do a lot more than you or others believe. Be honest with yourself about what you can do and learn to ask for help (and directions).

If you get "stumped," take it as a challenge and charge on.

Chapter 5
The Phantom

One of the things which screwed with my mind the most when my arm was lopped off was to have it hurt but not be there. The pain I was used to, but for the arm to be gone and still hurt just didn't make sense, based on my life experience. The hand, forearm, elbow, and the missing part of the upper arm hurt.

Less than four years before my amputation, amputees who admitted to having Phantom or Ghost Pain were routinely being placed in insane asylums. They were considered "out of their minds." If the limb was gone, then the pain had to be gone – out of sight, out of mind – or so the doctors thought.

Rubberman

If the Phantom Pain wasn't bad enough, my hand was traveling around the hospital room. It was on the opposite wall, under the bed, on the ceiling, inside my stomach, and moving. It was as if it was trying to find its form – the missing arm. It reminded me of the comic character "Rubberman." Try playing that game while you're on mind altering drugs.

The Body Aura

It did occur to me, "common knowledge of the day" had not prepared me for the results of the amputation, the missing part hurting and the room wide movement of the hand. Trying not to give too much thought to the traveling arm, although it was a bit disturbing, and having more experience with the traveling arm, I related it to the only thing which might explain the phenomenon – the body's Aura.

As life experiences being an amputee compounded, I eventually began to look at the human body differently. When it's thought of as a machine, many things are easier to explain. For example, besides the basic genetic code, what animates this machine? The soul is the animator. How is this soul displayed – can it be seen? The soul is the Aura, it surrounds the machine and can be seen by some people. Are there any other indications of the Aura/soul? I heard when the human body is on a scale and it dies, it loses six ounces/21 grams. Doctors admit to this, but basically say, "Yes the body does lose six ounces when it dies, something leaves which has mass and weight, but we can't see it, so whatever it is doesn't exist."

Psychics, who observe human death, describe the Soul/Aura as lifting out of the body. The conclusion is the soul has mass and weight, even if the doctors can't explain it because they can't "see" it.

The Russians did a lot of research on the "super-natural" and eventually were able to photograph Auras, using Kirilian Photography. In fact, all living things have Auras, and if a piece of a plant or animal is cut off, the Aura remains in the original shape. With the sensitive electronic equipment developed by the Russians, the "meridians" of the body can also be seen and tracked. These are the same "meridians" that the Chinese Chi Master's can see. These are the meridians the Chi Masters read and use acupuncture to "balance" the body's Aura to heal disease.

One day in a theatre, just for grins and giggles, I moved the Phantom Arm close to a stranger sitting next to me, and he moved away from it. In every instance where I approached a person with the Phantom Arm, when it reached their Aura, they moved away from it. Everyone needs their "personal space" at least the size of their Aura.

And then it became a game, especially whenever I could maneuver a woman to my left side. I'd explain, "Every amputee has a Phantom, but mine is unique. My Phantom has a distinct advantage, I feel with it, but you can't feel me feeling you, and damn, you feel good!"

Of course they would reply, "Oh, you can't either feel with your Phantom."

I'd say, "And if I could feel with it, where do you think my hand would be right now, and are you sure you can't feel it?"

With that, they'd usually laugh nervously and move out of range of a normal arm. Then I'd mention the Rubberman thing. Another way I flaunt the missing arm, and the responses are fun.

Psychic

Love County Fairs, especially the long aisles of booths where people are hawking all kinds of goodies. While enjoying the "This knife is the greatest, sharpest and most flexible knife in the world" show, I felt something and noticed a woman at the far end of the aisle, staring intently at me. I looked around to be sure it was me she had singled out. Then she almost ran towards me.

As she stopped in front of me, staring at my stump, she said, "I can see your Phantom."

I said, "Ok, describe what you see."

She said, "Well the hand is partially closed with the fingers together, and positioned at the end of your stump like so," as she positioned her hand to look like my Phantom.

I said, "You're absolutely correct."

"But," She said, "that's not what caught my attention, it was the Aura around your other arm. It's the largest, brightest and most colorful Aura I've ever seen."

I smiled and said, "Well that explains why my good arm became so devastatingly strong and fast. The bio-energy from the missing arm transferred to the good arm after the amputation."

We continued the conversation as we walked to her booth. Of course, she was a psychic. I've never questioned my experiences, but I do enjoy confirmation of the discoveries I made.

Form & Substance

One of the impressive things I noticed when putting on a prosthesis, was the phantom hand going to the fake hand or hook. In fact, I could almost feel with the prosthetic hand or hook. The Phantom needs a substance to provide form, otherwise it's just a "formless" vapor. A "Ghost?"

Other Amputees

Down through the years, having made it a point to talk to many amputees, one of my favorite questions is, "How's your Phantom?" This question elicited many different answers, but never a denial of there being a Phantom.

The discovery, as a result of the question, is I'm among the very few amputees who can move their Phantom. I'm not sure why the distinction, but there's definitely a difference in our experiences.

When foot amputees are asked if they have to buy the right size shoes, they answer, "Yes, if I don't buy the right sized shoe to fit the amputated foot, it hurts."

This is well known, and if I were the least bit curious about it, I'd get some foot amputees together, some Aura reading psychics, with Kirilian Photography and do some experiments. Gee we might find out some new things about the body. But no, anything new is risky, and who wants to be criticized?

Although, I do wonder if to the Soul's, aura feet stink.

Doctors

In the first 15 years after my arm was amputated, I saw 32 general medicine doctors, three orthopedic doctors, and two neurologists. Every single one of those doctors asked me the same question, "Do you have Phantom Pain?"

My answer, "Every amputee has Phantom Pain. Whether they'll admit it to a doctor or not, they admit it to me."

What amazed me was at the amputee ward of the Miami, Florida VA Hospital, the doctors there asked me the same question. My answer eventually became, "I think every doctor who asks that question should have an arm and a leg amputated so they can make up their own minds about Phantom Pain."

Summary

In my experience, the soul is represented by the Aura, some people can see it and modern technology can photograph it.

Few amputees can move their Phantom, but all amputees have a Phantom. Most foot amputees must use shoes that "fit" the Phantom foot to avoid pain.

Is there more to this than meets the "normal" eye? Yes! Considering the effect of the bio-energy transfer from my left arm to the right arm and people moving away from it, what is the aura capable of doing? I've never really taken the time to try long enough to make it happen, but I believe I could move objects with the Phantom. If I could, then the real test would be to try moving an object out of my normal reach, using the Rubberman effect. But since no one seems interested, I've lost motivation.

Watch the Star Wars movies, Sci Fi predicts the future. Whatever we can conceive we can achieve.

Chapter 6
The Nerves and Regeneration

The gas gangrene which infected my left, upper quadrant hurt, big time. The Demerol given as an anesthetic, caused me to throw-up. Try heaving your guts out with a broken collarbone and all your left side ribs separated from your sternum. That was painful! So I told the doctors to quit giving me pain shots, and learned to shut off the pain – mentally.

Due to the gas gangrene infection, the left arm swelled up to approximately three times its normal size and became cherry red. Because of the swelling, the doctors did a Guillotine Amputation, cut it straight off at mid upper arm. The end of the stump was left open so it could drain. The raw meat, bone-end, artery, and nerve tube were identifiable when the arm dressing was changed. (I was going to put in a picture of my open stump, but figured if anyone was eating and reading at the same time, they might have a problem.)

The doctors tied a suture around the main artery, but did not tie off the nerve tube. Eight days after the accident the arm was amputated. The day after the amputation, the main artery suture came off and I bled to death.

Eight days after the amputation, I was released from the hospital to go home, but went back to work. Eight weeks later, a skin graft was taken from my hip to close the open end of the stump. The day the stitches were removed from the skin graft, I dived down to the habitat.

The initial, infection-caused pain decreased, and the amputation pain went away, but the broken collar bone and separated ribs pain never completely stopped, I just shut it off mentally.

The First Nerve Regeneration

Nerves are the fastest regenerating organ of your body. If a nerve is terminated in your big toe, it will take approximately two years to regenerate again, before you would get the feeling back, as long as the nerve tube conduit is intact.

It took about five months for the nerves to degenerate to my brain stem and then regenerate back down the stump. As the nerves exited the open nerve tube, they tried to get to the parts of the arm they had originally operated, were stopped by the skin graft and started to spread out and attach to the skin. Touching different spots on the skin graft would "light-up" different parts of my missing hand, forearm, elbow and upper-arm. Initially the sensation was entertaining, but it didn't take long before the skin graft became super sensitive.

If the stump was bumped, it would take up to 45 minutes for it to calm down. The feeling was like hitting your "crazy bone," but many times worse. A bump felt like subjecting the whole missing arm to electrocution using 220 volts of electricity.

With three young, active boys playing and running, bumps to the stump were inevitable. With the strength and speed of the good arm, it's a wonder my boys survived. All of them got knocked across the room for bumping the stump. It was an automatic, defensive reaction to the extreme pain.

It didn't take long, before I could "sense" when anyone got close to my left side. Even if not seen or heard, I knew they were there. The problem: when anyone approached the left side, I automatically clenched my right fist and got ready to punch without any rationale decision made, purely reactionary. I knew it was just a matter of time, before some little, old, blue-haired lady in a department store bumped my stump, and I killed her with a punch that would have destroyed a heavyweight boxer.

It was obvious if I were going to function in society, I'd have to have a "stump revision." Having already filed my Medical Malpractice Law Suit, I didn't think it would be a good idea to let the Puerto Rican doctors have another chance to finish what they had started. So, I quit my job and moved my family to Florida to get the nerve thing fixed.

Stump Revision

The stump revision at the VA Hospital – where they should have had a lot of experience – was fraught with more problems. Just the attitude of the doctors and their questions was a clue, but something had to be done.

The first thing the doctors had to "check" was whether the pain at the skin graft was "real" or "in my head." This was one of the best/worst tortures ever invented. The doctor dug around with the needle, about halfway up the stump, until he found the nerve conduit. When he finally pushed the needle into the tube, it was worse than having the stump bumped. The pain-killer was injected into the nerve tube to see if the procedure would in fact deaden the nerve sensation on the skin graft. Of course the injection deadened the nerves and feeling at the end of the stump.

Once the torture was completed, and they determined the pain was physical and not mental (I'm not sure they know the difference), the stump revision was scheduled.

The stump revision operation involved removing the skin graft (which actually worked and looked good), cutting off an additional ½" of bone, pulling the nerve tube out and cutting it off about three inches shorter – but it was not sutured off – again. The skin was pulled together across the end of the stump and stitched. A tube was left in one corner of the stitched together skin to drain the blood. I was released to go home after one night in the hospital. From the standpoint of the nerve pain, the operation was a success – the pain was gone, but the Phantom remained.

While redressing the stump at home, I noticed the side of the stitched area which did not have a drain tube in it was swollen, cold, hard and purple. Opening the corner of the patched stump and using a muscle vibrator, I worked ½ a teacup of blood clots out of the end of the stump. That part of the stump is still cold sensitive. Any temperature less than 80 degrees and the nerves start firing off.

The sutured stump end now had two nipples, and was never comfortable when I tried to use my new, working prosthesis.

I went to the head of surgery, and asked to have the surgeon who operated on me brought in, but it seems he'd been transferred.

"Too bad," I said, "I was going to beat the living S__T out of him right here."

Explaining to the head surgeon the arm lose was due to medical malpractice and showing him the nipples, I described how I milked the blood clots out of the stump. He blanched white. You do know blood clots can give you a stroke or kill you. You realize this was the third malpractice.

The Second Nerve Regeneration

Five months later, the nerves regenerated, and since the nerve tube had not been sealed the nerves got loose again. But this time some of them started attaching to the muscles in my upper arm. Now the whole stump became sensitive, not just the end, and whenever the muscles in the stump are flexed, different parts of my missing arm will come alive. Worse yet, the "fighting" of the multiple nerves trying to get control of the muscles, causes the muscles to vibrate (shake) and hurt. This makes wearing and using a prosthesis impossible.

I returned to the Miami VA Hospital for the same reason I had gone there to begin with, the regenerated nerve problem. The surgeons said there was nothing they could do. Because having already performed a stump revision and a nervectomy, they doubted they could even find the nerve tube to block it off. Then I was referred to another doctor on staff for a review.

The sign over the door said "Psychiatric Department." I was pissed.

When I walked into the doctor's office, he immediately asked, "Why are you so angry?"

I explained about my experience: The malpractice causing the arm lose, first nerve regeneration, the torture, stump revision, blood clots, nerve tube not being sealed off, nipples on my stump, second nerve regeneration, and that the surgeons said nothing could be done to correct *their* mistake. He's been the only doctor who listened intently to what I had to say about both nerves and Phantoms. He even asked good questions.

I finally asked him, "Well, am I crazy?"

He said, "You're the sanest person I've talked to in months. There's nothing mentally wrong with you, and your suggestion about amputating the arms and legs of doctors may be the only solution to them understanding nerve regeneration and Phantom pain."

Summary

Terminated nerves regenerate as long as the nerve tube conduit is in tact. How long it takes a given nerve to regenerate is a simple function of the distance from the termination point to the brain.

Doctors have been and apparently are still confusing nerve pain and Phantom pain. I'll attest both are real. The Phantom (Soul) puts on the body as a virtual reality machine and "feels" what the body feels.

I have attempted to pass on my personal experience to medical doctors, but have been ignored or rebuffed, because they know it all. NOT!

The only one so far who has listened is my son Kirk. Kirk did his PhD in heart capillary cell regeneration, is a MD, and his specialty is pediatric cardiology. Because of his "reputation" he has had some luck in getting the word out.

What about using prosthetic nerve conduit or transplants from cadavers to replace/repair human machines when their nerve tubes are damaged. Could paraplegics walk and function again after two years of nerve regeneration?

Never mind, don't fix them, think of all the money lost to the medical profession and the jobs lost building handicapped access ramps. And besides, they're someone you can be better than.

Chapter 7
Basic Programming

Every computer has a "basic operating system." Since you're an android, a computerized machine, you have a basic operating system. Doom on Lance, he was given this super computer without an operations manual. What kind of a joke is that? Why do I have to stumble down through life trying to figure it out? Where's that book, *The Human Brain for Dummies?*

Survival

One thing's for sure, the most basic of our programs is "Survive." For those who've found the secret, survival equates to food, clothing, shelter, and procreation (sex). The circumstances you've chosen to live under will determine whether that's a handful of rice a day or three gourmet meals, rags or Armani suits, a cave or a 10,000 square foot mansion, sex only for reproduction or exotic and sensual experiences.

But without the basics of survival being taken care of, you can forget art. Only, when the basics of survival are taken care of, can you afford to be artistic.

Consider the problem. Birth is a death sentence and our basic programming is to survive. There has to be a cosmic joker, why else would that dichotomy have been scripted?

Ostracism

The problem with basic survival, the media has figured it out. I'm going to refer you to a book/movie; *Clan of the Cave Bear*. When humans had to band together for protection and survival, a program was implanted and reinforced which says, "Join up or die!" Conform to a society/group or be ostracized. If you're ostracized, kicked out of the cave, you die.

The basic Conform survival program has been manipulated to mean; wear the right clothes, have the right hair cut, go to the right schools, attend the right church, drive the right car, conform to your peer group (body piercing and tattoos?), smell a certain way, eat a certain brand of food, walk a certain way, shake hands a certain way, etc. Remember our basic programming, if you don't conform, you'll be ostracized from society and you'll die.

If you don't put your make-up on right, do the hair, wear enhancing clothes, smile just right and/or move sensuously you'll not be competitive and aren't going to have sexual experiences, which allow you to procreate and ensure the "survival" of your genes.

Oops, that's going to make you laugh at others (and hopefully yourself) when you catch them "preening." You/they are just trying to get laid.

Survival, Ostracism and Ego

When our computer brain considers Survival with Ostracism and combines in Ego, some very interesting thoughts can occur. Constantly confronted with worrying about what other people thought about me, caused concern about acting foolish, looking different, or not having the correct answer to a question and being ostracized from society.

High school was a dangerous place, because it seemed everyone was trying to catch me in some act allowing them to make fun of me and kick me out of the "cave." I was deathly afraid to answer a teacher's question for fear of answering wrong and be made fun of. I was almost physically sick every time I had to give a speech in my public speaking class. I felt it necessary to wear the right clothes to fit in, and my parents were poor.

During high school, the only thing I wanted to be was a mountain-man, isolated from society, hidden away in a cave. I was coming from a place of personal insecurity, little self-confidence and less self-esteem. I had very few friends, pulled into my shell, and just tried to survive till graduation. As soon as I was 18, I joined the Navy to get away.

Given the current pressures on teenagers, it's a wonder there aren't more Columbines and teenage suicides.

When you see the TV ads, ads in teen magazines, and the fads kids are going through, have some empathy for why kids are the way they are. If you want to do them a favor, build their self-confidence and self-esteem. Give them attention. As if you could look the other way when you see tattoos, purple and green hair, nose rings and pants riding so low, if the weather turns cold they're going to fall down (shrinkage – you know the only thing that's holding those boys' pants up are their peckers). The boys who have to keep pulling up their pants, in warm weather, have little peckers.

Let me give you an example (I know you just can't wait). Take the current body piercing and tattooing rage. Is this just a way to prove your man/womanhood? Does this prove your ability to deal with pain? Are you just trying to fit in with a certain group? Is this a new way for you to show-off your "religion" – belief system? Maybe you're just trying to get attention by standing out in a crowd, because you can't get enough attention by being "normal."

Amputations-R-Us

Have I got a deal for you. Be the first in your neighborhood to start a new craze, be a distinctive leader, stand out in a crowd and/or prove how tough you are – no pain, no gain. We guarantee you'll get the recognition you deserve. If you really love him/her, send them an ear. If you've pissed of someone, repent by sending a finger. If you have an accident, call us first, we'll remove a body part so you can get some real money.

You're appalled? Come on, that last paragraph makes just as much sense as almost anything teenagers do, so why not? I've thought about this enough to write it down, standby to see it in action. It'll be advertised on TV and billboards – 1-800- Amputations-R-Us – MC/VISA/AMEX. Call us and we'll chop off something. Jerry Springer will interview the amputees – it won't be long now.

Damn, and then I won't stand out in a crowd as much any more.

It took becoming a SCUBA Instructor to come out of my shell. When I started college at the age of 28, I had put most of the childishness behind me. Thank God or me – whichever.

The Soul and the Body

When you buy a car, it has purpose. It gives you the opportunity to move in two dimensions on this earth. It may be limited in where it can go, but you can get close to almost anywhere on the land using your car. It allows you to have experiences which are impossible without a vehicle. You drive it, care for it, and replace it when it becomes damaged beyond repair. Or you trade it in when you think it's time for a change – a new model.

Sure sounds like you "reincarnate" into your next vehicle for a variety of reasons. Now that's a good explanation of how souls view their use of a human body.

The body is a "machine," made from dirt which allows the soul to have experiences in the playing field of life. The soul cares for the body because of the experiences. When the body wears out and/or the experiences the soul wants to have or is here to provide for other souls, is completed, the soul comes up with some ingenious way to shed the body (kill it), so it can get a new model and have different experiences.

The souls really don't care about bodies, they only care for the experiences. For the souls, the body is just a "Virtual Reality Machine." So physical pain, emotional trauma, physical damage, handicaps and physical defects are all part of the experiential script you (Soul) wrote to learn some important lessons about who you are and help you to change your behavior and personality.

Advancement

The advancements of human kind in the last two-hundred years have been phenomenal: automobiles, planes, trains, ships, construction, agriculture, science, exploration, computers, and space travel to name but a few.

But just how far have we really advanced? Can we control the weather, the tides, volcanoes, earthquakes, meteors, or gravity? Can we even predict these with some degree of accuracy? As an animal species are we really any better off than the hunter-gathers of old?

As spiritual beings, have we learned our lessons or are we still greedy, religious fanatics going about the job of converting, controlling or killing the "non-believers." Show me don't tell me. Demonstrate the personal changes we need to make to really advance as a species.

Legacy

In order to control my youthful activities, my mother used to say, "Don't do anything in the 'barn' you wouldn't do in the open – remember God is watching."

Yea, God and everyone else is watching – so what? If we don't have the experiences or watch them on the media presented programs or read about them how are we going to learn and change our behavior?

In the overall scheme of things, every lifetime is important. Every bit of data collected by every person for every second of their lives is stored in the "Library of Experiences" (the Akashic Records) in the big computer in the sky.

Everything you've done, felt and thought is recorded for all the souls to review – God is watching you – so are all the other Gods – and you (God) are able to review all the experiences of the other humans.

The things we consider to be unimportant and those things we consider to be important are/aren't important. It just depends on who's reviewing your/their experiences.

The experiences had, lessons learned and behaviors changed are all there is. They are our legacy. So the *legacy* we give to our offspring and everyone else is our own behavioral changes – it's all that really matters.

Life Programs

The decisions you make are based on the data you have in your memory banks and the programs (software) which analyzes the data. Incorrect, insufficient or emotionally biased data will render an incorrect decision – mis-take. So the data is important. Of more importance to making good decisions are the programs used to analyze the data.

In addition to the human basic operating system, you also received 2 million years of proven programming pertaining to the human experience. We all know snakes are dangerous, breathing water will kill you, fire hurts and injuries or death result from falling off cliffs. Our ancestors learned this from experience and passed it on to us in our DNA, along with many other "instinctual survival programs." Our brains use these programs to analyze our DNA, ancestral and life experience data instantaneously, based on the current event.

If you hear a snake rattle – before your conscious brain can register the sound – you jump out of the way. Then your brain registers the danger. Your brain has done its job, reacted automatically to save your life. After you're clear, you can analyze the danger and make a rational decision about what to do next. Hold that thought.

You run out of eggs needed to make a cake– before your conscious brain can register – you head for the bathroom to put on your make-up before going to the store. Your brain has done its job, reacted automatically to save your life. The program your brain used to provide you the decision is based on ostracism. If people see you without your make-up on, you'll be kicked out of the cave (ostracized) and you'll die.

May I suggest the historical survival programming you're using has been skewed by the media being paid by the greedy cosmetics industry to sell you make-up. There's a big difference between a rattle snake's danger to your life and being seen by complete strangers without your make-up. Your brain works automatically not rationally when it senses a survival threat.

This is just two of thousands of automatic, reactionary programs your brain uses to protect your life. Many of these programs no longer serve your best interest. These programs are based on the fear of not surviving. Down through the years, the essential survival programs have been expanded into all aspects of your life by the sharp promotion and marketing moguls.

You've been programmed to believe that if you don't wear Nike shoes, eat at McDonalds, drink only Coke, wash your clothes with Tide and thousands of similar concepts, you'll be ostracized from society and therefore die!

Programs are "habits" which only take 22 to 54 repetitions to be created in your subconscious. Programs can also be installed by physical and/or emotional pain. Someone outside of your self can "install" a program with voice, tone, emphasis and emotional power. Any repetition of: music, voice, written word, picture, symbol, logo, etc. can create a program.

Once identified, programs can be "uninstalled," modified or overwritten to gain control of your life. Read ***Body/Brain – Soul/Mind – Two Entities, With Different Agendas, Equals War.***

Summary

Appreciate your journey, learn your lessons, and make sure you leave a legacy of behavioral changes for review.

I wonder how the tattoos and body piercing are going to play for the Gods. And then there are the amputations to come. Makes you wonder what's going on. No, not really, just remember who's doing the casting, the Cosmic Joker. Look around, how can you take any of it serious? The more bazaar, the better. If you don't think so, just look at the movies and TV shows. Do they pattern life?

And to think you were taking you serious.

Identify the skewed programs running your life, and change them!

Chapter 8
I'm a Little Short Handed
(The Working Title of This Book)

Returning home from Florida International University, in Miami to my home in Jensen Beach (150 miles) from one of my late-night education class, I stopped at the turnpike restaurant to get a snack and some coffee to make it through the commute.

As I approached the counter, the waitress hollered "Coffee?"

I nodded my head and sat down.

She came whizzing by, slid a cup of coffee to me and continued on toward the kitchen. Looking over her shoulder, she said, "I see you're a little short handed tonight."

Well I almost fell off my stool laughing, and so did the other 15 or so customers. From then on it was a weekly stop on my way home. Every time I stopped, she had another "one-armed" joke. Regardless of how rough my week at the university had been, she'd have me laughing in just a few minutes. I've never forgotten her and I owe her a lot, I stole a lot of those jokes.

OK, I heard you say, "So, Lance what does that have to do with anything?"

It has to do with not taking yourself serious. If you can't laugh at yourself, and at yourself with others, you'll be laughed at anyway – behind your back. If you find your life funny (regardless of how bad it may seem), living it will be a lot more fun. All you have to do is step back and get a good perspective on it – from outer space if necessary – and you can't help but laugh. The worst thing which could happen to you is death, right? And that's just wonderful, so stop worrying!

After Arm Lose (AAL) Awareness

When I woke up minus an arm, I accepted it as a challenge and immediately began to problem solve. *How am I going to tie my shoes?* I thought. *Cutting a steak, that'll be interesting. Oh, I can hold the fork in my teeth.* I reasoned. *Cutting my fingernails? I can use my teeth to operate the clippers.*

Each problem was mulled over in my head until I had figured out a solution. As long as I was problem solving, I was fine.

The realizations of the effect of losing an arm began as I lay in the hospital bed recuperating? My whole life I had been a doer, and I could make things happen through force of will. But with the loss of the arm:

I lost my vanity – I was a cripple.

I lost my self-confidence – non-competitive in the job market.

I lost my self-esteem – all my licensed trained vocations and avocations were impacted by the missing arm.

I didn't have sufficient education to do something "mental" – I thought.

I'd been strong mentally, physically and I was cocky, but my ego had taken a serious blow.

Eight days after the amputation, with the arm still draining puss and without a skin graft, I was released from the hospital to go home. I went straight to work to make sure the habitat was ready for the next mission and provide input as to how to sink it. I didn't stay at work long, too weak. Now, I was an under achiever, over achieving, headed for mediocrity. The more strength I gained, the longer I could stay at work.

Eight weeks post amputation, a skin graft was taken from my left hip to cover the raw meat. The day the stitches were removed from the skin graft, I went back in the water. I never allowed myself to whine, complain or blame. The stump became my new ego. Being short handed was just another problem to be solved.

The Castle Vision

Several years AAL, I asked, "What am I supposed to learn from losing the arm?"

"It took you long enough to ask the really important question." The Counselor replied. "Observe."

NOTE: My visions occur while I'm wide-awake, and appear as if they're playing in a surround theatre. I'm not just an observer, but actually involved, at least emotionally.

I was enveloped in a cloud of smoke, and as the smoke drifted down, I was standing on a mountaintop. Looking out over the area, I saw green hills in the distance. There was nothing but smoke in the immediate area. As the smoke moved down farther, surrounding me were ruins, which appeared to be the remains of a castle.

In my right hand was a broken sword. My left arm was still attached to the shield lying at my feet. It was obvious I had been in a tremendous battle from the bodies in the courtyard. Around me lay my armor, bent and damaged. Shouts and moans of the attackers came from the smoke. I had won the battle, but the result was my maiming and the destruction of my castle. I knew, as soon as the smoke cleared and the attackers could see the condition of the castle, there would be another attack.

Looking around me, I could see my wife and three sons were safe. I had protected them from the sure disaster which had been planned by the attacking force.

I noticed "Bravery" written on my shield. When located, the inscription on the broken sword blade read, "Courage." Throughout my life I was always the first to volunteer and always took the most dangerous job or position.

I quickly inspected my damaged armor. Each piece was inscribed, through the blood and dirt I read; "Self-confidence," "Self-esteem," "Self-righteous," "Quick-minded," "Physically-strong," "Hunter-gatherer," "Provider," "Compassionate," "Responsible," "Dependable," and "Honorable."

Coming from the smoke were threats and curses, the attackers would be back to seek vengeance for the slaying of their companions. To protect my family before the next attack, the defenses had to be rebuilt.

Chiseled in the different stones of the destroyed castle walls were all the things I had done during this life to earn money. They were displayed for all to see. The problem now was the stones were toppled and provided no security.

My educational background, the foundation of the castle, had not been destroyed. All my education, seminars, training programs and certificates of completion were inscribed on the foundation. What I knew, was still intact.

The shouts and noise from the smoke signaled impending disaster. It was obvious, with just one arm and only my family for help we could not rebuild the castle in time to defend from the coming attack.

The only thing I could think of was to bluff the attackers. "Hurry," I summoned my helpers, "We must build a façade." Poles were placed next to the foundation and stabilized with loose rocks. All of the bedding and linens were hung from ropes strung between the poles. Paint was used to draw in lines so the façade looked like the former castle. We worked quickly to complete the work before the smoke cleared.

"Help me prepare my armor." I ordered. When assembled we began to hammer out the dents and repair the damage as much as possible. I was dressed in my armor. The sword was backed with a stick, and bound together with rope. The shield was tied to my body to hide my missing arm. I was as ready as possible to attempt the charade on the assembling attackers.

As the smoke cleared from the valley, the hoards were assembling in their camp. Strewn about the grounds were the dead and dying.

Stepping out of the castle with the sun at my back, and raising the sword high, I shouted, "I'll give you one hour to leave this valley, never to return, or I'll come among you and destroy you. As you can see, you've caused no damage to my castle, to me, or to my family. Look at the devastation I've wrought."

Turning, I went back inside the castle and collapsed.

The attackers wasted no time in departing the area. The charade had worked.

"So what is the primary lesson you're to learn from losing an arm?" The Counselor asked.

Then the meaning of the vision began to settle in. "The only real thing which had lasted after the battle and losing the arm, had been what I knew." I said. "What I could do had been destroyed. My personal attributes, my ego, had been built around the do part of my life and are now in question. I'm not competitive in the job market. Even though I can still do most of the things I did in the past, I can't do them as fast. After loosing the arm, I threw up a facade to protect my ego."

"Solomon was right! Vanity, vanity, all is vanity." The Counselor said. "It took the two by four up-side your head multiple times, beating you severely about the head a shoulders with the missing arm and a vivid vision to make you aware of how alive and well your ego/vanity is."

"Thank you." I said, "I just realized most of my life has been a façade."

Whenever my ego would go on a trip (ego trip), I'd be allowed a little slack, then whack, up-side-the-head again and a reminder from my counselor, "Remember the castle?"

Chicken Fights

While I was recuperating from the amputation, I got a chance to watch lots of little roosters. Chicken fights abound in Puerto Rico and our neighbors raised fighting cocks.

I hope you've had a chance to watch baby chicks grow up. At about half grown, the roosters – males – start having "Chicken Fights." They fluff out their feathers to look bigger, dance around flapping their wings showing off, and start the "I'm bigger, better looker, better fighter than you" game.

Sound like human males?

The male chicks will begin to peck each other in their fights, and as soon as one starts bleeding, the others gang up and kill it. In fact, if you're going to raise male chickens, you better eat the males while they're fairly young, or you'll end up with just one left.

As I began to interface with more and more people after the amputation, I noticed a not too subtle change in how men interfaced with me. The ritual human "chicken fight" which goes on anytime men meet wasn't happening. There's really only two things men talk about to each other; "Mines bigger than yours," or "God, ain't it awful."

Well, men didn't play those games with me anymore. It seemed they intuitively knew a fight with me was a "no win" for them. If they won, they'd beat up a cripple, and if they lost, their ego would never recover.

Even if theirs was bigger than mine, they couldn't take the chance of challenging me and being proven lacking. And they didn't even try the "God ain't it awful" because my missing arm was right in front of them and I didn't cut anyone any slack (as you'll read later).

So the little roosters taught me a good lesson and gave me a "leg-up" or should I say "arm off" on other males.

Who are You, Really?

Traveling my life path, eventually an awareness began to form, *Who I am is determined by who I'm with.*

I "acted" different when interfacing with different people. My personality changed, I talked different and used different words. At times I was boastful sometimes not talkative at all. Other times I'd be aggressive then again friendly. Standing up for what I believed or backing down from what I knew was right.

I wondered, *Why do I act so different around different people? Am I trying to impress them, be like them or be different from them? Am I demonstrating my hidden agendas?*

And then a new word – Synergy. It's what happens when people interact. This meant something happens between people, which is not just a result of what they think, say or do. There is some kind of "connection," a melding together, which defies the normal communications techniques I had been taught.

I questioned again, *Could it be, Mind Reading? Was it a Spiritual Connection of the Souls? How could the influence of another person change me so much? Will I ever be able to be myself? Who am I, really?*

I'm still not sure who I am, really. However, the evolution has begun and I like myself a lot better, now, than before. I realize this is a process and not a destination. Beyond survival instincts, life is about developing character. We're shown our character options by everything we experience. Our job is to fix the flaws we observe in ourselves.

Summary

Loosing the arm demonstrated that what you can do can be taken away in an instant. So your physical abilities are great, but can never be depended upon. "Study to show yourself approved, a workman that need not be ashamed." All you have is what you know.

What you learn, know, and experience are what is really important in life – learn on!

Be careful what you base your Ego on, because if the base is destroyed, so is the ego. With the ego goes your self-esteem and self-confidence. The building and destroying of your ego is an ever on-going and changing process. If your ego is attacked, you will do anything to try to protect it. I threw up a façade of competence and ability. I compensated by trying harder, doing the impossible and reaching objectives in spite of difficulties.

Most of who we think we are is a façade. Understanding this part of your life will cause you to want to change.

The next time you're around two men meeting for the first time, be an observer and listen to the conversations. Enjoy the "Chicken Fight" and listen carefully to determine who's using the "Mine's bigger than yours" or "God ain't it awful" approach to one-upsmanship.

Notice how **you** change as you interface with different people – voice gestures, words, tone, attitudes, and personality.

Identify the character traits you admire and make them you.

Chapter 9
Patience

"God, I want patience, and I want it right now!"

I don't suppose you've said something like that.

I have. Be careful what you ask for!

The last time I was masochistic (self punishing) enough to even think that thought, I was sent to Hawaii (or I sent myself). Hawaii has a posted, maximum speed limit of 55 miles per hour. The posted minimum speed limit is 40 miles per hour. Hawaii is the only state of the 48 I've been in where you can depend on doing the minimum speed. In every other state, you can expect to drive over the posted maximum speed or get run over.

In Hawaii, no one is ever on time for anything. If the surfs up, almost everything comes to a standstill. If you're working on patience, may I recommend a move to Hawaii.

One of the things I bought with my arm money was a 1 ¼ acre lot in Hawaii. I dreamed of building a house on the lot from before buying it, had it cleared, prepared for building twice and drew multiple plot and house plans.

After paying off the lot, I moved to Hawaii to start the building process. However, both of the partners who owned the lot died, and it took over 2 ½ years to get clear title. I didn't build on the lot, in fact it just sold – what a relief.

Impatience is its own reward (learning experience). If you want things to run smoothly, you must be patient. If you want everything in the world to cause delays and try your patience, be impatient.

This is another Universal Law – Impatience creates delays. There is a time for everything and everything in its own time. It's obvious, one of the life lessons and behavioral changes needed by virtually everyone is patience.

Learn patience quickly, or it will take a long time. There you go, thinking again. Are you going to go sit in a corner and try figuring that out?

You can have everything you're passionate about, you just can't have it all at once. So establish your priorities, write your goals including dates, make a plan, get started fulfilling your dreams by taking action, but be patient.

Adulthood

The difference between the young and adults is the ability to put off, delay, gratification (Notice this is not doing without). Adulthood is about deciding what you want, setting your priorities and working towards rewarding yourself for being an adult.

I've never heard an older person say they wished they'd spent more time at work. What I've noticed in myself and others is, at the point in time you get life fairly well figured out, you have time to do what you want and you have the money to really enjoy your life, you can no longer physically do what you would like to do.

In the process of making a living and just living most people damage their bodies to the point they have a difficult time functioning physically as they get older.

"If I knew I was going to live this long, I'd have taken better care of my body" the lament of most of the older people. Even if their bodies are in fairly good shape, life experiences have built up fears of taking risks and they won't do things they wouldn't have given a second thought about when younger. There should be a way to retire during your youth, when you're physically fit and adventuresome, then work until you die, that would make a lot more sense.

Another difference between the young and old is the ability to withstand pain. The older you get, the more pain you've dealt with and the easier it is to deal with it.

Aging Gracefully

Bull Shit! I'm going fighting into my senior years. My soul is about 16 years of age, and as I continue to grow older, it keeps writing checks my ass has a difficult time cashing. Gravity has taken over and pulled hair from on top of my head to some very strange places on my body; nose, ears and other unmentionable locations where I would not chose to put hair. Gravity has also pulled my organs down and the more writing and less physical activity, the bigger my belly gets.

This process is so gradual it took walking by a full-length mirror, before I was aware of how much my once youthful body had changed. I was really pissed at myself for letting my body deteriorate so much.

Just when I determined to start on a reduced intake of food and an exercise program, I managed to give myself a hernia. The reduced diet helped, but it's difficult to exercise with your belly lining ripped open. It took over ten years of nursing a hernia and ripping it to the point of having to have it repaired before I'd let the guys in white coats work on me again.

But that's another story, maybe even a book.

Work

Work is you trading life energy for money. You can also "barter" your life energy for what you want by doing what you're capable of in exchange for someone doing what they're good at for you. The IRS will expect you to put a dollar amount on your "barter" and pay taxes – yea right. Pay taxes on what you traded, what you got in exchange, or both? And if you declare the barter, you'll have to name the one you bartered with, and if they don't declare it, will they go to jail and/or get fined? Barter away, the more you can barter, the less you pay in federal, state, and local taxes.

As of this writing, Americans are paying out over 50% of their wages in taxes. We're paying taxes on taxes on taxes. Historically, at 50% taxes, the economic system fails.

Between local, county, state and federal bureaucracies; people on welfare and the retired people; over 50% of the potential working-population are non-producers.

This means less than 50% of the population is supporting over 50%. Historically, when this happens, the society fails!

Our nation is at a critical place where the next step is anarchy, every man for himself. The 50% rule – you check it out, or you could just put your head in the sand. About the only reason anarchy hasn't happened yet is the bureaucracies are in control of the police forces and the military.

I like to work! I enjoy building things, making things work, solving problems, teaching, and managing people. My most productive time at a new job is the first three months. Because of my diverse background, I can identify most of the problems and offer several solutions for each problem. However, repetitive tasks bore me to tears.

Most employers pick out just one of my talents and pigeon-hole me. I don't last long on the job after that. The more challenging the job, the more problems to solve, the more diverse the tasks, the more I like the work.

You must remember the "job" is owned by the employer and is worth a certain wage. The company pays you what the "job" is worth, not what you're worth. To verify this, answer this question, "If you leave the company, do you take the job with you?"

When it comes to a problem needing to be fixed, I'm one of the best at "jury-rigging" something so the job can continue. However, that's just a stop-gap measure. Once back in operation and the immediate problem repaired, I start figuring out how to **_fix_** the problem so it can't happen again. I'm really good at the repair, but even better at fixing things. I hate repairs, because I know the same problem is going to happen again. I want fixes so a given problem never happens again.

These "fixes" include me and other people as well as things.

Work Ethic

Your attitude about work is your work ethic. In the past everyone expected to work long and hard just to make a living. For children, who lived on ranches or farms, work started in the form of chores as soon as they could walk. For others, it was actual factory or mine work starting as young as age six. Many adults labored for 12 to 16 hours per day seven days per week to make enough money or produce enough food just to survive.

In the mid 1800s, 70+ percent, of the population of the US, were African slaves (20%) or Indentured Servants (50+%) - all *slaves*. Hold that thought.

For another percentage of the population, once they started to work for a company, they bought all of their needs from the "company store" on credit, and once in debt, they could never get out. Most of the population in the first 150 years or so after the independence of the US "owed their soul to the company store." They were virtual *slaves* of the "company." They couldn't quit until the debt was paid, and they could never make enough to pay off the debt. The workers children, as soon as they were old enough, had to go to work for the company just to help pay for the child's food and clothing.

So debt (indentured servitude) enslaved most of our nation. Once caught in the trap, there was very little chance out of the slavery.

Bad working conditions, no hope and no future for the working class made Unionization the only recourse for the majority of the working force. However, the government was for the industrialists because they owned property, voted, and generated the government's money. In fact, in the beginning, government troops were used to put down union strikes.

Then a whole series of laws were put into place: to let people without property vote (even women – go figure), control child labor, establish a minimum wage, make business owners responsible for safety in the work place, legislate Compulsory Schooling, etc. But have things changed all that much?

Who are you a slave for? If you're in debt, who is "living big" on the interest you're paying?

The Great American Dream! Own your own home. Own your own car. Have a dozen credit cards to buy whatever you want. Immediate gratification for your desires!

Who really owns your home? If you fail to make the payments on the loan on your house, who's going to take it away from you? If you own your house and you don't pay the property taxes, who's going to take it away from you?

Then you don't own your house, someone else does – the finance company. If you don't pay your property taxes, the county will take it away. You're just renting the ground.

If you don't make the payment on your vehicle, who's going to take it away from you? If you own your vehicle and you don't license it, who's going to fine you and impound your vehicle?

So ownership is "virtual reality" not reality. Slavery (Indentured Servitude) is alive and well today!

Did you know the finance companies (actually you pay for it) carry bankruptcy insurance on all of your unsecured debt and as soon as you declare bankruptcy, they get paid what they loaned you.

The people with money have "hedged their bets" so they don't lose, but remember they also answer to someone. You and generations before you have not paid attention, because you were programmed by the Government Legislated Compulsory Schooling System.

There's plenty of information available for you to learn how money works and what to do to make money work for you.

If you were born in a coal-mining town in West Virginia, what do you think would be the focus of your primary and secondary Compulsory Schooling in the local school district? Maybe how to be a good miner? Now do you think education in a given community is "designed" to keep the working force doing the work of the community?

Given the above information, if you had money, you would want control of the stores, the financial institutions and the educational system. WEEEELLLL, isn't that exactly what has and is happening?

I heard you say, "But what can I do, I'm just a worker bee?"

OK, this means you want my advice, so here goes. First, Grow-up and implement delayed gratification! Second, you must be Self-motivated to learn! Begin right now to decide what's really important to you, then prioritize your needs, wants and desires. Get out of debt ASAP! Learn about money and Financial Intelligence by reading **Rich Dad, Poor Dad** and **The Millionaire Next Door**. Start your own business so you're in control of your own destiny, and pay attention.

Remember, change is inevitable and if you don't change, you'll get left behind – in slavery. If you keep doing and thinking what you've always been doing and thinking, you'll keep getting what you've always been getting. Change!!!

JOB stands for Just Over Broke. Most people have JUBs Just Under Broke – slavery. There are ways out of slavery, but you have to grow up and change your programming.

Enjoy the process!

Workers

I've noticed a change over the years. It appears, in general, the American work force is doing less and less work and expecting more and more money. I estimate the average American worker is actually producing less than 50% of what they're capable of doing. This means they're getting paid over twice as much as they should be paid for the actual work they're doing.

This is good for me, because all I have to do is find some "piece" work which has been valued at the 50% work rate, then do 150% of what everyone else is doing and I make three-times the money they do. That only works for a short time and two things happen: the other workers are embarrassed and the management cuts the piece rate. The workers then make me an offer I can't afford to refuse – leave or else. It was good money while it lasted

My Grandparent's Advice

While I was in high school, I confided to my grandfather, "I can't figure out what I want to do when I grow up. All I want to do is hunt and SCUBA dive."

He said, "When I was your age, hunting was about all I could think about too. But just remember, whatever you want to do now, will change with time."

Whenever I was having a rough time, my grandmother used to tell me what her mother told her, "This to, will pass." That little statement usually didn't help much, but it got repeated enough times it stuck, and it is true – you can depend upon change.

So from a very young age, I knew my wants, needs and desires would change with time, and regardless of what kind of a time (good, bad or indifferent) I was having in the present, it would get better or worse in the future.

Career Choices

I went to work for PADI International College as a SCUBA Instructor Trainer and started my first program assisting one of the staff who was leaving.

The first day we went to lunch was a real revelation. George was a former college football tackle. He was 6 foot 5 inches tall and weighed 275 pounds. He was huge! For lunch, he ordered two double cheeseburgers, two large fries, two milkshakes, and two apple pies. I ordered a single cheeseburger, small fries, and a medium soda.

It cost him at least three times what it cost me for food, just to support his size. I knew his SCUBA equipment all cost more than mine due to the size. His clothes all cost more than mine. And his vehicle had cost more, because it had been modified to accept his frame.

In everything he did, it cost him more money than the same activity cost me.

The reason he was leaving the diving profession was to make more money. He had to, just to survive. Hold that thought.

At one time, I was a career planner. And one of my responsibilities was to "assess" different careers. As practice, I tended to do this wherever I was. The exercise was to break a job down into its basic sub-jobs. In this way, skills from one job could be related to other unrelated jobs allowing people to move into other trades without complete retraining.

One morning I was having breakfast at Denny's, and decided to analyze the waiting job. I mentally broke down the job skills of the waitress who was serving me. That evening, Judy and I went to one of the fancy restaurants near Sea World. This was a high end, cook at your table, wear fancy clothes, charge a lot of money place. I again applied my craft, and analyzed the waiter's skills.

The end result surprised me. The basic job skills of the Denny's waitress and the fancy restaurant waiter were exactly the same. The difference was the amount of money they made.

Then I had the privilege to break down the "job skills" of a housewife. This person told me she had no work experience or job skills. As we began to look at what job skills were required of a housewife and the time involved, even I was amazed.

Let me list just a few of the required and integrated skills a housewife must develop to do her "job." These jobs include: banking, basic accounting, planning, teaching, negotiating, food preparation, dietician, nursing, management, janitorial, entertaining and many more. One of the things most employers want to know is how much experience you have. Considering their reference is a forty-hour week, the housewife works at least 12 hours per day, seven days per week or over 84 hours per week. The housewife was ecstatic! She not only had saleable skills, but a long work history.

No, I won't do career planning or write your resume for you – do your own.

How Much Will You Allow Yourself to Earn?

As I began to look at the jobs and earnings of different people, it was evident, how much money you make is controlled by what believe you're worth. You have a built-in (programmed-in) limit as to what you think you and your skills are worth. You also have a belief about how much a given job skill is worth. And a basic belief (taught to you) about money. Then embedded deep, is what education or training you believe is required to "get ahead" in today's market.

What you tend to do when looking for a job is compare the job description with your "qualifications." You discount transferable skills, work experience, ability to learn (change), and your work ethic – attitude. You then pull a number out of your head, and that's what you'll work for. The number is there, it was programmed/taught into to you by your family, peers, schooling and life experience. If the number is low, you'll work for Denny's, but if it is high, you'll make much more doing the same job working for a high-class restaurant.

If you want to make more money, you have to "change your programming" – first.

Does experience count? Yes! Does education count? Yes! Does skills training and expertise count? Yes! But you will still limit how much you make – mentally, because it's programmed in your hard drive.

Lock in your brain, that the most important thing and the thing you have control of are your attitude and thoughts. You must reprogram your android computer to earn more money.

When you marry and need more money you'll find a way to earn it by reprogramming. If you set a goal, focus, and work towards the goal, you'll attain it if it's programmed in. You can reprogram your basic internal drive. If you don't change what your program is, even if you get a "windfall" of money, you'll get rid of it - somehow.

Shit Happens

I've never liked whiners and complainers. I put up with a lot less of it now than I used to.

I believe the Souls script their own lives. If so, then why are people complaining about what they wrote, directed, and are acting out in their own life's movie?

I'll admit, while your movie is going on, some of the things are not necessarily "fun." But have you ever seen anyone pitch a fit over going to the bathroom to take a dump? Have you ever heard them say, "I hate taking a dump. I don't like the way it feels coming out, I don't like the way it smells, and that wiping thing is awful, if you poke through the paper your finger gets stinky."

NO! They just go do their job – careful to fold the paper several times.

OK, so some of life is like taking a dump. Just do it and get on with the learning process. Someone has to clean the house, do the laundry, buy and cook the food, go to work, do the dishes, take out the garbage, etc.

Every job has things which have to be done, so why complain? If you don't like something, fix it or re-script it. Quit Bitching!

Whatever you do, avoid putting one of those stickers on your car, or you'll have "Shit Happen." That's scripting for everyone to see and act on. Did you ever notice the vehicles displaying "shit happens" stickers have been in accidents?

The Buddhists have a saying about seeking enlightenment, "When on the road to nirvana chop wood, carry water. When you reach nirvana, chop wood, carry water." In other words, just do what needs to be done.

Sometime good shit happens to good/bad people.

Sometimes bad shit happens to good/bad people.

Question not shit, just live with it – or learn your lessons and move on. Shit has a purpose in the bigger plan - to create opportunities to change your behavior.

If you get involved with shit, pay attention!

Summary

Learn to be patient, now, or it can take you a long time and be very frustrating.

Learn to delay gratification and deal with pain.

Get out of debt and stay out of debt!

Remember the employer doesn't owe you a job and the government doesn't owe you a living. You chose this life, so make the best you can of your circumstances. If you don't like the work, change your occupation. You can change your occupation by gaining knowledge and learning new skills.

When you work – trade your life energy for money – work! Try to always give your employer at least 110% for what they're paying you. You need to do this for you, for your self-esteem, and for the person who has provided you with the opportunity to earn a living.

Pay attention, be ready to change when necessary, and know whatever is going on is going to pass.

Quit your bitching! Chop wood, carry water! Work is a part of the learning experiences you scripted into your life's movie - enjoy.

Attitudes of Wealth

As a result of our life experiences, a program has been developed and then through reinforcement become a habit. This program controls how much Wealth we will allow ourselves to have. Programmed into the cells of our body is a $ amount we will allow ourselves to have. The 22 to 54 repetitions of your Money Blueprint started while you were still forming in the womb and continues throughout your life. Until you change the program, you will not allow yourself to earn more money. You will sabotage any effort, or job, or business, or commission or source of income. This is why the vast majority of Lottery winners are bankrupt within two years of winning a lottery. If you do not change your brain/memory/programming, you will not change! If you keep doing what you've always been done, you'll keep getting what you've always gotten.

I'm going to suggest a book and from the book a program that will dramatically change your stored-memory limit on what you will allow yourself to have financially. *Secrets of the Millionaire Mind* by T. Harv Eker and the *Millionaire Mind Intensive Seminar.*

If you really want to increase your wealth while on this planet with infinite possibilities, and infinite abundance read the book and attend the seminar.

For further info and a testimonial, contact me.

Enough said?

Chapter 10
Why do You Believe What You Believe?

Everyone has a belief system! So how did you end up with your belief system? What makes your belief system different from or the same as other belief systems? Why is what you believe important, and to whom is it important? What do you really believe? Just when you thought you had some answers, more questions.

At one time I believed in Santa Claus, the tooth fairy, the Easter bunny and the Bible (all Myths). After finding out the "truth" it was difficult to believe anything adults told me ever again – thanks UI! Keeping the doubt to myself, I relied only on those things which could be proven (though not necessarily by scientific means).

What things in your belief system have changed as you collected more data and life experiences?

Here's a simple "template" you can use to determine the validity of anything, *"Works – Doesn't Work."* You can use these three words to validate anything – science, thoughts, dreams, beliefs (religions) and more. Works – Doesn't Work – ***works***!

So, you *can* change your belief system with more data and life experiences, you've been doing it your whole life.

Depending on viewpoint, every "belief system" is a myth. Myths are a combination of fact and fiction – "faction." Originally I tried writing non-fiction, but discovered it was virtually impossible to make it interesting. I took a non-fiction writing class, and the freedom to write came with one word – faction – a combination of fact and fiction. But then I realized that's exactly how humans write/describe everything – faction. Talk to a fisherman – the fish gets bigger with each telling.

The purpose of this chapter is to help you gain some perspective on where your Belief/Myth System came from. May the "Force" be with you!

What you have been taught

In your formative years, you received data pertaining to your beliefs from your parents, family, friends, teachers, enemies, religionists (ministers, preachers, priests, mullahs, oracles, gurus, monks, rabbis, etc.).

Without additional input, you bought into what you were told. So the questions are, "Why do *they* (the people who taught you) believe in their myths?" and "*Who* taught them to believe their myths?"

What you have read

When you grew older, you began to read and collect data from books. Which religious books did you read? Which "version" of the religious books did you read? As your readings expanded, you received additional information about science, life, and universal laws. Who "interpreted," explained the meaning of the information you read in the books? How much of the explanation was biased by the myth of the interpreter?

What you have experienced

Life creates Myths, which, when coupled with Religious and Spiritual events, insights, and communications with God (your wee small voice), lock into your psyche.

Since you filter the data from your experiences through your box of filter screens, you don't collect all of the truth, including all of the spiritual truths. You develop your own special, skewed myths.

For example: How would original man, without books and preachers, with just personal experiences, have developed a concept of God? Can you define God without using what you've been taught? Can you back off and look at everything – cosmic dust to all existing life – and have an "original" thought about the creator of all that exists? Could an entity, powerful enough to create all that exists, "need" anything from us? Could this entity which created all life be vengeful?

What if . . . the creator is just "playing" with life in all its forms to gather data – a laboratory experiment?

What if . . . the human perception of God is the result of applying human nature to God, and the reverse, applying God's nature to humans is what's supposed to be happening?

What if . . . all the "messages" sent by God, via humans were skewed by the humans receiving and passing on the messages? Did you ever play telephone?

What if . . . in all the God messages, a simple common thread actually exists but it's distorted by humans due to interpretation, presentation and hidden human agendas?

What if . . . the concept of God is so encompassing – "God is all things and benevolent" – it's difficult for humans to accept?

What if . . . all of our attempts to define God, i.e. what God needs from us, what we must do to please God, punishment and reward via God are not true?

What if . . . our most basic beliefs in God are not true? Could these skewed beliefs be the reason for the problems between nations and religions – therefore the problems on earth? Could these skewed ideas about God be why we have no respect for the earth's eco system?

Works – Doesn't Work – applied!

If we're a part of God and God is everything, then we're part and parcel with everything. This includes all humans – we are all ONE organism. Do you think if that concept/belief was universal then peace and ecological recovery would happen?

But, OH my, who would you have to be better than? Who would be your enemy? What would happen to the churches and their leaders? Without lying, cheating, stealing, murder and greed – what would we do, what would we do?

OK, time for that corner thing again – take fluids and snacks.

What has been "quickened" to you

When presented with special life lessons, all of us have experienced goose bumps, deep feelings, epiphanies, a "calling," visions, and/or confirmations (tests for God to perform) and you know truth has just been presented to you. Couple these "special" occurrences with death and/or out of body experiences and you can develop a powerful myth. You do know this book is my Myth.

The Written Word

The Bible was written 400 years **after** Jesus died, commissioned by an idol worshiper with a hidden agenda. Did you ever play "telephone" and have the original message so modified through several tellings, it was unrecognizable? You do know there are several different "versions" of the bible. So which "version" of "The Word of God," edited by which human(s) with a personal "box of reference," an agenda and specific motivation do you believe?

I believe the Bible was written by God/man. I believe there are many universal truths in the bible. I believe a force, outside of the human, influences us to do many things (Soul/God). I don't believe "God" stopped talking to and influencing humans 2,000 years ago.

Life is a dynamic process, and human evolution is much more than the "decent from monkeys" theory.

I believe every single human/soul/God has a purpose/reason/message to share. From the best to the worst, youngest to oldest, we get to see and experience the yin/yang of the human possibilities. Through this data we're able to decide how we wish to be and develop our own myth/belief. How do you wish to be? Can you define the "perfect" you? What would your ideal myth be?

Can a 2,000 year-old book of myths really suffice in the age of e-mail, e-commerce, science, air travel, space exploration, cloning and worldwide communications? When is mankind going to take the important evolutionary step back/forward to an increased spirituality and utilization of the inherent Soul/God we are and the Mind/Brain-power available to it?

What if, the basic concept of God as presented in **_ALL_** of the religious books of all of the different religions and interpreted by the leaders of those varied religions is wrong? What if God is not vengeful, needy, or separated from us? Would that change how we conduct our lives? Why have myths (beliefs) been changed with the selection of a new Pope? Why did we stop the crusades? Did we stop the crusades?

NOTE: Whenever I refer to the Bible, I include all other published, "religious" works. When I reference "religions" I include them all. (I have my own myths based on past history also.)

Expectations

A universal truth, what you believe in manifests itself in your life – regardless of or because of your belief/myth. So as you build your own personal myth/belief system throughout your life, it becomes "true" for you. The universe lines up, because of your expectations, to provide proof to you, your system is true. Therefore, every belief system which has ever been, is, and ever will be has been or will be proven "true" to the believer(s).

The Universal Law is: "What is in your brain reveals itself in your reality." What you expect through faith – happens. What you focus on happens. What you put emotional power to will be created.

Mythical Guideline

Those things which are comfortable for you mentally, physically and emotionally, make them a part of your life. Those things which are uncomfortable for you mentally, physically and emotionally, eliminate them from your life. If it hurts, quit doing it – DA! This is your job, which you wrote into your plan before you took on your body. You find out about the yin/yang of the human possibilities through interface with other humans, observation of other humans and personal experiences. So interface often and pay attention to everything which happens to and around you.

Question Your Belief System

Identify and question your beliefs. Change and modify your belief system often. Are you absolutely sure you have the truth, the whole truth, and all the truth so help you, you/God?

Is it possible for you to have all the truth, and others to have none?

Are you wasting away your now time dreaming, hoping you're going to make it to heaven and live happily ever after? What if this is heaven/hell and after you transition, everything is just wonderful? What if *Dante's Inferno* (hell fire and damnation) was just a figment of Dante's imagination, which has served the churches to hold you in slavery?

What if "heaven" is just someone's wishful imagination and the promise of a reward to manipulate you, and you bought into the dream of something better to come – the carrot – when in reality, you're going to experience it anyway.

What if your belief system is not all correct? Can you come up with an alternative?

What if your religion is not the one that's got a place in heaven?

Why, after 2 million years of existence on this planet, are humans now down-breeding, positioned to destroy all life on this planet and regressing mentally and spiritually? Could the problem be, what we believe, because of what we've been taught, is WRONG?

You can put your head in the sand (watch your ass) or question everything – just a choice.

Summary

OK, are you at least open to new data? Are you thinking about what your belief systems are based on? Will you pay more attention to your own "wee small voice?" Do you know how to personally prove the difference between truth, fiction and myth?

Simply put, does what you believe in work for the overall good of **_ALL_** life on this planet or doesn't it work. Works or Doesn't Work can be used as a "truth" template for virtually everything – try it, you'll like it.

Can you identify the yin/yang in your life, actions, thoughts and myth?

I hope you said yes to at least most of these questions. Ya done good! You're on your way to making you the way you want to be.

Enjoy the heaven/hell you've created here on earth as you have your experiences.

See you at the feast!

Situations and Circumstances

Given: Everyone's life is a series of situations and circumstances from which they are offered the opportunity to learn and change their behavior. The overall purpose of life is to create the you, you want you to be – personality and character.

The Problem: Given everyone could have exactly the same event at the same time in their life, what they would learn (behavioral change) would be different due to individual perception (what you were taught), individual perspective (how you view life) and the individual emotional response to the event. Therefore, a given event will elicit an infinite number of responses based on the humans experiencing it.

Future Response: If it were possible to have exactly the same event in the future, each individual would have a different response, due to life experience and behavioral changes. If the response was close to the original response, then learning (behavioral change) did not occur the first time.

Programmed-in-Responses: Similar responses to similar events are indications that habitual programs are running your life. If the responses are not advancing you as a human being, then a programming change is necessary.

Chapter11
Esotericness

You knew this was coming. There'd be no reason to bring you this far if it wasn't going to get weirder. So get yourself something to drink and a snack, you may need the energy.

I've found, in order to see/understand something clearly, it's best to look at both ends of the spectrum: good-bad, right-wrong, left-right, black-white, works-doesn't work, best case-worst case, etc.

Since in my opinion, life is about learning and changing my behavior, I have to know what my options are. Since I have a definite aversion to anyone telling me what I should believe, I must explore the possibilities myself. Since I know about the 50% rule, I know my best guess will be less than expected because of incorrect, slanted and incomplete data. I also know the results of my taking a risk and doing something will provide more data upon which I can base wiser decisions.

So my normal way of trying to learn is to look at the extremes. By looking at the best case versus the worst case, I have options in my choice. If there's only one answer, I have no options.

I like to think about a pendulum. It reaches each side of its extreme swing ½ as many times as it passes the center. What I try to do is "center" myself, my thoughts, and my decisions. If you think I compromise everything, you're right or left or center.

As I am writing this, the Israelis and Palestinians are having at each other – again. Because of what each side has been *"taught"* to believe about the One God there's no workable solution for either side.

The only solution is just what was supposed to happen when the Jews first returned from Egypt – genocide of all people in the "Promised Land." One or the other side must be wiped out – completely. Unlike in the time of the bible, this is virtually impossible now, because of how far a field they're spread in other nations. This same "battle" has been being fought for thousands of years. No one's learning. So I guess the only solution is the elimination of all mankind so there can be peace on earth. Then the spirits can start the game over again, maybe they'll just go back to dinosaurs.

The New Revelations

A little timeline, my arm was amputated January 8th, 1973 and I'm editing this section of the book January 8th, 2005 my 32nd year anniversary of the arm amputation. It has taken time for me to accumulate my life experiences, to gather information and confirmation from books and other people, and learn to write.

I just completed reading **The New Revelations – A Conversation With God** by Neale Donald Walsch. I believe what he has written is absolutely right-on. I refer you to this book at this point, because from my perspective, what it says about God is correct. This is, I believe, an important reading reference for you – get it and read it, it will help you to find truth and gain understanding

Neale, thanks for the confirmation.

Now let's explore what life is about, and how everything could turn around if we would just pay attention to why we're here on this planet. The solution to all of the world's problems! And for the price of this one book – uh, make it two books.

Mistakes

Mistakes? Well maybe not. Your life is your movie. You write the script, you direct, you act, and other people play bit parts in your drama. The spirit world is the "casting director" for your movie. Since this is true, then they're not "mistakes" – errors, but "mis-takes"– do-overs – just another "take" in your life's movie.

An event didn't turn out the way you think you scripted it, so, given the new data you received as a result of the mis-take, try it again (another take), and again until you get it right by learning your lesson demonstrated by your positive behavioral changes, or die.

It's OK to have mis-takes in your life's movie. How else are you going to learn? Life's not about getting a good GPA where you have to get good grades to advance. Life is the "school of hard knocks" where you often get the test before you get the text. The problem with life is with each lesson **not** learned – behavioral modification – the more "intense" the lesson's going to be the next time. So whenever you have an uncomfortable experience, stop, pay attention, analyze, ponder, learn, change your behavior, and get on with life.

Consider the woman who marries a man who abuses her. She gets a divorce and then marries another man who abuses her, only this time the abuse is worse. She's not learning her lessons.

My brother John was going through his second divorce and was having a pretty rough time. He looked up to heaven and said, "God, I don't care how bad this has to be, I want to learn my lesson this time. I don't ever want to go through this again."

That's the best explanation of life I've ever heard, and the best prayer you could voice. He didn't blame his spouse, he didn't ask God to "Take this learning lesson away." He asked for help in learning his lesson so he could change **<u>his</u>** behavior – not the behavior of someone else.

I've never worried about making mistakes when I was doing something new. But if I make the same mistake over, I get real pissed – at myself. It means I'm not paying attention – my fault.

I've always warned people who worked for me, "I don't care if you're making mistakes when you're first learning to do something. However, if you want to see me real pissed, just keep making the same mistakes over and over." Several people have passed out from under my guidance for repeating mistakes.

The Devil Made Me Do It

The Devil/Satan, God, boss, parents, peers, race, society, religion, politics, laws, rules, weather, natural disasters nor anything else made you do anything! The sooner you accept this, the faster you can quit blaming things outside of yourself and take responsibility for how you scripted your movie. You chose to take on a body, you chose your parents, you chose to concentrate on this frame of time, and you chose to be in a certain place at a given time. You scripted your movie, and sometimes it just doesn't turn out the way you "think" you planned it. Well there's more to you living your life than just you. While others are playing bit parts in your life movie, you're playing bit parts in other peoples' movies. And Mother Nature is working with the Cosmic Joker to make it all interesting and help us to learn life lessons.

There are physical, spiritual, and universal laws, which we function within, but each individual's life is like the ball in a pinball machine. We all intuitively know what the objective is, return to the spirit world – get to the escape hole – death. But the pinball game of life really is fun. You can just be born and return immediately (father and mother learn some life lessons) you managed to make it straight to the exit hole – your choice/agreement with the souls you interfaced with in the "Planning Room." You can live an adventure-filled, long and changing life gathering data so you can make wise decisions. Sit in front of the TV and eat yourself to death. Or live anything in between. Your choice!

You can have life anyway you really want it. If you don't like the way your life is, change it! And quit asking to win the lottery. You don't really want to win it or you would. I know you've been thinking, "I would really like to win the lottery and be rich and that would solve everything."

Apparently being rich is not what you scripted into your life's movie this time around. You scripted in lessons and until you learn those lessons, how are you going to script in anymore? In other words, if you want to change your scripted life, learn the "now" lessons quick. Then you can have whatever you want.

"Really?" you said.

"Really!"

So if you don't have what you think you want, it's because you have unfinished business in the behavior category – change you brain and your behavior.

What is, *IS*. Accept it and get on with your life. If you don't like it, learn, and change it.

If you want to do yourself a real favor, do an "Insight Seminar" www.insightseminars.org. They're based out of Santa Monica, California. I was privileged to attend two of these seminars, and they taught me to take responsibility and love myself.

Empathy

One of the amazing things I learned from loosing an arm was empathy. In my Before Arm Loss (BAL) life, I could find it in myself to "feel sorry for" others less fortunate than myself – sympathy. But sympathy means you're "better than" those you're feeling sympathy for. That's an ego thing. You can always find someone somewhere "worse off" (in your perception) than you are, to feel sympathy for (better than).

Once you understand the body has no meaning except as a vehicle to transport the soul, and the body is expendable, a lot changes in your perception of things. It really changes when you accept you're the writer, director, and primary actor in your life's movie. Whatever happens to you (your body), you have scripted into your life – everything.

I've walked up to people in wheelchairs and asked, "So what life lessons are you trying to learn from doing this to yourself?" (I don't do it to everyone, only those I'm lead to ask the question.)

NOTE: these are complete strangers.

They have in each instance reacted as if someone had just hit them with a ball bat. Their mouths drop open, and they get a real far away look in their eyes. I have yet to have gotten an answer, but I'm sure the question was not for me, but for the other person to pay attention to the real reason they chose to be in the wheelchair.

What have you chosen to put yourself through?

This section is about empathy, so what does the above have to do with it? I can look at someone and understand what they're putting themselves through to learn who they are. With the physical pain, the frustration, the emotional upheavals, the examples to others, and the lessons learned. Everyone has their own "special" way to create an environment in which to learn. Should you feel sorry for them?

NO!!

Admire them for their inventiveness and script writing ability.

When I was involved in "Evangelistic Training" I came to understand every single person, regardless of affliction can be made whole (be healed) through the "laying on of hands." What amazed me was some people were healed, and within a short time, they were afflicted again. The answer seems simple now, they hadn't learned their lessons yet. They hadn't finished the process of modifying their behavior the affliction provided them.

Wisdom

Solomon of the bible was "doin' good," and God decided to reward him. God said, "Solomon, choose whatever you want."

Solomon said, "I'll take wisdom."

God made him the richest man in the world, and gave him 700 wives and 300 concubines.

Following Solomon's example, I've been asking, "God give me wisdom!"

You know, in order to make wise decisions, you must have experiences in which you screw up so you can gather new data, correct the incorrect data and learn to control your emotions. Solomon didn't write about his screw-ups, but with all his interpersonal relationships, he certainly had lots of chances to learn his lessons and become wise.

Cutting Others Some Slack

"Beep, Beep, Beep, Beep!" You shut off the alarm, and go back to sleep.

Angry at having to hurry so you won't be late for work and have the threat of losing your job – a survival threat – you're driving aggressively. Ahead of you, a driverless car, is doing the "minimum" allowed speed. Your anger builds. Finally, you manage to pass the "no driver" car. Your angry glance at the driver revels a little, old, blue-haired lady wearing thick glasses, and navigating via the power lines, because there is no way she can see over the hood. You swerve in front of her, to vent your anger, causing her to brake. You yell, "Why does she still have a driver's license?"

And then someone in the far left lane cuts across three lanes of traffic to make an off ramp, causing you to brake and stimulating your anger again – because again your survival was threatened. Of course the offender was just daydreaming, almost missed his exit, and if he's late to work again, he will be fired.

I know this has never happened to you, but go along for the ride a bit more.

You, they, and everyone always make 100% correct decisions. If their decision is 100% correct, then why are you angry with them? You caused this problem by shutting off the alarm and going back to sleep.

Take some responsibility! If you're making 100% correct decisions, then you must give the same consideration to others. Understand about survival and its relationship with anger and cut yourself some slack, get up when the alarm goes off!

I hope you can expand this example to encompass all aspects of your life, otherwise, this book will have to be 10,000,000 pages long. The next time you see that "blue-haired lady," just laugh – it's funny –avoid an accident having fun.

Need

As the Aquatics Sports Director at a resort in Haiti, I had an opportunity to observe a very different culture from the one in which I was raised. Haiti is the only nation in existence today, formed as the result of a slave revolt.

The first noticeable thing was the Haitians appeared to be happy. They had a good work ethic, worked hard, and were helpful to each other. They'd get together after work every night, to tell "tourist stories" and belly laugh for hours. I have never seen a happier group of people. In spite of the "do gooder" religious groups in the area, the local Voodoo priest was the one who visited and cared for the local workers.

Even though they worked in a fairly "high class" resort with toilets, showers, beds, walls, windows, screens, furniture, hot and cold running water, electricity, etc. they didn't appear to want, need, or expect anything more than their grandfather had. Their basic accommodations in the villages were stick houses with palm frond roofs and covered around the outside, about half way up, with banana or royal palm "sheets" with the upper portion open to the breeze. They made fences out of coconut palm fronds buried into the ground and woven together. Almost everything which grew provided building materials, food or medicine. In the tropics, very few if any clothes are required to stay warm, so the Haitians' basic survival needs were taken care of with little work.

Yes they were poor by our standards. With what little money they made working in the resort, they lived "the good life." Sooner or later they would make the cardinal mistake, buy a portable radio. Now they had "Need" for batteries to make it work. Technology had them, and there was no turning back. They now had to make money to support their "Need." Worse yet were the radio advertisements, which lead them to become dissatisfied with their place in life and created in them the desire (programs) for "stuff" which they could not take from Nature or manufacture with simple hand tools.

The more you "Need" the more of a slave you become – to someone. The more you "Need," the more others are in control of your life.

Have you ever wondered why people would move to a cabin in the woods or buy a sailboat to get away? They're trying to reduce the deadly clutches of "Need" – talk about an addicting drug.

Stuff and Things

My mother said many times, "Oh, that's just stuff and things. You won't be taking it with you when you die." All of our things: toys, props, vehicles, structures, clothes, tools, food, etc. are created from nature. Given time, all of these things will be recycled back into nature, including our bodies. So all this "stuff" we put so much value on is just "stuff and things" which are going to be recycled. Just how important can any of it be? When you die, you're not going to take any of it with you. It may serve you here and now, but not where we're going to end up. Perhaps a different perspective is in order?

Oops, if you quit buying the stuff, think of all the people who're going to be on unemployment.

The fastest growing and most profitable commercial real estate right now is "Storage Facilities." When people accumulate more stuff than their garages can hold, they need a place to store the overflow. When the renters of the storage units, the owners of way too much stuff (some of it never used), die, their heirs have to deal with the deceased's stuff. The most often asked question by the heirs when they show up at the storage facility is, "Where's the nearest dump?"

Someone to be against

There's a psychological precept which basically says we gain our "identity" by who/what we're against. It says, in order for us to advance we must have an "enemy" and conflict. We need a "War" to feel secure in ourselves, to have an identity. The more substantial the enemy, the better we feel about ourselves.

Our "war" can be anyone or anything we can "be against." This "enemy" you chose to go to war with can be another religious belief, another country, a personal enemy, a sports team, or a different race or culture. Your war could also be any number of causes: pro or anti abortion, environmental concerns, civil rights, a given war, drugs, drunk drivers, crime, the criminal justice system, the death penalty, the rich/poor, the stock market, the government, political party, president, etc.

Keep in mind, today's hated enemy is tomorrow's trusted and loyal friend, and today's friend may be tomorrow's enemy. You automatically go to war against your competitors for a mate. You may hate and fight the IRS. Whatever you chose to be at war with, you'll tend to be engaged in one "War" or many at any point in time. The choice of your "War" is demonstrated by what you say. Listen carefully to you, pay attention.

Figure out if this is your war, or if you're just trying to "fit into a group" so you won't be "kicked out of the cave." Is your war dependant on your view through your box and filters, i.e. perspective, perception and your emotions? Did you go to war for your mate, family, church, or political party? Did the government force you (by conscription) to go to war? Is the government's enemy really your enemy? Does your war change based on who you're with?

If you step back, kick some holes in your box and gather objective data can the "reason" for your war go away? If the war goes away, can you make "peace" with your enemy? Do you really want peace?

The Bible says, when you hear everyone talking about peace, war is imminent. Choose your "War" carefully and realize what it's really all about – your identity and self esteem. The "I Am" of your ego. Dealing with your Ego is a big enough war – trust me on this.

Someone to be Better Than

Now you have a war/cause, you need someone to be "better than." This is an interesting program, because it's the "little rooster" thing, which involves "pecking order." Regardless of how far down the pecking order you find yourself, you have to find at least one person you can be "better" than.

This is another part of the basic survival programs. If looks and/or physical prowess don't set you apart as "better than," then it may be played out by being: uglier, dumber, fatter (bigger), worse, weaker, sicker, poorer, smaller or some other extreme just so you can be better or worse than someone.

Different From

In order to "stand out in a crowd" you need to be different than the norm. Individualism is a part of our basic programming. "Different from" others is part of the survival instinct, because if we don't "stand-out" we don't get to breed. If everyone is the same, then there's no choice. Hair, jewelry, clothing, make-up, body condition, tattoos, and how we talk, walk, or gesture can set us apart from others.

Be Right

Deep inside you need to be "right." If you're not right, then you must be wrong and that goes against survival. Have you ever witnessed someone do every thing possible including lie, to prove they were right about something they knew was wrong? It's "Basic Programming" at work. You can be right or you can be rich. You can be right or you can be happy. Your choice!

Join-up

Conform to and join a group to avoid ostracism. Every "group" has its own initiation and rules. To be a part of a group, you must: pass the initiation phase, follow the rules, look similar to the others, and do something. You may belong to several different groups at the same time – just to make life interesting. When the different group activities are in conflict, the fun begins. If the groups go to war, then you have to make choices.

Confusion

So you need – are programmed – to go to war, be better than someone, be different from the norm, be right, conform to and join-up to a group. I don't know about you, but I'm confused. Maybe its time for some reprogramming.

No Respecter of Persons

You're a unique, special God, a part of the all-encompassing God from which we all came and to which we will all return. You don't need to bow to, defer to, pay honor to, or take a back seat to anyone! And this includes because of money, political position, religion, race, education, skill, or physical ability. Give each person their due, which they "earn," but also honor yourself for why and what you're doing here.

Natural Disasters

I heard you say, "But what about Natural Disasters? Surely I didn't create these things – hurricanes, tornados, floods, lightning, tidal waves, volcanic eruptions, avalanches, earth quakes, ice storms, etc."

You agreed with the other souls to let them happen and put yourself in the place where you would be affected. You didn't have to move there, you could have left, you could have changed your plans (written your script differently).

Accept responsibility for where you are and when you're there. It makes a big difference in how you view the world. It also makes a difference in how you view what happens to you and to others. A different viewpoint makes disasters take on a whole new meaning. Disasters are radical opportunities for you to learn some very important life lessons and have them stick. Maybe it takes a disaster to get through to you and others. It took one to get my attention, and the actual learning is still going on.

One example; Think about the lessons learned by the people who live in a trailer park when they're hit by a tornado. Just how important is all your "stuff" if it can be gone in an instant? (You know Mother Nature hates trailers, right?)

If you were involved in this experience, when the tornado is over, what's your reaction going to be? Would you be pissed at God or Mother Nature or would you accept responsibility for choosing where you live? Would you feel sympathy or empathy for the people who put themselves through the adventure? How would you deal with the radical emotional swings immediately before, during, and after? Would you cry out to God to save you? Would you "cut a deal" with God if she saves your life? What kind of a deal? What would those emotions be like for you? If you survived, would you be worried about finding as much of your stuff as possible, or helping the injured and looking for the dead? Would you buy another mobile home in "tornado alley" or move to a different location so you could have a different kind of "Natural Disaster?" How would you feel about having your home destroyed by a tornado in a place where there had never been a tornado before? And then, how would you feel to find out your "home owners" insurance policy didn't cover tornado damage?

You know you can't hide from Mother Nature (or yourself).

I've spent a large portion of my life in California. When I'm in any other location and I mention California, the locals always say, "I wouldn't live in California, there are too many earthquakes."

You know what? I've been a lot of places, and it really doesn't matter where you live, there's always something natural you have to put up with. The strongest earthquake in the US happened on the upper Mississippi River – a major fault zone. Make peace with Mother Nature, and be ready to run, or stay for the adventure.

In the over eight years I lived in Florida, we had torrential rains, hurricanes, and tornadoes. The one time we decided to leave the keys because of a hurricane, as we drove north, it followed us up the coast.

You may be able to run, but you can't hide. The weather people are getting better, but they don't know what's going to happen, because they don't even look outside. 50% chance of rain, yea right.

When I was young, we lived in Southeastern Colorado. We were snowed in, for 30 days – nothing in or out. I've experienced ice storms, floods, lightning storms, earthquakes, rode out two hurricanes at sea, and witnessed volcanoes in Hawaii.

With what I've been through, I'm a fatalist. If I choose to go, then I'm gone. If I choose to stay, then nothing could kill me. Stuff doesn't matter, the body doesn't matter, and only the memory of the experiences and what I can learn from them is important.

In Mother Nature there are neither punishments nor rewards – there are consequences.

Don't Tempt Fate

What does "Don't tempt fate" mean? Does it mean my fate is already predestined, and I'm not supposed to go against the plan? Does it mean I'm just to go along for the ride? If I tempt fate, did I script it or am I now outside of my plan? If you're afraid of something, and you move through the fear, is that tempting fate? If you don't tempt fate, how are you going to exit this life? Are smokers tempting fate? Is driving a vehicle tempting fate?

Tempt away, get out there, take some risks, have some adventures, face your fears, learn, and change.

That's Impossible

In the not too distant past, if you wanted to get me going, tell me I couldn't do something with one arm. "Lance, you'll never be able to fly a plane again, that's impossible with only one arm." "Lance, you can never be a SCUBA Instructor Trainer, because you'll have to be a First Aid Instructor, CPR Instructor, and Water Safety Instructor first, and to do those with one arm is impossible." "You'll never be able to rewire your vehicle with one hand, that's impossible."

You know, they were right, but I put myself through hell to prove "them" wrong, and did those things and a lot more. Writing this book on my computer should also tell you something, I cut no one slack.

After discarding my arm for the experiences it would provide me, I went back to college. One of the courses I took was "Computer Programming" – the old punch card method. The professor gave us our assignment, and immediately several students started complaining about having to type. (let's see, taking computer programming but can't type.) I was sitting in the front row, stood up, turned around and said, "I suggest you shut up or get out. If I can do it so can you," I turned back around and sat down. The professor's jaw was almost on the floor. Suffice to say there were no more complaints. Damn, I hate whiners.

"Would'a, could'a, should'a, if"

"I would'a done so and so, if such and such hadn't happened." "I could'a done this and that, if my mate had supported me." "I should'a done this wonderful event, only that horrible thing happened."

Give these statements up! Cut them out of your vocabulary. These are all excuses for a lack of action. If you really want to do something – do it! But quit complaining and making excuses. If you say something like that to me, I'm going to ask you, "Who is in charge of your life, you, something, or someone else?"

You're either in charge, or something/someone else is. If you start to do something (not just sit around and watch TV), and something, some event, or someone interferes – there just may be a reason. I've been interfered with many times down through my life.

People have for one reason or another failed to board planes, trains, buses, ships, and automobiles which had accidents where everyone was killed. Go with the flow, appreciate the dynamics of the universal plan to protect or not protect you for your own good. Serendipity works for all of us and it's very interesting.

I want, I wish, I hope

Every time you use one of these phrases, you're just wasting time. These get you nothing but wanting, wishing, and hoping. Just create it – do it.

The problem is hope tends to sink those hoping without action. The more you hope for change in your station in life, the more things remain the same or decline. Give up hope, and do something. Any move in the direction you "hope" you'll go is a thousand times more effective than just hoping.

If you hope you'll change your behavior, nothing happens that's good. Just change your behavior. Consciously determine what behavior needs to be changed, and make an effort to change. It may take a little time to change, but it took a long time to develop the "habit" you want to change. A habit must be replaced by a habit. It takes 22 to 55 repetitions to create a new habit. Avoid the trap, if you "hope it" it will happen. All that will happen is you'll just hope more but nothing good will come from the hoping.

Be careful what you ask for and how you ask for it – you might get it. Setting a goal of earning $60,000 in one year (back when that was a lot of money), I put my head down, and worked. When the year was over, I asked my accountant wife, "Did I reach my goal?"

Her answer was, "Well, yes and no. You grossed over 60K, but netted almost nothing. You spent everything you earned, earning it."

I got what I set as my goal – earn 60K, I just asked for it wrong. If you want to know how to develop your goals – so they will happen, read **The 11th Element**.

"The grass is always greener on the other side of the fence." Have you ever observed cattle risking their hides by putting their heads through a barbed wire fence to get a few bites of grass? Have you ever thought about another job, and started to imagine how the job would be? Soon you've worked out the people, the environment, the type of work, the pay and what you'll do with it. If you get the job, all you get is disappointment. Your "Expectations" are not met.

Maintenance

Always look at the "maintenance" before settling on a dream. You have an idea about what you want – location, job, car, house, mate, toys, clothes, food, etc., but before you make the commitment, consider the maintenance.

Location – One of your critical "lifestyle choices" will be where you live and work. It might be a good idea to include the logistics between the two in the formula – avoid a long commute. Remember the three top priorities in selecting real estate – location, location, location. There are many considerations in this choice – family, extended family, educational opportunities, recreational potentials, climate, potential pollution, etc.

Regardless of where you decide to land, you must remember Mother Nature will be trying to recycle everything you own. No place is immune to natural disasters. Weather will exact its toll. And different climates create different and unique ways of dealing with you and your stuff.

Job – Consider the commute, the wear and tear on your vehicle, fuel and oil. Are you going to be "thinking about your job" at home? If so, add the thinking hours to the hours you work. Will you be getting calls at home about work – more work hours. Will you be required at social events – more work hours. Of course you'll consider the benefits package as part of your income, it is. Now add how many hours you'll work and drive and divide them into your salary to determine your true wage. The environment you'll work in, the wardrobe you'll need, the people you'll work with, the tools you have to use, and additional training you'll need must also be considered.

Car – Consider what you want, the price tag, and then the true cost including the price, interest, service, repairs, fuel and insurance. How much per month does this really look like?

House – Take the total cost of your house including: Down Payment, Closing Costs, Principle, Interest, Taxes and Insurance, then divide by the number of months. Remember to include the monthly services: pool and landscaping (even if you do it, it costs in supplies and time). Even if this is a new house, you'll have service and maintenance expenses: paint, window, electrical, flooring, plumbing and sewer. Yearly you'll have carpet, window covering, and gutter cleaning. And at some time there will be appliance repair and replacement. The older the house is/gets, the more maintenance will be required. Can you really handle the maintenance?

Mate – When you choose your mate, you must consider the maintenance. What are they used to, i.e. food, drink, clothes, car, house, travel, entertainment, tools, toys, sex, etc., plus the time demands to maintain your relationship.

Clothes – The environment, work, home, and entertainment all get included in the clothes formula. You must consider seasonal clothing changes, initial cost, duration, replacement and maintenance, i.e. repair, dry cleaning, and laundry.

Food – What is it going to take for you to survive or "live the good life?" What do you and your mate plan to spend on food, drink, and going out to eat?

Money – How much money are you going to make, how much time is it going to take to make the money, how much money do you need to take home to afford all of this, and are you really sure you need all of this? What about taxes? Are you willing to spend the time (life energy traded for money) to maintain your possessions? If you're working a 60 to 80 hour week to earn money, then coming home to cook, clean, do laundry, mow lawns, shovel snow, wash the car, and walk the dog – what kind of a life is that? Don't answer. I wouldn't want you to evaluate your value system, just a question.

Summary

Give other people the consideration of making 100% correct decisions, even if their actions as a result of their decisions conflict with you or because they do.

Seek wisdom and develop empathy. Appreciate the inventiveness of the Spirit.

Choose your wars carefully.

Never be a Respecter of Persons unless they earn it directly.

Enjoy Nature including the disasters.

Tempt Fate, how else are you going to change and have fun?

Nothing is impossible.

Quit talking about it and "just do it!"

When you think you just can't live without something, consider the maintenance.

Life is a lot of fun in all of its variety. Spice your life up, open up your peripheral vision, there's a lot more going on around you than you imagine. Get out there and have some adventures so you can share with us.

Chapter 12
Personal Relationships

This chapter is a "brain dump." The overall purpose of this book is to help you get rid of your programmed-in box-of-reference so you can see what is actually going on around you. As you read this, remember, you were taught your belief system. If your belief system causes you to become angry at anything written here, ask yourself what you're afraid of. What's included in this chapter are some of the most controversial topics of the day, on the front page of the news papers, and around which most of the guilt and conflict in a given life occur. These topics are keys in the sitcoms and soap operas we're acting out. Each topic is multiple books and university studies in its own right.

Crank-up your brain, be honest with yourself, and if something in here offends or angers you, spend some time in the corner thinking. The Meaning of Life is learning and changing your behavior to become the you, you want you to be. You can ignore these topics, but you can't avoid them, because they 're what living on Planet Ocean is all about.

The freedom to make your own decisions and the freedom of choice is the concept this country was founded on. The basis of our laws is "Do unto others as you would have others do unto you." Do you treat others the way you want to be treated? If not, change!

The Mating Ritual

The belief there's only "one-man-for-one-woman" and "one-woman-for-one man" is a modern romantic myth. In the not to distant past and in some cultures now, when you were born, available mates, and which culture/religion your parents came from would determine how you would be mated. Getting to choose your mate is a modern phenomenon.

Now let your mind wander, just think of the possibilities as you consider this suggestion. Let the Mother Nature based natural instincts do their thing. Human mating as occurs in nature.

How about we take all of the "eligible for mating" males and females, strip them naked, put them all in a big stadium, and let the games begin. Got the picture? Want to be in the stands watching or on the field playing? How much would you pay to watch or participate?

How would you pick a mate if you were one of the participants? Would you cover-up some part/parts of your anatomy? What criteria would you use to select your mate? How would body condition and looks play into your decision? How would you demonstrate your best attributes? How would you get attention? Would you use paint/colors to stand-out in the crowd? How about body adornments – tattoos, hair-dos, and body piercing adorned with jewelry (ears, nose rings, eye-brow, lips, belly button, tongue, penis, and clitoris).

What attributes would you look for in a mate? Would the selection be made based purely on the physical outcome of your offspring, would it be how well the two of you could care for the offspring or would the selection be a simple matter of animal lust?

Do you think the males would compete with each other for a mate? Would the females compete for a mate? Wow, the human mating ritual revisited. What do you think goes on at schools, malls, sporting events, bars and dances?

For a really good laugh, read **The Human Ape** by Desmond Morris – a zoologist's assessment of humans.

It's for certain, some of the best learning experiences come from interpersonal relationships. Nothing is more personal than mating with someone. Some of your best and hardest lessons happen after you're mated.

Marriage - Mating

What is marriage? Is it a religious ceremony, a legal contract, a legal ceremony, a myth, a commitment between two people or something else? I guarantee you if it's not a commitment between two people, it will be fraught with problems and possible divorce. The two biggest problems in marriages are ego and control. The partners' egos will not allow them to admit personal change is necessary, and/or one feels they must control the other one and the one being controlled resists.

Let's review. Life is about becoming the person *you* want to be. To do this requires *you* to change, not someone else to change. If you keep thinking your partner needs to change but you're OK, there's going to be trouble. No doubt your mate needs to change – that's what life is about, but you can't change them. Just like you, they must be self-motivated to want to change.

If you're a control freak, you'll create all kinds of trouble for yourself. Who are you really trying to control and why? Are you trying to control others because you're "out-of-control" in your own life?

Aw, now don't go and start analyzing yourself, you might change and then you could just let others learn their own lessons and do their own changing – like you need to do.

Who are You?

The thing which defines you the most is who you're with. Who you're with affects your thoughts, personality, action/reaction and behavior. You're different around your parents, extended family, in-laws, friends, members of the opposite sex, bosses, co-workers, strangers, etc.

Wouldn't it be nice to be able to just be "yourself?" The problem, who you are changes with who you're with.

Polygamy

The people who constructed the US Constitution did so based on what they knew. They based it on their beliefs in the Bible. There was never intended to be "separation of church and state." Several belief systems (churches) in the world believe in polygamy. Solomon, of Bible fame (you know – the wisest man in the world) had a whole bunch of wives. In fact, the Moslem faith, which has the most believers worldwide, believes in polygamy. Why did the US legislative system (the State) make polygamy illegal? Why in the world did we not separate church and state and allow Polygamy? Polygamy is in the Bible – upon which we based our constitution – Da!

If we kill off the men in war, then we have another dilemma, what happens to the extra women? If there are fewer men than women, how do the women breed? I guess they can just go to a sperm bank or utilize another woman's man. The problem: the best way to learn some of life's most important lessons is living with a mate.

I can understand how this law came about. In our past, men out numbered the women. So for a man to have more than one mate just wasn't fair to the other men. Watch **Paint Your Wagons**.

Now women outnumber the men, maybe we should rethink the law. Oh, but then women would want to marry two men so they could have more money to spend at the mall. Maybe we could just change the bigamy law like we tried to do the equal rights amendment – equal but different. Men could have any number of wives, but women could only have one husband. (Knowing women read more than men, I put that in here just to get your juices going. However, you women know you can share a lot easier than the guys can – it's the male chicken-fighting thing.)

If the US really believes in "freedom of religion" and polygamy is a part of a given church's belief system, how can the "State" make polygamy illegal? If someone is emigrating from a foreign country, with a belief system which allows polygamy, and has more than one spouse, can they only bring one spouse into the US? What happens to the other spouses? What if they're only visiting the US, can they bring all their spouses?

In the Muslim religion, a man can have up to four wives. Because of our federal law, a Muslim can't practice his faith, as it is written in the Koran (his holy religious book given by God), in the US without being discriminated against by the State.

We're a nation that says it believes in religious freedom, but creates laws to control the religious beliefs of everyone in this country through application of laws. Therefore separation of church and state is a figment of our imagination, not what is really going on – nor was it intended that way.

By the way, for Muslims, if you can't afford a wife, you don't get one – they're still up-breeding. Think about that.

Personally, I don't care one way or the other. I don't want to deal with more than one spouse/mate at a time. I don't need all those lessons at once. Although it would put me on the fast track for behavioral changes predicated on interpersonal relationships. And it works if one wife stays home to take care of the children and the others work for money – four wage earners, one dwelling, and you could all live the good life.

Can I get an Amen! Now salute the flag!

Love

I spent the major portion of my younger life being confused about love. I was hammered with the "love" thing: love God, love your family, love yourself, love your spouse, love your neighbor, love your enemy, love your dog, love the environment and work towards unconditional, God-like love.

You spend time trying to make all of those things fit under the definition of one word, and welcome to confusion. At times I was fairly successful at loving, when I was alone. Whenever there were people around, I was sorely tried. It became obvious there was more than one type of love and/or the definition I was taught was wrong. I gave up trying to figure it out and just tried to do the best I could.

Dazed and confused as usual, I asked, "What is the real meaning of love?"

"Love is: **Wanting spiritual growth for yourself and others**." The Counselor said. "Spiritual growth is behavioral modification, the result of learning from your life lessons."

Given my new awareness of life as an experiential learning exercise with everyone playing a bit part in my scripted movie, I simply had to realize everyone was there for me to learn from. I was there to help others learn. WALA!! Love became understandable, simple, and something I could not only understand, but also participate in.

I raised three boys. I wish I could do it again with my new insight. I was pretty good at the "Hard Love" by withholding love if they were making too many mis-takes. I did however let them learn their own lessons. I supported them with their "Props," let them make their own decisions, and then made them live their decisions. They became fairly cautious when it came to decision time. They tried to collect all the data they could, they corrected any errors, and if it didn't turn out the way they expected, they learned and tried their best not to repeat mistakes (I had little tolerance for repeats).

It took many years to determine that Love and Hate are not opposites but in fact very close together, emotionally-charged events. The opposite of love and hate is indifference. It took years for me to put a word to the feelings I had for my mate – indifference. It wasn't hate and it wasn't love. When finally realizing and accepting how I felt, the relationship was over and we split.

I've had the privilege to interface with quite a few young people recently. I was stunned by the difference between how we perceive the world. To the youth of today everything is love/hate, black/white, right/wrong, good/bad, left/right or some other set of opposites. It's interesting I almost never think in opposite terms. To me everything is gray. To have an opinion about anything limits my ability to see all sides, to receive more data, to learn/love.

Marriage and Taxes

You did know this was coming, right? When Shellie and I first got together, one of the things she looked at was what affect getting married would have on our federal income taxes. Shellie's an accountant, so she looked at it from all angles. To my surprise, it would cost us more in taxes if we married than if we just lived together and filed separately.

It appeared, the federal government didn't believe in marriage. I know people who got divorces during this time to save taxes. I don't know who wrote the laws, but it sure made me question the government, and their entity the IRS.

Being confused, I sought higher counsel (be careful what you ask for). "Why is our government against marriage?"

Understanding from the Counselor, "The government, through discouraging marriages, is trying to control the birth rate."

I understood the biggest problem we have on Planet Ocean is overpopulation of humans. Now some states are granting "same-sex" marriages, which again controls reproduction and births – that's good. However, the churches, governmental parties, and states have different ideas about birth, pregnancy, abortion, same-sex marriages, and taxes.

So, depending on where you live, what church you go to, and your sexual orientation, the "laws," which control your behavior, are different. Isn't that discrimination? I thought discrimination was against Federal law.

I believe in freedom to exercise my own will as long as it doesn't hurt someone else physically and/or mentally. I believe in the freedom to never do guilt.

If everyone is afforded this kind of freedom, then where is the problem, and why do I need so many different people, churches, and governmental agencies telling me what to do? I make my decisions and I take responsibility for those decisions, then what's the problem? As long as my spouse/mate/sex partner(s) is(are) adult(s), by their own free will and without coercion, why should anyone else object? Maybe jealousy?

Women's Rights

Before "women's liberation" I had a chance to live in Norway and then Morocco. This was like swinging the pendulum to both sides.

In Norway, the women outnumbered the men almost five to one. For anything to get done, women had to work. Before women's liberation started in the US, the Norwegian women were liberated. They worked as seamen, engineers, laborers, etc.

In Morocco, the women also worked, pulling plows alongside horses, cattle, donkeys and camels, carrying loads of firewood on their heads, and other labor beneath men. In 1972, 16 to 20 year old female virgins were for sale in the marketplace for $100US. These women were just a commodity to and a drain on the economy of their families. When in public, most of the women showed only their eyes. There were few if any paying jobs available to the Moroccan women, and little in the way of training or education. Most of the women, from birth to death, lived behind walls and never had a chance for any kind of a social life. A man could have a harem of up to four wives, and as many concubines as he could afford. To survive, non-virgins and ex-wives could become concubines (slaves) or prostitutes.

This life experience taught me slavery was alive and well. It was also apparent that 50% of the brainpower of Morocco was being wasted by not educating the women. By enslaving the women, the labor and contribution the women could have made was keeping Morocco in "Third World" status. The laws of Morocco were based on a religious book – no separation of mosque (church) and politics (state) there either.

Since I believe in freedom, I believe in equal pay for equal work. If a woman is going to do a man's job, then they need to do the full job and not just part of it, if they expect the same pay. If you want an example, visit Norway.

Nature and Sex

"What is sex all about?" I asked.

"Nature has three basic programs pertaining to procreation." The Counselor said, "In these breeding programs, the fittest of both sexes are the ones who breed – genetic selection.

- Males compete, the winner is the one who breeds and when done, the female splits and cares for the offspring = Breed and Run.
- The dominant (Alpha) male gathers up a herd of females and fights off other males while he breeds the females = The Herd Instinct.
- After the competition (by both the male & female) to prove fitness to breed = Pair for Life."

"Why is sex such a strong drive?" I asked.

"The drive to breed – procreate – is the program 'Go forth, multiply, bring forth after your own kind.' It was instituted, from the beginning, in all living organisms." The Counselor explained.

"Why do humans demonstrate all three of the programs?" I asked.

"In humans, the observant, thinking and parroting creation; procreation evolved into the sex act and was useful to reunite couples separated for periods of time due to their survival activities." The Counselor explained. "The 'observe and parrot' aspect of human programming caused the adoption of all three of the natural animal mating programs."

Sex and Men

Climb inside a man's head, and you'll find all three of the animal-breeding programs deep in the survival instinct. Listen to uninhibited conversations between men, and you may hear all three of these breeding programs expressed in just one paragraph. No wonder men are confused. They're operating three different programs pertaining to breeding and women.

Watch men compete for a woman's attention in a bar, and you know the animal instincts are alive and well. The bar "winner" gets to plant his genetic seed then leave (the one night stand – Screw and Run).

Take a man to a well populated beach and watch his wandering eyes. You know he believes every woman wants him – he for sure wants them (the Herd).

After two million years of programming, he's expected to pair up – "till death do us part"– never look at another woman and support a family. Based on the collusion between church and state and forced on him through laws and guilt, he's expected to deny his basic, animal, genetic programming (Pair for Life).

I didn't do the programming. All I did was look, listen and report. Better yet, I represent those remarks. The basic program can be modified or stuffed but never erased – it's millions of years old.

Sex and Women

It took me many years, but eventually the "board up side my head" actually got my attention. Sorry, but women have all three of the programs also. Watch a group of women get together when they have children (herd protection).

You know what young girls are like at a live band concert. If that's not a herd instinct, what is?

When a woman has a child, she will usually exclude the male from care – screw and run – and take care of the child alone. Quite a few women demonstrate this in that once they're mothers, they're never again a wife. The male takes last place in all their decisions (even after the cat/dog). They would prefer if the male would go to work and send a check in the mail. (Go hunting, throw the meat into the cave and leave.)

And of course, the instinct to pair for life with the male "taking care of them" is always deep down.

I know, I know, you're not like that, you're liberated. You wouldn't like to be part of a harem (herd), or would you if the man had enough wealth? You of course would entertain having a baby without any interference from the male, if you had a means of support. And when you think about pairing for life, you expect equal participation by the male in all aspects of the relationship (and he better not even look at another woman).

For women, there's a program which messes them up for any monogamous relationship. Deep in the human programming is, "Genetic diversity is necessary to advance the human species." Soooo, the female of the species is always considering how her genes would "mix" with other males' genes. Maybe not consciously, but subconsciously, women are always on the "look-out" for the perfect DNA match to produce the optimal offspring.

Well we're evolving, but it'll take a long time to counter the 2 million year-old basic animal/human programming. So what you say and what you feel deep down may not be the same. Are women confused a little too? Why are women always looking at and making comments about good-looking men's butts.

Do women have a conflict when choosing a mate? Is it because the tough stud they would really like to produce a baby with, they know is not the one they would like to pair with for life?

Human Breeding

All a man has to do is get down wind of a woman in heat (laying eggs) and it's all over but the breeding. The chemistry thing, which has been talked about for so many generations, is real. Remember the 50% rule, don't believe me, figure it out for yourself. The problem: women are only "in heat" for three days out of every 28 day cycle, and men have to be ready to breed all the time. What are the odds, that in a group of women one is "in heat?" No wonder men are horny all the time. Men, a suggestion, stay up-wind of all women.

The perfume manufacturers have figured it out. The problem now is, how are men supposed to know when to make babies if the "chemistry" can just be sprayed on. And if a woman is wearing the "chemistry" and a man makes a breeding advance to her, who is really responsible?

Sex

Sex for procreation, that's what animals do, but for humans it was also meant as a "Toy of Joy" to keep a relationship from falling apart and as a reward to the male for risking his life to "bring home the bacon" (meat). Because of our national religious beliefs: sexuality, sex, premarital sex, homosexuality, extramarital affairs, and the human body have been "off limits." Different religions even specify "correct positions." Whenever we go against natural urges, we're in trouble, example, the catholic priests and their sexual problems. Also, if we point out anything with a negative, the majority of the population – 60+% – will go against the edict. "Thou shalt not . . . " The Cosmic Joker at work!

Our religions and our society have made sexuality a "taboo" and thereby forced sex to be internalized and to go underground. They've made two-million-year-old, natural, animal, urges illegal, and made criminals out of many people. Thank God for Playboy!

I think sex education in school is teaching some of the right stuff, but missing a great opportunity to provide real guidance for our young people. The churches could have done this, but no, they had to make sex a sin so they could run guilt trips on their congregation to control them and get their money. In general, the priests and pastors are so screwed up sexually, they can't think or act correctly. Works – Doesn't Work! Maybe it's time to bring Isis – the Goddess of Fertility – back.

Homosexuality

In my opinion, homosexuality is great, at least they won't reproduce. What's done in private, by consenting adults, is their business. I have my choices, and because I do, I honor everyone else's.

At least 10% of every animal population has "same sex" orientation. This phenomenon has been recognized from the beginning of recorded history. If you're choosing homosexuality as your "war" is it because it's going to hurt you, you've been brainwashed or because you have tendencies? Be careful around closets.

The Egg & Sperm War

The female ovulates, laying an egg. The sperm swims up to the egg, the acid on its head eats through the calcium shell of the egg, procreation begins and so the war.

Let's consider the make-up of the new human being. How are the sex, color of hair, height, weight, shape of the body, skin tone, number of fingers and toes, smarts, and a zillion other factors going to be included in the DNA of the new baby? Through WAR!

The DNA of the sperm and the DNA of the egg must fight over which part of their DNA will be in the new DNA. You only get a part – not a whole. The new one is a combination of the two – a new make and model.

Children

Children are the natural result of mating. Given what we now know, they don't have to be automatic or an accident. There's a basic driving force programmed into your subconscious – survive. To survive, you'll go to any length to try to pass on your genes – make babies.

What a dichotomy, when you're the most physically motivated and strongest to have children is when you're the least prepared mentally, emotionally, financially, and experientially – when you're young. A fact – older parents produce smarter children (more knowledge to pass-on in the DNA). If you insist on procreating when young, then pick out the best older person you can find to raise your child, you go back to work. The older person may be a relative or someone you hire, but if you're young, you don't have the experience to give the first child what they really need – understanding and proper behavior training.

Babies are learning machines. Their only problems are learning to communicate and developing discipline – finding out what they may and may not do. They must learn to operate by societies rules. What if you could teach a baby, before they learn to talk and walk, to communicate their wants, needs and desires. Would it surprise you to learn babies are capable of body language and hand signals way before they're able to talk? 50% rule, check it out. Watch **Meet the Fockers.**

Babies don't have a lot of habits, and they need to learn the parameters of life. When you say, "Baby, don't touch that, it's hot." You do know, the only way they're going to learn about "hot" is by getting burned. Your decision is how to let them learn their life lessons, let them explore the possibilities, and try to minimize the injuries. Notice, I didn't say eliminate the injuries. Pain's a real good learning experience. To find out about how pain programs your mind, read **Dienetics** by L. Ron Hubbard. Raising children is "Damage Control." You know there's going to be damage, just try to minimize the damage.

Why Are Breasts So Important?

Breasts, tits, teats, boobs, ta tas, melons or whatever you call them are vitally important to both males and females. They represent survival, because they provide a baby's first survival food.

Females are infatuated with breasts because they represent maturity and draw in mates.

Males are infatuated with breasts because they represent the best chance for the survival of their genes. This explains bigger is better – the assumption – right or wrong – is bigger breasts give more milk.

I hope this doesn't ruin breasts for you, but think about the problem of prosthetics – fake breasts and padded bras – false advertising.

Does this information explain a little about men's and women's fixations on breasts? Consider the impact a mastectomy has on a woman's psyche. One of the most important things in her life has been surgically removed.

Butts

Yes, I have to go there. A recent Discovery Channel animal behavior show, explains how a certain type of female ape's buttock swells up when she's in heat. She presents her swollen buttock to the dominate male to stimulate the breeding process.

Now, consider the human female and how she "presents" her buttock to stimulate the human male to breed: the tightness and shape of her clothing, the maximum allowable exposure ("T" back bikinis), the shortness of the skirt, short-topped pants with buttock cleavage showing and the "shapeliness" of the form.

Why do women "present" their butts to men? Why do men look at women's butts? Is it because sexual intercourse from behind is how almost all "animals" breed? Isn't this position the "best" way to insure procreation occurs (the egg and sperm meet)?

The sink gets stopped up, help is called for and the "Plumber" arrives. As soon as he stoops over, part of his butt is exposed and the cleavage between his butt cheeks comes into view. Women go berserk.

"Why?" You ask. You did ask, didn't you?

Competition!

You say, "No way, it's just ugly."

OK, hang-on, I haven't finished with butts or breasts yet. In current society, it's not Politically Correct, in fact it was absolutely against the law for females to expose their butts in public, until the invention of the "anal floss" swim suits.

Why do women expose their breast cleavage? Could the breast cleavage remind men of the buttock cleavage, subconsciously stimulating men's urge to breed, reminding them the opportunity to procreate is close. Why do men's and women's hands end-up on their mate's butt?

If you think not, think again, and be real and practical. If it's just the shape of the breasts, then why not allow them to hang natural? Why bras at all? Why "lift and separate" or "lift and push together" bras?

Would a blouse or sweater do the same job, have the same effect, if it didn't show the cleavage? Why do women's exposed breasts have such a predictable effect on men?

Do partially exposed breast cleavages remind us of "Plumbers" butts? Maybe? But Plumbers' butt cleavages would only stimulate the sexual response in about 10% of the males.

Obviously some of the girls need two mirrors, because their breast cleavages don't match their butt cleavages.

A suggestion: don't patronize Plastic Surgeons who don't understand a "Matched Set" or eventually you'll be found out when your breast cleavage doesn't match your butt cleavage – false advertising.

I'll bet that revelation will bring many smiles to your face as you travel through a crowd or call the "Plumber" – you're welcome. Just remember, it's all about getting laid.

Just Say No!

I just found out the US Government is now on an "abstain only" kick. This is to be the "new" edict if your school district wants federal "sex education" money. Is "no" a negative to be filtered?

How stupid is that. Turn on TV anytime of the day or night, and even the PG shows show more than abstaining. With 60+% of high school graduates *admitting* to having sex, abstaining is not going to work.

Be real, remember for over two million years, human females were mated by the time they were 10-12 years old. With that as part of the human "passed down" genetic code and programming, laws will not change the hormonal drives to mate.

We could just give all the boys vasectomies at age ten then reverse it if or when they're mentally, physically, emotionally and financially ready to have a family. How about free neutering clinics like we have for pets. In fact, why not let the vets perform the neutering?

Did I just hear you say, "That's a good idea, but not my son – everyone else's son."

When the teenagers start dating, have a medical check-up for VD before every date. Before the boy can take your daughter out of the house, he has to show his doctor's OK slip. Before the boy leaves with his girl friend, he has to see her doctor's OK slip.

There are solutions for the two main problems of teenage sex – pregnancies and VD. You may trust your children to not have sex before marriage, but I don't. I understand the combination of raging hormones, basic programming and chemistry (smell). Watch **Blue Lagoon**.

Do I think young people should have children? NO! Neither do I think people who are unsuited to have children; chemically, financially, physically, mentally or emotionally should procreate.

You decide and figure it out. You make decisions considering the guilt trips, emotional fear, and the drive to have offspring to carry on your genes. Educate the children truthfully about sex and procreation including all the disease preventative measures, masturbation, contraception, adoption, and abortion options available. Then let them make their own decisions. You'll never be able to prevent them from having sex. Just say no - yea right.

Thanks to President Bill Clinton and our compulsory education system, the youth of today believe oral-sex is not sex – read the dictionary definition. That belief will get you a lot of dates.

Have all young people read the **Tao of Sexology**. This is Eastern wisdom denied western society for thousands of years.

My mother, in all her young wisdom, had started warning me about sex when I was only eight years old. She told me, "If you have sex out of wedlock, two things are going to happen. You're going to get venereal disease, and the girl is going to get pregnant. Then you're going to have to get married and support her and your child."

My hormones were raging. I was horny as a three-peckered, billy-goat, but scared to death of women. After over a year in the Navy, I finally got up the courage to have sex. Then I waited for the inevitable, my dick to rot off, her to get pregnant and marriage. Well nothing happened, except my horns got trimmed. I began to doubt my mother. Yea, I joined the Navy when sex was safe and SCUBA diving was dangerous.

Later, I met my wife, we were both in the Navy, lonely and in lust. We married at the age of twenty, so I didn't even have a chance at the bar scene. She was a virgin, and I wasn't much more. We did what we both had learned from our parents (not much), but there were a few books available and soon we had three sons.

After 28 years of marriage (kids out of the nest), with several years off for my bad behavior (that depends on whose perspective), we looked at each other and saw someone we had nothing in common with.

I asked myself, *Would you let a 20 year old tell you what to do or direct your life now?* The answer was obvious, and we split for the last time. We still respect each other, but we're not together.

As for my mother's other advice, she was right when she told me, "If you ever stick your finger in a girl, it will rot off." I didn't believe her, and it rotted all the way to mid-upper arm.

That was a joke – pay better attention.

Abortion

It's estimated up to 75% of pregnancies end up in abortions, either natural (most with just a heavier period) or otherwise.

Let's review. The biggest problem on earth is too many humans. You better hope the abortion percentage doesn't drop, or we'll over populate the earth even faster, and quickly wipe out the human race completely

Some religions are teaching it's Gods Will for the congregation to produce more humans so the Spirits will have more bodies to incarnate. This is their reason for being against abortions? The souls don't need the human bodies, there're plenty of other planets to play on and life forms to play with to have "physical" experiences. This is just a stage, there is only so much room on the stage and the planet will only support so much life – sustained yield. If more "Body Toys" are needed, more planets and bodies can be created with just a word from UI.

When it comes to abortion, why are men telling women what they can and can't do? If it weren't for religions, would abortions be OK? If it weren't for religions, would contraception be OK? If people get overly emotional about abortions, then what are they afraid of? Could the fear be as simple, as basic, as survival of their genes? But why are they so emotional when it's not them or their offspring who are pregnant?

If God got you pregnant (God's will) then where is your free will and scripting in the sit-com? If the sexual drive wasn't so intense during the early hormonal changes, children would not be driven to the point of madness about having sex, something which only lasts for a few minutes or just seconds, and they wouldn't get pregnant or cause pregnancies.

Currently our two major national parties are at odds about abortion. I suggest the vast majority of people running this nation are men. I also believe the major push against abortion is caused by the religious organizations. Hummm, so overly religious men are trying to control women – interesting.

What about separation of church and state? Who's trying to control whom, and why? Why are churches telling me what to do? What makes anyone (especially church goers who are taught to "Do unto others," "not kill" and "Love your neighbor" get so worked up trying to control my life (impose their will) they think it's OK to destroy property and kill people who don't believe the way they do?

Now we're either free, or we're slaves. We either have free will, or someone else is telling us what to do – slavery.

When a fetus is born, when does life start? When it breathes in its first breath! If the baby doesn't start breathing, it's "still born," born dead. So it appears from a simply logical viewpoint the fetus must be considered a moving and growing "tumor" until it takes its first breath.

Does the fetus record data and learn in the womb? Yes! So what? All atoms are receiving and recording data. It isn't "alive" until it begins to breathe.

NOTE: The Soul (the Operator/animator) enters the baby slightly before, with its first breath or soon after birth.

Eliminating a tumor is not murder! If it is, then we're going to have to kill a lot of surgeons.

My solution is very simplistic. Forget religious beliefs, which simply want more converts so they can reap more wealth from them. Forget the government, run by men, who are trying to keep women in slavery and using religion as an excuse to do so. Let each woman decide for herself whether or not to carry a pregnancy to full term.

I'm really tired of all of the psycho-babble surrounding abortions. What does a woman do if she has a natural abortion? Get over it, and go on with her life.

If a woman gets pregnant (by whatever means) and decides she doesn't want the baby, she has the right to make up her own mind about carrying it. Not the church, the government, her parents, the partner who participated, or anyone else. She's the one who has to carry the tumor for nine months, go through the labor, and take care of the child for at least 18 years after it's born. Or live with having chosen to have an abortion.

Anyone can gather all of the information necessary to make a reasonable, rationale decision about what to do with a pregnancy, with in six weeks, over the internet. Once the decision is made, live with it.

Take some responsibility for running your own life. If it wasn't illegal to have an abortion, there wouldn't be illegal abortion clinics and butchers. If 75% of pregnancies are aborted, then abortions must be much more "natural" by a factor of 3 to 1 than full term pregnancies.

Don't you just hate logic?

Determining Who Lives

If there's going to be a "Problem Birth" and a decision is to be made about whether the mother or the baby is going to survive, who gets to make that decision? Is it the church, the pregnant woman, the father, the doctor or the immediate family?

If you were the woman, what would your decision be? If the woman decides to sacrifice her life for the unborn tumor, isn't that premeditated suicide? Does her "suicide" mean the Life Insurance Company doesn't have to pay the premium to the surviving spouse? Does that act make the doctor a killer – either way?

Whatever the decision, at least it would be your decision, and your lessons to learn. There's at least one religion which believes in sacrificing the mother to save the "tumor." After all, she's had her chance at life.

Parents Who Kill Their Children

In the news, on a regular basis, is startling information about parents who kill their children. You do know, in nature, killing offspring is a pretty normal thing. It's one way animal populations are controlled. Because of the human drive for the survival of their genes, many humans procreate who should never have children. Some of these people are known to be at risk chemically (drugs), physically, emotionally, mentally and financially and yet they make babies.

In our society, procreation is supposed to be a joint, male/female, responsibility for the care and raising of the child.

What if . . . when a non-wed woman becomes pregnant and can't find someone to marry her and/or take legal responsibility for the baby, an abortion was legally performed?

What if . . . a couple, in front of witnesses says, "Till Death Do Us Part," has children, then decides on divorce, should the children be legally eliminated (killed) in front of their parents and extended families, and to consummate the divorce, the married couple are eliminated?

What if . . . when parents are found to be unsuitable to raise their children, the children were eliminated in front of them, not given over to someone else to raise?

What if . . . when a child gets in trouble with the law, you punish them and their whole family, parents and siblings equally with physical punishment, jail, probation or death?

What if . . . the law said, in the event your child was born with a defect, even a blemish, it was to be immediately destroyed? Watch the movie *Hawaii*.

Do you think people might make better and more informed choices? Would people tend to take more responsibility about marriage, having babies and raising their children?

Disobedience and Punishment

And then we come to Bill Crosby's famous saying where he quotes his father, "I brought you into this world, I'll take you out of this world, I'll make another one just like you!"

That's exactly what I told my three boys, and I'm pretty sure I meant it. At least they thought I did.

In the Old Testament of the Bible, if a child was disobedient or even disrespectful to its parents or caused trouble in the camp, the child would be killed by the family or group/tribe. If the problem was considered to be genetic, the whole extended family was eliminated – killed. The Israelites were exercising "genetic selection" and it also tended to keep order.

If we could redefine "cruel and unusual punishment" then maybe the courts could specify public whippings, and make the parents punish their own children with a cat-of-nine-tails with bits of metal to tear the flesh and make them bleed. The number of strokes specified by the judge based on the offence. If the parents (both would have to administer the strokes) refused, not only the child but also both parents would be whipped. The parents would also have to pay monetary restitution for any of their child's offences. I don't know, do you think that might be a deterrent to juvenile crime?

Now days, parents are jailed for meeting out corporal punishment to their children. And yet, the Bible says, "Spare the rod and spoil the child." Go figure. Finally, we have the legal system vs. the church – separation of church and state happening. You know the shape our country and the world is in concerning crimes against society. So maybe we need to re-think what's best for society and not take into consideration the church or the state.

Works – Doesn't Work!

My boys were allowed to discuss my decisions to a point. I was a lot more flexible than my dad. But they knew, from an early age, my final decision would be final. They also knew if I provided food, clothing and shelter, they played by my rules. They could always pack and leave – anytime at any age. If the law had ever tried to interfere with me administering appropriate punishment to my sons, the government would have been raising them.

Children's Rights

I don't believe in any kind of "Child Abuse." But I have a little different viewpoint than some of our more "modern" thinking parents. I do believe in "object lessons" and if some pain is involved in those lessons, the results are dramatic. Leaving marks on a child is against your survival (now), so you have to get a little inventive. Talking back and trash talking seems to be a big thing with kids now days. Well forget the bar of soap, use dish washing liquid – that really works. You want real leverage? Take away their CD players, cell phones, game boys and trips to the mall to hang-out and shop-lift.

It's one thing to deny children an education in order to work them or to injure them in that work, but remember children are "in training" to be adults. The whole first 18 years of their life, until they're of age, they're supposed to be learning how to take responsibility and work. In the past, when we lived in villages and on small farms, everyone worked. From the earliest age, the children had chores to do. The children did what they were physically able to do. Now kids can't legally work for money until age 15. That only gives them maybe three years to learn how to work, and limits our country's productivity.

Maybe a part of all school curriculums should be a "Child Labor Program." Design the learning process to involve productivity, attitude, cooperation, problem solving, quality of the product, mental and physical activity, financial responsibility and rewards. Who knows, maybe the productivity of the children might generate enough money to give the teachers a raise. The better the teacher, the more money their students earn and the more the teacher earns.

Kids Pitching Fits

I see kids pitching fits in public, and parents giving in to the brats. Who's in control, the kid or the parents? What kind of a president are the parents setting? What kinds of behavior are the kids learning? The brats are going to be the next generation of juvenile delinquents. How are they going to act when they go to school and then to work?

My youngest son, Brad, saw a display of "fit throwing," by a kid about his same age. You know the kind, ask for something, mommy says no, so flop down on the floor in a department store, cry, scream, kick your feet and beat your hands on the floor until mommy gives in.

A few aisles later, Brad spotted a toy, asked for it, was told no, and he proceeded to pitch a fit. I told him to stop, and when he continued, I picked him up by the back of the pants, walked to the front of the store, found a trash can, removed the lid and threw him into the can – hard.

I told him, "What you pulled was trash, and this is where trash belongs, never do that again! No, means no!"

About three months later, Brad tried the little trick again. Picking him up by the pants, I walked around behind the store, to the large trash containers, opened a lid, heaved him over my head and down hard into the container (without looking to see what was inside) and slammed the lid. All he did was whimper for awhile.

I said, "I told you last time, pitching a fit anywhere, especially in a store was trash. When I or your Mom says No, it means No! Trash containers are where that kind of fit belongs. If you ever pitch a fit again, you'll stay in the trash." He never pitched a fit again.

For those little buggers throwing fits in restaurants, I found a glass of cold water in the face just as they start to inhale stops the crying (a little coughing occurs), gets their attention and the water is fairly easy to clean up. I've also sent the boys out to the car while we finished dinner. They weren't allowed to eat when we got home – they didn't starve to death, they're still alive and well and they do much better when taken out to dinner.

Remember, the punishment must be **grossly** more than the crime (mis-behavior) or the crime (mis-behavior) will continue. If a kid is hurt, and they're crying, that's legitimate to a point. For a kid to cry for attention or because they don't like your decision, isn't allowed. That's unless you like a kid to run your life and annoy everyone around you.

Mothers need to get this. The child is the center of your attention until a maximum age two. No later than two, the mother needs to become the disciplinarian and center of the child's attention. The mother no longer follows the child around catering to its every whim. The child is to follow the mother around and help her in all the family chores – learn to work. The child is to do **exactly** what the mother says or receive punishment and get no food – learn obedience.

Have you ever trained an animal yourself or seen someone else train one? They do it by rewards, not punishment. Children are animals, and they'll respond to training just like any other animal. When they do something right, reward them and praise them. When they do something wrong, ignore them and don't feed them. Treats and food used as rewards and punishments – do you think it would work?

Once you have kids, you've a lot invested – time, effort, money, emotions, hassle, and of course love (remember the definition). With this kind of investment, it's no wonder you want to "Protect" your kids. But don't forget the biggest drive is for _**"you"**_ to survive through your genes (kids) and it warps your decisions. You must get everything into perspective, step back, and be real about what life is about – modifying behavior. Do the best you know how, learn from the experience, and enjoy. Your job is to love your children – modify their behavior! Start early, by the time they're teenagers, it may be too late. Keep in mind Dr. Spock apologized for his theories.

Until the children are 18 years old, the parents are responsible for them. If they pose a problem, the parents should take care of it.

If the parents are unable to handle their responsibility – for whatever reason – then just maybe, the child should be eliminated – in front of the parents. Always keep in mind the biggest problem on earth is over population. Unruly children being eliminated could be a beginning.

Extend that to adults to catch up with what should have happened in the past and it's a start.

A Casual Survey

In a non-formal survey of women, 90+ percent admitted, by the time their youngest child was out of high school at least one of the following had happed to them or their children: rape, molestation, incest, physical abuse and/or mental abuse.

Since this appears to be the case, it's amazing we're not more warped than we are. It's also amazing there aren't more revenge murders. In nature, many animal mothers will kill the offender or die defending their offspring.

I'm a man, I know I don't understand all of the intricacies of this dynamic, but the guy has to sleep sometime. The first time any abuse incident occurs, report it to the police, videotape the damage, and use your biggest and heaviest frying pan on the perpetrator – when he's asleep.

Come-on women, you've got to give out more than you get or it will continue.

I know about the Bobbitt thing, but if all of you women banded together and kicked some butt, the authorities would have to pay attention – you are the majority.

And if you cut it off, run it through the Incinerator. Get a female judge and a female jury, show the police report and video tape, claim it was your "time of the month" and I'll bet there'll be a different outcome.

The Oldest Occupation

Why is the oldest profession on earth (prostitution) illegal in most states? Is it because of jealousy? When money will buy anything else, should it be illegal to purchase sexual favors? If prostitution was legal, it could be taxed. If wives were taking care of their men, why would the men need to pay for sex? If men were satisfying their wives, why would women need to pay for sex? If the churches didn't make the use of contraception, tubule legations and vasectomies a sin, then maybe the wives would be more likely to service their men. If there were sex schools where men and women could learn how to pleasure themselves and their mates, maybe they wouldn't have to flounder around for years or for life trying to; be satisfied, satisfy their mate and enjoy sex.

I learned a very important lesson when I was teaching High School. The standard verbiage of the day was/is "Get a good education so you can get a good job, work hard and you'll be taken care of in your old age."

Several of the 14 year old girls pointed out they were making over $40K a year working part time, on their backs, with no taxes (= $80K in working wages). Their 15 year-old pimp was driving a new car and he didn't even have a driver's license.

I know, what you're thinking, "There's no future in prostitution."

They were making way more money part-time than any of the 'educated' teachers working full-time! They didn't care about the future or death, and you would have had to provide them with money now and guarantee them a lot more in the future to even get their attention.

They know what the professional athletes are making, they know most of the millionaires in the US come from the working class and barely have a high school education. They also had daily contact with school dropouts who were making lots of money selling a commodity – drugs.

If the females even thought about marriage, it was in how much money they would get to spend, and the potential to get a lot when they divorced. They equated being wives to prostitution and slavery.

Where do they get that kind of a perspective? They get it from talking to relatives and friends, in the checkout line at the super market, newspapers, and from TV programs – daily input. And that's not even considering the risk of marital abuse.

The guys looked at marriage as prison. If they generated a child, it was an eighteen-year sentence, even if they didn't get married. If they were married and then divorced, it could cost them up to 80% of what they had earned. Watch *War of the Roses.*

So how would you respond to young people with that as a point of view? I found my education, life experiences, upbringing and the standard replies left me with no answers.

Divorce and Separation

Mates – married or not – go into relationships with "Expectations." Expectations are those things, which, because of culture or a picture in your mind, you think should happen the way you expect. Normally these things are not voiced, and they go unfulfilled. Persons from different families, cultures, religions, races, etc. have different expectations from a relationship.

It's amazing to me any relationships last.

Talk to each other, voice those things you expect and work out how you BOTH can get what you want. Keep in mind you both must change for the relationship to work. Enjoy the process, refuse to do guilt, admit when you've made a mis-take in your movie, learn and change your behavior.

If you go into a relationship, but in the other person you recognize some traits as "different" than you would like, but you know you can "fix" whatever is wrong. I have news for you, it isn't going to happen. You can never fix someone else.

Even if the person you hooked up with is everything you ever wanted, their interests are going to change with time and experience, then what? What they once liked: food, sex, entertainment, recreation, spiritual growth, occupation, etc. may all change. How are you going to adapt, learn and change *your* behavior?

A relationship is almost always over when you can't communicate – because of ego. (Can't is one of two things – don't know how or not willing to.) You're right, they're wrong, and you won't talk about it. If this happens, either reestablish communications, or move on. What's the point of continuing the torture?

Middle Aged Crazy

There's another time that's critical in a long term relationship – the "middle" years when people have to face up to their "mortality." The "Middle Aged Crazy" times are extremely entertaining if you don't take them serious and just learn and enjoy them.

Many relationships end with neither mate knowing why. This can be as simple as the learning slows too much in one or both partners. One partner "out-grows" the other partner – changes their behavior. When you're not learning from each other, it takes a particularly intense effort to keep the relationship going.

Summary

If this piqued your interest, pissed you off, made you think or rethink your beliefs about relationships, I done good. If you got anything out of my brain dump, if you learned something/changed your behavior, you done good.

I don't know the answer to raising kids, but you must apply the right kind of love if you want to avoid creating juvenile delinquents. If you're going to raise a delinquent, keep them out of the public so you won't look so stupid (The same thing goes for rowdy dogs.).

I don't know the answer to maintaining a relationship, other than communications and personal change. Pay attention, change, maintain control of your ego and stop trying to control your mate.

There are only two emotions: Love and Fear. From these, all other emotions are generated.

If you become angry at your mate, remember anger is fear. Ask yourself, "What am I afraid of?"

Both Parents' job is to prepare their offspring to function in society. Children must be prepared emotionally to deal with school, work and personal relationships with a mate. Is what you as a parent are doing, preparing your child to be a positive influence in the world or not? Is that a simple enough question? Works – Doesn't work.

Chapter 13
Death

Birth is a death sentence. The death and recycling of the body is guaranteed. So, death is a big deal because survival is our most basic and longest running program. Cosmic Joker – survive but die – go figure.

The biggest problem we have on earth today is too many people. We're fighting the survival race and destroying the quality of life on earth by continuing to produce more humans and keeping "defective" humans alive to breed (they pass on their genes).

OK, I know that upset you, but consider what's in the best interest of not only the humans, but all life on this little, blue marble. We should be "breeding" smart, tough humans – up-breeding the stock – the same way agribusiness has evolved livestock and plants.

Death is just a transition of the soul from the sitcoms and soap operas of this world back to where it came from. The Soul, 99+ percent of what we see in the mirror, is going to live forever, and the body is going to get recycled back into cosmic dust. Death is just change.

Living life in reverse

I believe we have life backwards. If we could live life differently, what would the ideal life be like? Come dream with me for awhile.

Scientific proof has verified; children who play a lot, have varied experiences, keep their curiosity working, pay attention to events, and broaden their horizons are by far smarter than "normal" kids. It would seem, then, the longer a person can extend their childhood, the better off they would be.

So the ideal life would allow people to "retire" during childhood till say 30 years old – full maturity. This childhood would include fun, toys, adventures, worldwide travel, self-motivated learning experiences, interfaces with all cultures and religions with a variety of interpersonal relationships. There would be no worries about pregnancy or venereal disease.

This period of a life is the risk taking, fearless times. It's the time when humans are in the best physical shape, have the greatest endurance, learn fast and heal quickly.

At full maturity, you would choose your occupation and your role in society (a result of your youthful experiences). Then the formal education and job training would start, but be very short and fast. Read *21st Century Learning – Faster, Easier, Simpler, Better.*

Once you start to work, you would select your mate and, if you choose, start a family. You would have money, maturity, and experience.

Maturity is the time of caution and fears resulting from the physical and emotional pain learned from the youthful experiences.

You would then work until you decided it is time to exit this earthly plain, when you would start to shrink down, and eventually enter a womb – a nice, warm, safe, protective and loving environment. By reversing the womb experience you would becoming less and less over nine months until the finale, the ultimate orgasm and your gone.

No bodies to dispose of, all the cosmic dust recycled, a full, productive and fun life. In the end you have chosen your experiences, wrote your life script, played your part, and the parting is one of the most fun and stimulating aspects of life on earth.

Ready to sign-up, or is it already too late for you to play?

Population Control

Now let's have some fun. Step way back until we get through this.

Dis – ease is what we call Mother Nature's way of controlling the population. Now man is coming up with ways to offset Mother Nature's diseases with drugs.

Why?

Starvation – Let's look at starvation in animals and see what causes it. If it's a good, productive food year, and/or the predators have a reduction in their numbers, there can be a population explosion of "weed eaters." If this goes on for several years, the protein converter populations can double. When this has occurred in the past, two things have happened: the food sources were unable to support the population growth and animals began to starve. With the decrease in food, the weaker animals contracted diseases and died. Soon the population decreased to below the level when it had its explosion. The survivors were the toughest animals, resistant to disease and capable of dealing with diminished food. Starvation is one of Mother Natures' ways of "thinning the herd."

Humans can last about 30 days without food, as long as they have water. So starvation is a fairly long process, it takes time. For those people subjected to starvation, there's time to learn many lessons before they die. Starvation takes longer and is a lot more painful and debilitating than a bullet. I'll take a bullet anytime. If humans continue to overpopulate the earth, we can standby for starvation.

Suicide – Suicide is a legitimate way to exit this life. Most religions preach against suicide (the longer you live, the more money you give them), and at least in the US, it's against the law to commit suicide.

Was it the church or state that came up with the suicide rule first, and what about the separation thing?

One of the main reasons for the law against suicide has to do with insurance. Since suicide is "against the law," if you commit suicide, the insurance companies, by law, don't have to pay the insurance premium, you paid for.

Is this collusion between the insurance companies and the government? Now that would never happen.

If our problem is over population, and someone is ready to reduce the population by killing themselves, why should we care. The law against suicide only matters to the person who's unsuccessful. If they're successful, they don't care if it is against the law.

I believe if someone wants out of this life, we should do everything in our power to make the death possible, and this applies to assisted deaths. Let's take a vote about Kevorkian. For people who are ill or injured and want out of their situation, why are the doctors so adamant about keeping them alive? Is it because it's so lucrative to have people under medical attention and taking drugs? When the money runs out, *then* they pull the plug.

There are many ways to commit suicide, some more successful than others. In fact, if you believe the way I do, then, by definition, *every* death is a suicide because you wrote the script.

Many people "play" at suicide, but set up the game so they'll be "saved" before they actually make the transition. Many suicides and suicide attempts are just for the manipulation of others. If you don't want to be here to have your experiences and change your behavior, don't miss, goodbye!

If I decide I've had enough experiences this time around, I damage my vehicle (body) beyond repair or my quality-of-life becomes intolerable – I'm gone! I'm going to give the human race another parking place.

I would suggest you don't put me on the suicide hot line. My answer to a call, "Shut up and pull the trigger already!"

Automobiles - Over 50,000 people die with 500,000 people injured in the US each year from automobile accidents. This number has held fairly consistent for years. If we want to save people, why not outlaw automobiles?

Thinning the Herd – The food we're told is safe is now mostly under the control of the tobacco companies who can add 10,000+ "chemicals" to our food without listing them on the labels. The "food additives" make us "addicted" to the food so we become fat and eat more (who owns the food industry?).

Over 700,000 people die from arteriolosclerosis (heart attacks and strokes) each year from eating the food that is "safe" and drinking water with Chlorine added. Chlorine changes the good fat to bad fat and causes it to stick inside your blood vessels.

Fluoride, a toxic poison, is in drinking water & toothpaste and responsible for over 100,000 deaths each year.

Medical mis-adventures (malpractice) kill over 100,000 people each year.

FDA approved prescription drugs kill over 180,000 people each year.

And who do you think is in charge of all of this collusion and allowing this to continue in full knowledge of what's happening? Could it be the Food & Drug Administration, Federal Trade Commission, Environmental Protection Agency, the Medical Profession, Pharmaceutical Companies, Tobacco Companies, US Department of Agriculture and Agri-Businesses?

Could the reason this is allowed to continue, even though it's known, is for "Thinning Of The Herd," especially the elderly, so Social Security and Medicare survive and so the big businesses involved (and who "contribute" to the politicians) can prosper?

Can't you just see the US Population heads down, munching away like cattle on the chemically altered food and drinking government-sponsored poison (chlorinated and fluorinated water). People believe the advertisements put out by the media, paid for by the government and huge businesses, "propagandizing" us to believe what they are producing is in our "best interest." Watch **Super Size Me**.

Oops, do you think "they're" going to build an "L" shaped cross and hang me up (kill me), like they have done to other whistle blowers. Maybe they'll put me in jail like they did the guy who discovered the sonic means of curing all terminal cancers and other people who came up with natural cures in competition with the drug companies.

Tobacco – I'm not sure we should do anything to inform people about the hazards of smoking. Tobacco is one of the most addicting of drugs. We know smoking related deaths kill about 2,000,000 people in the US each year, and its legal – go figure. If it weren't for tobacco, how else could we "legally" kill that many people each year?

Is the reason our government subsidizes the tobacco industry is to control the population? Let's eliminate the filters and increase the nicotine (a very toxic poison) so we can get rid of more people. If people want to smoke in public, they should wear a jug over their heads to take full advantage of the tars and nicotine, don't waste any of it.

I'm amazed the life insurance companies are not refusing, legally, to pay if a smoker dies of a smoking related disease. I would assume, given the available information, a "suicide case" could be made against anyone who has ever smoked.

It's estimated that smoking related illnesses and deaths cost the general public over $2.00 per cigarette smoked. Shouldn't there be at least a $3.00 per cigarette tax? I don't like the smell of tobacco, the butts and containers polluting the environment or the spitting of tobacco juice in public. If you keep it away from me and clean up after yourself, you have the freedom and right to kill yourself. Smoke on!

Drugs – Nicotine is one of the most toxic poisons in the world, it is also one of the most addicting drugs and it's legal.

Alcohol is a known poison – a drug. There is a physical law about alcohol; if you drink, you're going to hurt. We outlawed alcohol until we discovered the law only made criminals rich. We then legalized alcohol again, and taxed it. The reasons it was made illegal have not changed. It still kills its share of humans each year. (For the people killed by drunk drivers refer to the Death Sentence section.)

We've already lost the war on drugs. We need to legalize **all** drugs, make them available to anyone who wants to buy them, **_gets neutered_** and registers as a user. This would take the criminal element out of the drug business, save us billions of dollars in enforcement, get a lot of people out of prison and back to work and we would derive taxes from the sales (same as the legal drugs; alcohol and tobacco). The quality of the drugs could also be controlled. And, none of the drug users (tobacco users, alcohol drinkers and recreation drug users) would be reproducing – at least some population control.

I believe if someone overdoses on drugs, we should let them die. Why waste time or resources on someone who has decided to violate their own body? The only time anyone should intervene is if someone overdoses someone else, and then refer to the Death Sentence section. As these people remove themselves from this planet, we'll have less piss-laced drinking water, cleaner air and more parking spaces.

Because of our basic nature, whenever we're told we can't do something (rules and laws), we're drawn to try it – just for spite, the experience, the adventure.

Life is about making choices. How are we to experience life and learn from it if we have no free will or choices? Smoking, drinking alcohol and taking drugs is a choice. Every choice we make has consequences. Gain knowledge up-front, and if you want to violate your body and interfere with your brain, get neutered first!

Other Deaths – Sports kill a few more people each year: mountain climbing, hiking, snow skiing, SCUBA diving, swimming, biking, surfing, water skiing, boating, and sports competition in high school and college.

Think about floods, hurricanes, tornadoes, hot and cold weather, fires, earthquakes, lightning, volcanoes, snakes, and bugs. And, quite a few people die each year from falls in showers or bath tubs – maybe we should outlaw bathing.

We are about to see another way Mother Nature will help to reduce the human population – killer bees from Africa have invaded the US, stand-by.

These are just a few of the many ways people die each year.

Thou Shalt Not Kill (A negative statement being filtered?)

If I am in fear for my life and I defend myself by killing the person who poses a threat, is that murder?

If the person posing the threat is a policeman, is it murder?

What if the policeman is committing a crime against me?

If a mother kills someone who is raping her young daughter is that murder?

If I kill as an act of war against the enemy of my country is it murder?

So murder, killing people, is another of those "relative" things. It just depends on the situations and circumstances. We have as many different possibilities of murder and killing as we have murderers.

Take a stand (go to War)! And remember it really doesn't matter which stand you take, you'll be tried by the extreme possibilities.

Can you come up with one justifiable reason to kill another human being? Consider war, terrorism, torture, family, possessions, religion, revenge or a threat to your life. Just look at all of the media produced options. Listen to the news every day. Isn't there something you would kill for?

Death Sentence

I know our legal system is just as warped as my view, and some innocents are convicted. However, we've swung the pendulum way to far the wrong way. Currently, criminals have more rights than their victims. Since Birth is a Death Sentence – are mothers who give birth guilty of murder? If a birth didn't occur, then a death couldn't happen.

If you *really* want to stop drunk drivers on our highways, pull the drunk over, if they fail the breath-a-lizer test, put a bullet in their head, have their car towed to a demolition yard with them in it and turn the whole mess into rebar.

How many people would risk drinking and driving when that word got out? And it cost less than $.50 cents to dispose of the culprit, less people, less cars, more parking spots, crowd control, more rebar and thinning of the herd in one.

Our constitution established there should be no "unusual punishment." The courts, lawyers, do-gooders and the CLU have managed to get this twisted around until there are way too many restrictions on punishment. We should have public: hands cut off for steeling, beheadings, firing squads, burning at the stake, forehead brandings (sex offenders), genitals cut off (incest, rape child molestation), boiling in oil and whippings on CNN prime time.

I'll bet we could charge admission to these events – remember the Roman Coliseum? If you want to stop crime, quit screwing around! Make the criminal pay and pay dearly for their crimes.

If you really want to get people's attention, round up all the convicted person's immediate family – men, women and children, and execute them – in front of the criminal, before the criminal is executed.

The Jews believed in "bad seed." The bible talks about the sins of the father carrying forward for seven generations. Let's get these people out of the gene pool **before** they make any more like them.

Read the Old Testament of the Bible, for yourself, like a novel, not one verse at a time, to see how crime was handled in the good ole days.

Check out the past history of the US for how the righteous, religious leaders of New England dealt with criminals and witches.

If that's not enough, research what the Catholic Church did during the inquisition.

In some Moslem countries today, if you're caught stealing, your hand will be cut off in public.

In the news was a story of an American who was "caned" with a flexible stick in public for violating a foreign country's law – Great!

Or, we could just **kill** all the criminals and let God sort them out. You violate the law in anyway, boom, goodbye. The punishment must be **grossly** more than the crime if you want crime to stop!

War

Whether war is the result of greed or religion, it serves a purpose – thinning out the herd. The problem: it's mostly men who go to war and are killed. Come on girls, hold up your end!

When war occurs over natural resources or land, we can relate to that - greed. One wants to take away a resource and another one wants to keep it.

When war occurs over a difference in beliefs – religion, it gets to be rather interesting, because both sides believe they're right. Their God has decreed this is to be a holy war, and all the rules are thrown out. The losers will either convert or be destroyed – genocide.

Americans are not going to like this, but oh well. The attack on the World Trade Center and the Pentagon on September 11, 2001, was a legitimate attack of war. This was not the first attack by this religious belief on the same target. We call it "terrorism" the perpetrators see it as a holy war – a jihad. The ones who sacrificed their lives in the effort will be rewarded by their God – so they were taught!

The US is now "going to war" on terrorism. Right, wrong, or indifferent, large or small, here or abroad, it's war. In a war, both soldiers and civilians are killed. That's what war is all about.

The problem with 9-11, it was more of a political statement than a real attack. Those planes could just as easily have targeted the nuclear power plants. That would have caused a lot more deaths, bigger disruptions of our economies, and made some of our country's most expensive real estate uninhabitable for 10,000 years.

If you want to find out how this war is going to proceed, Mao Tse Sung wrote a book on how to "ramp up" attacks. The book explains how a revolution can occur. It shows how to "ratchet up" the attacks on a superior force until you win. It's how his rag tag army defeated the superior Imperialist Chinese army, backed by the US. Mao eventually took over the whole of China. This same technique was used in Vietnam against the French and eventually the allies of the United Nations.

As long as people are willing to sacrifice their lives for their beliefs, the only way to stop them, is to kill them. If you kill terrorists who are planning to destroy your city, before they attack, does that make you a murder or a patriot?

Were the American Indians or the Whiteman the "terrorists?" What is a "Freedom Fighter?" Which side would you be on today? Would your choice of sides depend on whether or not you won in the Indian casino?

Quality-of-Life

To me, quality-of-life is more important than life. I have an established minimum standard which I will tolerate, and beyond that, I'm gone. Have you established your minimum standard for Quality-of-Life?

A suggestion – Plan now, so you don't trash your: brain, muscles, bones, organs, joints, cartilage, ligaments, and tendons. Each different part of your body, created for different reasons, from different building blocks needs different kinds of "food" (building block material) to replicate the cells according to the perfect DNA blueprint. "Premeditate" *now* to create a Program (habit) so as you age, you will continue, automatically, the proper diet and exercise for wellness.

Due to the FDA, Tobacco Companies (that now own the companies that process most of the food we eat), the Medical industry (profiting from sickness), and Agri-business collusion – you have a very difficult time finding food which will actually sustain life.

Death Has No Hold

Do you believe, in your heart of hearts, there's life after death? If not, just throw this book away. If yes, then hang on for some heavy stuff.

Survival is the basic program embedded in humans at the deepest level. You don't have to do anything about it, it's in you, and will manifest itself whenever your survival is threatened. Learn to control the survival drive when fear based.

Just recently, a hiker was trapped by a landslide and amputated his own arm to survive. What would you have done?

Things which threaten your survival are considered "dangerous." Many things, which you consider dangerous because of culture, myth, family, religion, or media – are not really dangerous or threatening to your survival. Wearing the right deodorant does not really mater in the overall scheme of the universe, but it might get you laid.

Longevity – how long you live – is not a matter of time, but what you learn in how you want you to be. So quit worrying about how long you're going to live, live today as if it were your last day and pay attention to what's going on – learn – change your behavior.

Death – the act of the soul leaving the body. The soul weighs six ounces/21 grams, and if the body is on a scale at the time of death, this weight/mass loss is evident. This is the point when your soul leaves for a review, before you get another shot at life to get *"IT"* right, and when Mother Nature begins to recycle the body back into dirt.

Transition – is the soul going from being trapped in a body, trapped in gravity, trapped in two dimensions to the freedom of three dimensional mobility and infinite wisdom.

Funerals – a place where people who have not made the transition yet, feel sorry for themselves and not glad for the soul who just left. The survivors stand around, look at a chunk of dirt and shed tears. When the souls, who have been the entertainers and data collectors on this plane, make the transition, there should be a celebration.

Reincarnation – when a soul wins at dice and gets to come back to earth and play with a new body in the "Playing Field of Life." "Except you die, you cannot be born again."

Writing Your Own Epitaph

A very interesting exercise is to write your epitaph, your eulogy, what you would want to be remembered about you when you exit this life. Try this exercise and consider your: family, friends, employers, co-workers, occupation, recreation, accomplishments and how you would like to die. Write it all down, edit it several times over a month, and then try to read it to a group of people. That should kick in some strong emotions. It will revel what you consider to be important.

Summary

There are too many humans on earth today. We need to re-establish the rules, and violators need to be eliminated quickly and cheaply – protect the human "gene pool!"

For "sustained yield" of our resources to happen, we've got to "thin the herd." From all indications, there's collusion to that effect going on.

No one will ever get a chance to play enough – you need to get out there, find the child in you and play more.

Birth is a death sentence. The soul is going to live on after it kills the body. The body is going to get recycled back into dirt.

Write your epitaph, it is a great life exposing adventure.

Chapter 14
Reincarnation

After my "death experiences," I was left with no doubt my soul had been here before and would come back again after it gave up the body. I had been reincarnated back into the same body in this same stream of time.

This new revelation flew right in the face of my religious training and the beliefs my relatives had been taught and taught me. And yet they all believed their soul would continue after they died, or what's the reason for believing in salvation and heaven? With my new concept, many of the confusing things in the Bible began to make sense.

Just one example, when Jesus said, "Except you die, how can you be born again?"

There are many other things in the Bible, which finally made perfect sense to me after I accepted "Reincarnation" as a fact. It also helps explain: Ghosts, spirit guides, guardian angles, channeling, and dead family members consoling the living. The acceptance of Reincarnation also helps explain why some problems a person has in this life may have been carried forward from a previous life (Karma?), and it provides a way to "regress," eliminate the "carried over" problem(s) and get on with the lessons of this lifetime

Information From The Past

I don't care what you believe, but if you believe in life after death, then why not reincarnation? What makes you think you've only been here this one time? If you've been here before, then what didn't you learn you chose to come back and learn this time? If this concept is new to you, maybe your teachings were limited by people not thinking outside their box. Possibly it's time for you to look beyond the limited scope of your life experience and teachings – outside your box of reference. You do know more people on this earth believe in reincarnation than don't believe in it – should we take a vote? The Egyptians (mummies), Jews (Hassidic Tales), Hindus, Muslims and Buddhists believe in reincarnation. Then the Christians and Catholics, must have believed in reincarnation in the past – because of where their beliefs came from. Reincarnation is somehow tied to most of the world's religions, so who changed the belief/myth system of the Christians and why? Possibly crowd control?

After dying, getting my review, and "reincarnating" back into my body in the same time frame. I never questioned Reincarnation again.

It took several years after the death experience before I was willing to say anything to other people about what had happened. Not until I began getting confirmation to these things through books documenting other people's similar experiences did I open up. When talking to people, I found many were having similar things happen in their lives. Current opinion is approximately 25 percent of the population will **admit** to having death/near death and/or out of body experiences before they die. That's a lot of people confirming and testifying to my experiences.

Personal Experiences

Throughout my life, I always felt like I was being pulled from many different sides. I could never put my finger on it, but some things I did just seemed natural, like I had done them before.

Building to me was easy, building design made sense, and using concrete was exciting. But it was difficult for me to build small or leave anything like it was. I could see in my mind what it could be. I intuitively knew how to landscape for drainage.

The first time I tried to sail, it just seemed I knew how. With only 10 hours of sailing instruction, I became a sailing instructor, and taught for a whole summer. Boating, knots, splicing, navigation, the whole thing was just natural and made sense.

But what I really liked was being around water – any kind, anywhere. I especially loved the inner tidal zone, and tide pools were a constant source of entertainment.

Past Lives Reveled

When in the "psycho-babble" section of a bookstore, I spotted a book on how to do your own Past Life Regression. I took the book home and began reading. I'd heard about past life regression from several sources, and had read about it in L. Ron Hubbard's **Dienetics.**

NOTE: I suggest you read **Dienetics** for the information and technology about how the brain works. However, avoid giving the Scientologist your name – another religion trying to get your money. I had my run-in with them, and I "squirreled" (I refused to bow down to L. Ron Hubbard) so they kicked me out and they leave me alone – they better.

As I was reading the application sections at the ends of three of the Past Life Regression chapters, I had three separate and distinct visions.

The **first vision** showed me as the shaman of a village of Chumash Indians living near the Gaviota Pass north of Santa Barbara, California. This was in a time before the first white men arrived. These coastal Indians lived off the land and the bounty of the sea. It was my job to train the young to collect food from the inner-tidal zone and to fish offshore. I also taught them how to make and use traps, snares, spears, bows and arrows to take the land and ocean animals.

When the scene changed, I was leading a trading expedition traveling northeast across the San Joaquin valley. Everyone carried heavy packs. I recognized the terrain, because I had grown up in Taft, and looked out my bedroom window across Buena Vista Lake at the Sierra Nevada Mountains. The difference was the waist high grass and the profusion of wildlife.

While we were following a game trail, I came across my current wife, Shellie, who had been abandoned by her mate because she had a badly sprained ankle. I applied my knowledge of shamanic medicine, she quickly healed, was incorporated into our traveling group and soon became my mate.

It was several years later when I found out where we were headed and what we were trading. In a museum in Cody, Wyoming, I saw a buckskin blouse covered with beadwork and accompanied by a necklace. Worked into the beads of the blouse and necklace were bits of red abalone shell.

At one time, red abalone (a large snail) abounded in the inner-tidal zone of Central California, was part of the Chumash food and the shells were used as serving dishes. I also remembered a compulsion I've had most of my life to collect abalone shells which would nest inside each other. This is the most space-conserving way to pack them. With packs full of beautifully colored abalone shells, we could have traded for anything we wanted from the inland Indians.

I've lived in and around Santa Barbara multiple times, and it feels like home. I lived two miles from the south gate of Yellowstone, and it felt very familiar – a far off memory.

This was and is so vivid I've even thought of writing a book – similar to what Ariel has done with the *Clan of the Cave Bear* series of books.

My interest in the inner tidal zone, collecting food, hunting, teaching under water hunting, gathering shells which nested inside each other, and a book on my computer called *Inner Tidal Gourmet* – all made sense.

As I continued to read, I had a **second vision** in which I was first mate to Captain Morgan, a queen-commissioned Privateer (a good pirate?), sent to the Caribbean to harass Spanish shipping and raid their land based communities.

This past life explained why I have always felt like a pirate (but a good one, if such existed), knew how to sail, and why the Caribbean felt like a familiar place.

I lived and worked in Puerto Rico and Haiti, taught diving in the USVI, visited many of the other Caribbean islands. Was First Mate and Operations Officer on a 150' Ocean Going Salvage Tug, working for Mel Fisher looking for the Attochia, a sunken Spanish galleon 34 miles west of Key West, Florida. That story is going to be another of my books.

In the **third vision**, I was a city planner in Egypt. My job was highly respected and involved laying out complete cities. This vision explained my compulsion with construction, why it was so difficult to build "small" and why landscaping, drainage and concrete work was so automatic for me.

The question about why I had become a General Contractor in California was answered.

These Past Life Regression exercises not only made sense, but brought a lot of peace over things which had confused me. It explained my strong "pulls" towards careers appearing to be in conflict with each other.

Did these revelations change my life? NO! The revelations just made my life a lot more comprehendible and acceptable to me. I have noticed the "drives" of these three careers have diminished once I understood where they came from.

Would Past Life Regression help you? Maybe or maybe not, it would depend a lot on why you did it and your expectations. However, believing in reincarnation, will help explain many mysteries.

What OBEs Taught Me

If I can be functioning in my human role and at the same time be watching and communicating with the Body from outside, then there are two distinct and separate entities involved with who I am – Body and Soul.

If my body dies (clinical dead is when breathing stops and the heart stops beating) and I can see the body and what's going on with it, then the "observer" survives the body.

If the observer (soul) survives the body, then there's life after death. This is believed by all religions or what's the point.

If the observer returns to the dead body when the heart and breathing are restarted, then the observer re-incarnates into the once dead body in the same stream of time.

If the observer can reincarnate in the same stream of time into a once dead body, it's easy to believe the same observer can reincarnate into a new, future body once it sheds the current body.

And if the observer can reincarnate into a once dead body and can reincarnate into a future body, then it's certainly possible for the observer to have incarnated into previous bodies and participated in those past lives.

It was this reasoning, as a result of my actual experiences, which lead me to believe in reincarnation and past lives.

My past life regressions answered questions about knowledge, skills, remembrances, and urgings I had in this life.

Common sense and logic applied to my life experiences.

Once you have an OBE a question is fairly obvious, "What am I really?" If you're primarily concerned with and think you are the body and then are out-of-the-body but aware of the body, what are you? If the OBE occurs when you're unconscious, what and where is the consciousness? Is the conscious-self something other than the body? If there's a "you" that's not the body, what is it? If the body functions based on the five senses input, which are shut-down during unconsciousness, but something "sees and hears" from a totally different perspective and receives "impressions" (words and data) when unconscious, which it remembers when conscious, how did that occur? Where do intuitions, dreams, answers to questions posed before sleep, gut feelings and ideas come from?

The simple answer is the Soul, which lives beyond the body, this provides answers to all of the above questions. The Soul is connected directly to the Spirit world of Infinite Knowledge, Universal Intelligence, Spirit Guides and Counselors.

If the Soul is a Spirit incarnate in a body, and it is designed to forget its origin, it would become engaged in the game of life of the body. My grandmother used to say repeatedly, "The Spirit's willing, but the body's weak." How true that is. The Soul is unlimited in its possibilities, but the body is limited by the physical and natural laws. However, the human body is capable of more than has ever been imagined. The human brain potential is unbelievable in the computing power and problem solving it is capable of performing. The ideal is to work towards understanding the dichotomy of the Body/Brain and Soul/Mind interaction and focus on cooperation between the two entities.

One example should suffice if you will apply it to every decision you make in life: You approach a cliff and look down.

The Body says, "Back-up, the rapid stop at the bottom hurts."

The Soul says, "Jump, I can fly."

In every aspect of your decision making, there are two different entities providing multiple options (not just two options and not devil – angel). The Body is survival/fear based in its options and the Soul is seeking experience to add to its data base. The example is simplistic at best, but if you understand the different agendas of the two entities, you, whichever one you are at the time, can cooperate so both entities can gain from the experience.

The Soul cannot "deny the flesh," the flesh won't stand for it if it's going to survive. However, the flesh must overcome fear to give the Soul its "virtual-reality" ride. And they both have to cooperate to come up with a solution they'll agree on. The obvious answer for the cliff example is to use a para-glider to: jump, fly, enjoying the view and provide a safe landing.

From now on, consider both entities and work towards a cooperative solution in your decision making. If there's a question or problem to be solved, seek guidance – before you jump. You might even consider sleeping on the question or problem. You'll be amazed at the answers and solutions presented from a different perspective and dimension.

Summary

My death/out-of-body experiences set me up to believe in reincarnation. The Past Life Regressions proved to my satisfaction I've been here before, multiple times, playing different roles which have impacted this lifetime.

These experiences have helped to clarify and create a new "Belief System" for me. I find no conflict between what I've experienced and what I now believe.

There is a significant difference between what I now believe and what others tried to teach me.

Chapter 15
Learning

From the time you're born, you're learning. A learning objective goes like this: "By the end of this lesson, you will be able to _ _ _ ." What comes after "able to" is an action verb. To learn something, you must take in data, process it and do something with it – take action.

If our purpose is to have experiences, learn and change our behavior, then we need to know how to go about the process.

Do you ever remember being taught **how to learn** in school?

The Laws of Learning

Prerequisites – The first law of learning is; "You never learn anything new, you only add to existing knowledge and skills." Therefore, the people who can learn the easiest are those with the broadest knowledge and life experience. In other words "It's easy to teach an old dog new tricks." Well, maybe not an old dog, but certainly easier to teach older people than younger people, if they're motivated. Learning is FUN!

Primacy – How you do something the "first time" is how you'll do it in an emergency if it hasn't become a habit.

Recency – The more recent the learning occurred or was reviewed influences how much you remember (short term memory).

Repetition – The greater the number of repetitions the more you remember. Based on your prerequisites, it takes 22 to 54 repetitions of knowledge or skill to create a habit – automatic reactions to events.

Impressing the Data – The more you involve the senses the better the learning experience. The more pain (survival threat) involved, the "deeper" the data is impressed in your memory cells. Success and positive reinforcement increases self-motivation and so learning.

The Learning Pyramid

If you're going to build an Egyptian pyramid, the height will be determined by the size of the base, and so learning. The more you know, the more you can learn. Therefore, the best thing you can do for youngsters is to broaden their horizons and give them as many different life experiences as possible.

You Can Learn Anything

To learn requires only four things: Knowledge, Skill, Attitude and Time. K+S+A+T=L

Yes, to learn requires prerequisites – knowledge, experience and/or skill. But we can always back-up and develop the prerequisites. If a person maintains a positive mental attitude – is self-motivated – then learning can occur. If the person develops a bad attitude, oh well, give-up, it's their attitude, and besides we need lots of slaves who'll do what they're told without thinking.

The key to learning is time. Does the learner have enough time, in this lifetime, to learn the subject or skill? So, even if a severally, mentally-challenged individual maintains a positive mental attitude, they may not live long enough (Time) to learn a specific topic or skill.

You can learn anything by: insuring you have the prerequisite knowledge and skills, maintaining a positive mental attitude (self motivation) and giving yourself enough time. Remember you use less than 10% of your brainpower, imagine what you could do by just upping that a couple of percentage points.

Negatives

My brother was born five years younger. He never had a chance. Being the first born in a family of four aunts, I figured out how to get female attention and reveled in it. I was born grown up and the aunts made a big to do over me. John had to settle for "seconds." I learned, by going into the kitchen and volunteering to help with the cooking and dishes, I would seldom have to help, but always got rewarded with attention. My brother did what he could to compete for the attention, but had to resort to screwing up to get it.

John would take a beating to get attention. Any kind of attention was better than being ignored. He had a malady which afflicts most people ADD, so when his nickname became "Johnny Don't," he never had a chance. Whatever he tried, someone would yell, "Johnny, Don't!" Of course he went ahead and did it. Many years later, when I was being "edumacated" about education, I found out about Negatives. It seems the human android is programmed with an automatic, negative filter.

Multiple college research programs have proven this to be a fact. The human brain filters out negatives. If you see a sign which says "Wet Paint," you'll steer clear. If the sign says, "Wet Paint, Do Not Touch," 60% of you will walk right up and touch. What your mind saw was, "Wet Paint, Touch." So poor "Johnny Don't" didn't have a chance from about the age of two.

You don't have a chance either. Think about the written tests you've taken throughout your life having questions imbedded with negatives. If you're not extremely careful, and sometimes being careful doesn't help, you'll get the question wrong. What I've just told you is a basic human programming fact, which you can prove. Have you ever heard, "If you want 'so and so' to do something, tell them **not** to do it."

It makes me wonder who was programming whom to fail when they gave us the "Ten Commandments" that start off with, "Thou Shalt Not." Oops, religion again.

The more a thing is preached against using negatives, the more likely it is to happen (Jimmy Swaggart, Jimmy Baker and the Catholic Priests?). That's good for the churches, because they get to run guilt trips and leach out your money because of your "Sin." I'm not sure they want you to know about programming.

How Well a Student Does in School

During my Masters in Education program, I reviewed several (actually all available at the time) research papers on what factors affected the ability of students to learn. Out of all of the published papers, data collected, factors considered, there were only two things having any significant effect on how students learned – Parents and Peer Group. Location, teachers, educational supplies and materials, demographics of the student body, teaching technique, number of students in the classroom, etc. had "no significant effect" on student learning.

So, parents, if you want your kids to do better in school, you better be directly involved in making sure they do their work and attend school. The scary thing is, the kid's Peer Group – the kids they hang with – has a greater effect by far than the parents. Good luck in controlling who your kid's friends are. No I don't have any suggestions! Chain them up?

Self-motivated kids will learn in spite of the Compulsory Schooling System, not because of it. Home schooled kids are five to ten years ahead of their peers. Check my web site www.Lance-Rennka.com, for an article **K-12 Compulsory Schooling Doesn't Work.**

Teaching

The Romans had a saying, "Those that Can, Do. Those that can't Do, Teach." That saying has been expanded as modern educational institutions were formed, it now includes; "Those that can't Teach, Profess. Those that can't Profess, Administrate."

After loosing the arm (I thought I couldn't "do" any more), I decided to follow the advice of the Romans, and got a job teaching Oceanographic Equipment and Instrumentation at Florida Institute of Technology in Jensen Beach, Florida. Included in the Introduction to Oceanography course was a session on "knot tying." Around the water and especially on boats, you use lots of lines. I had already learned to align the students on each side of me at an angle (it looked like a V with me at the bottom) so they wouldn't "mirror" me (do things backwards).

I said, "Do with your hands exactly what I do."

The preverbal class 'smart ass' asked, "So Lance, what about the left hand?"

"Just fill in the blanks, use your imagination," I said.

I talked them through the tying of the Boland while demonstrating. "Right hand does this, and the left hand does that." We did it over and over, and no one could do it.

Finally, my 'smart ass' says, "I got it!"

"Great, come over here and show everyone how you did it." I stepped back and he replaced me, put his left hand in his back pocket, and tied the knot with one hand. I had an epiphany, bells rang, fireworks went off. I got it!

"OK, Enough of that," I said, "I just learned I can teach you to tie knots with one hand, but not with two."

Not a failure to communicate or a mistake. When mechanical skills are being learned they come primarily from "parroting." You need to see the skill from a similar perspective as if you were doing it. Face close to the same way the person demonstrating is facing or your mind has to reverse the process. All the individual steps must be included. When done slowly, correctly, and with explanations including why each step is necessary, the picture of the process is imbedded in your recording device.

Then it's simply a matter of doing the skill **exactly** the same way, slowly at first then speeding up, 22 to 54 repetitions to form a habit – never forgotten.

As a SCUBA Instructor, I tried to never demonstrate a skill. I'd get someone with two hands to do the skill. Think about the poor two-handed "students" having difficulty performing a skill, which a one armed person can do with ease. That will destroy an ego quick.

When I began training SCUBA Instructors as my primary, full-time occupation, I warned the candidates, "Leave your egos behind, and never flaunt them in front of me. You're paying me to train you to become an educator. If your ego gets in the way, I'll tear it to shreds. A good educator controls their ego." (Do as I say, not as I do?)

I recognized in them what was in me, and if not controlled the ego would ruin an instructor. When circumstances required I would give an object lesson (the best kind of lesson) by getting geared up quicker, entering or exiting the water better, doing a difficult skill with ease, performing a physically demanding rescue or any number of other tasks to demonstrate that a "cripple" could do easily what they were running their ego on.

A simple look was usually all that was necessary to let the "ego culprit" know they had a made a mis-take and to change their behavior – my job for which they paid me righteously.

Let Me Slow It Down For You

It's great to gain understanding, even if it comes from a child. Keep in mind we use less than 10 percent of our brain power. So there I was watching a child at play with a toy. I motioned to him and after making sure it was OK with his parents to talk with a complete strange, stranger, he sidled over. My first question was, "How old are you?"

A sly grin and then he answered, "Between five and seven."

I laughed. It was obvious he wasn't just answering. If I was going to quiz him, he was going to make me think. "When you were playing with your toy," I asked, "What were you thinking?"

"The turtle was swimming around chasing bad guys," he said.

"Show me what he was doing."

The turtle whizzed around, in front, over his head, up and down.

I said, "Whoa, that was too fast."

With a twinkle in his eyes, he said, "OK, let me slow it down, just for you," as he put the turtle through the same exercise, only in slow motion.

I thanked him between hilarious laughter by both myself and Rick Ford. The boy smiled and walked back to his parent's table.

It was obvious he understood at the age of "between five and seven," his mind moved much faster than our "old" minds did. I'm certain if his parents don't intervene, the school will have him on "slow down" drugs so they can keep up with him.

Subliminal

If you wonder why so many kids are diagnosed with ADD now days, watch commercials.

Some years back, the government cracked down on movie theaters for using subliminal suggestion. A single movie frame is 1/16th of a second – 16 frames per second. By experimenting, researchers determined the conscious brain can't see one individual frame. So in the lead-in to the movie, they put one frame per second of written suggestions with pictures, i.e. "drink soda," "eat candy," "eat popcorn," "eat hotdogs." Did it work? You bet! They experienced a 60+ percent increase in snack bar sales. So if you don't think subliminal programming works, think again. Movie theaters are restricted, *by law*, not to use this subliminal advertising technique on us.

Current video cameras record 30 frames per second. When one out of thirty frames was imbedded with "suggestions," an even greater subliminal effect was proven. If you need a little paranoia, ask yourself, "What are the commercials doing to my brain?"

In further "imbedded suggestion studies," it was found the brain is capable of picking up one image in one-thousand frames per second. That's a pretty good brain you have there. Your brain loves input, and the faster the better.

Now pay close attention to the next few commercials you see on TV. They're making ½ second "cuts" (changes from one scene to another twice a second). Why? Because it entertains your brain, and when you're receptive (entertained), it imbeds the information – sales pitch – in your brain.

Think carefully. Have you ever gone marketing and picked up something that wasn't on the shopping list and wondered why? Well watch those rug-rats in the baskets. They pick out only those items advertised on TV. Although they're entertaining – the best shows on TV – I dislike TV commercials, because I understand what they're doing to me – programming me to buy something.

Data Storage

Now we've established your brain is pretty quick, let's talk a little bit about how it stores data.

Close your eyes and think about walking into your parents' house. When you step through the front door, what's in the far right corner? OK, so what did you do? Pull up a picture? Then you must have a photographic memory. In fact, everyone has a photographic memory. That's how you record data, a picture along with over 52 other perspectives including; sight, sound, feel, smell, taste, temperature, emotions, body position, your alignment with Magnetic North, and much more. When we think, we think in pictures with all of this other sensory data included. Now hold that thought for the next section.

Filing Cabinet

Everyone experiences "Old Timers Disease," You know something, it's right on the tip of your tongue, It flashed through your brain and was gone.

So how do you get to the stored knowledge/data you know you have? In other words, "I know it all, I just can't remember it all at once." If you had all of your memories stored in filing cabinets, how would it look? Might it be multiple filing cabinets, with multiple drawers, with divider folders in the drawers? You would store everything about your immediate family in one cabinet. Each family would have a drawer. Each drawer would have folders with each person's name on it. The folders would contain the information you have on each individual. Put it all in alphabetical order, and if someone asks you a question about a specific relative, you go to the filing cabinet, to the drawer, to the person's folder, and all the information is right there.

That's precisely how you've stored your data. In fact you've gone many steps farther, you cross-reference (matrix) everything as well to make it both easier to find something, and easier for your brain to pull up extraneous information to solve a problem.

Your brain is a "similar to" master computer. It can store extraneous new information like history, but if you want to be able to get to the information and use it, you have to tie the new data to something you've already experienced – regardless of how far out it may seem. In other words, "You never learn anything new, you only ever add to existing knowledge or skill." So if you really need to learn something, have it available to use in the process of solving problems or taking tests, you **must** tie the new data to something you already know. This makes "remembering" the data (finding the right file folder in the right filing cabinet) much easier.

The key to this is to involve as many of your senses and strong emotions as possible during the "data acquisition" stage. Since smell and taste are your two most "locking" senses, use them to help store and retrieve data.

Let's say you're taking five classes in school. Pick out five different pleasant tasting jellybeans. Assign a flavor to each of the five classes and be consistent. Whenever you're in one of the classes, reading material about the class, talking to your classmates about the material, and doing homework, have the same jellybean in your mouth. Do this for the whole semester, and when it is time for the final test, pop the right jellybean into your mouth, and up comes the file folder for the subject.

Did you just say, "That's too easy, it can't possibly work."

Have you ever gotten a whiff of flowers or another smell and a movie started playing in your mind? "Yes!" Well the principle works great, try it. Read **Total Recall – How to Maximize Your Memory Power** by Joan Minninger.

Oh, and by the way ladies, some very good advice is coming. Avoid at all cost walking your mate through the perfume section of a department store. The mate will begin to run movies of any previous ladies he's been with as each of their perfumes are breathed in. Don't believe me. Try it and watch as the different movies play in his head. As the overlapping scenes with different movies play, he'll get very confused, and if you're not careful, he'll call you the wrong name.

Given what I've just disclosed, if you get angry or jealous, it's your own fault. When I explain this to couples, the women say, "No way." The men, however, say, "Absolutely!" (Why else would you stick to one perfume?)

Where is Memory Stored?

Where do you think memory is stored? "In the brain," you said? Well not exactly. The brain is the Central Processing Unit (CPU) of the android. Let's try cellular memory. We understand this, because people have had half their brains removed and retained their memory. You've heard of "Muscle Memory," where you program your muscles to perform a specific function, i.e. bike, swim, do a somersault, etc. There's physical as well as mental memory. The object of skills training is to gain consistent performance of a given skill/task by storing the "program" in the muscle tissues (muscle memory).

If memory is stored in your body's cells, do you think it might be of benefit if the nerve energy and circulation (the result of movement not sitting still) to those cells was working during storage and retrieval?

You've heard that people who receive transplants sometimes have memories and emotions of the people who donated the organs. Memory is stored in the cells of your body. So your cells are the filing cabinets not the brain. When you give cells from your body to someone else, they get some of your memories.

You just asked, "Oh, no – what about blood transfusions?"

Well I got a complete oil (blood) change in Puerto Rico, and when Caribbean music plays, my ass wiggles, I have no choice. Go figure. It gets better!!!

Thinking vs. Talking

So wouldn't it be nice to understand why we have such a difficult time communicating? Think of a painting or picture you have hanging on a wall. Now consider a master artist who's going to duplicate the painting, never having seen it. You're going to "tell" (in words) him/her enough about the picture so it can be duplicated exactly.

Good luck. "A picture is worth a thousand words?" More like ten thousand words if you want to get it close to right. So you think in pictures – moving pictures – and each "picture in your brain" is worth, let's say, just a thousand words. Your brain is speeding through the frames, but you can only talk at 120 words a minute. It's a wonder we ever get anything across.

What we're trying to do by communicating verbally is transfer the picture we have in our brain to the other person's brain using words. We use a series of words in a sentence, each sentence trying to bring up a part of the picture in the receiver's mind. By the end of the paragraph, we hope to have a completed picture at least similar to the one we see in our mind. If we use a word which brings up a different picture in the receiver's mind than the picture we see, we have miscommunications.

That's why men and women have such a difficult time communicating. A guy's definition of words is not the same as the gal's definition. Women invented language, back in the cave where hand and body signals didn't work in the dark. The problem is the women also came up with the definitions to the words, and just about the time a guy figures out what a word means, the woman changes the meaning. Women just want to be in control and do so by keeping men confused. (Not very difficult.)

Imagine how difficult it is to communicate with someone who has English as a second language. Each word in our dictionary has multiple meanings, while the person trying to understand what we mean only has the first definition as a picture of what we're trying to convey.

Now back to the boy who started all of this. You're his teacher. He enters the classroom, and what's the first thing you say to him? "Sit down, and shut up. I'm going to teach you something."

The next thing he hears from you, "Stop day dreaming!" His brain is playing pictures at a higher speed than yours, and you're trying to convey a thought/picture at 120 words per minute. That child could meditate and keep up with you. Remember what Einstein said, "Imagination is more important than knowledge." To educate someone in our current Compulsory Educational System, we have to turn off their learning switches, and slow down their brains. We speed up data in every other aspect of their lives, and then we subject them to school. They're being "hooked" on slowdown drugs, by adults while being bombarded with "Just Say No To Drugs." That makes a lot of sense. I'm sorry, I forgot. Schools are just a paid baby-sitting facility, to keep the kids out of the mall so they won't shop lift.

Depression

I know to gain knowledge I must read. The wisdom, from around the world, from the past to the present is stored in books. For years, the most depressing places I visited have been libraries and bookstores. There are over 195,000 new books being published each year. Divide that by 365 days a year and you'll see why I become depressed. How am I going to read this year's current books, let alone catch up on the books from the past?

Media and the Speed-up of Societies' Advancement

It's my opinion, the thing which may save society, is the current increase of media sources and the information age. When my parents started their lives together, other than radio and a few movies, there was no media. Now you can get any kind of interpersonal relationship you can imagine, and some you didn't even think about, on TV. If you're able to learn from others, you can advance at a rapid rate.

If you have to experience a love triangle, at least you have good examples to follow so it should be quicker than stabbing around in the dark. Interpersonal relationships are the best implements for behavioral modification, if you'll pay attention and let them. When you're the most upset, is when you need to step back or up and get a good look. Not at what someone else is doing, but what you're doing.

If **YOU** are not willing to change (never say you're not able), end the relationship – it doesn't matter what kind – boss, spouse, friend, associate. If they need to change, give it some time, you're playing a bit part, but let them know what your expectations are, and put a limit. Object lessons can help the learning experience immensely. It could be the only thing which will get their attention is you leaving.

Five years old

I love revelations, regardless of where they come from. I was having breakfast one morning, when a family sat down at a table next to me. Their son, about five, was just being a boy. He hadn't spilled anything, broken anything, or messed himself up too bad.

His mother, obviously having a bad day, grabbed him, shook him, and said, "Would you act like an adult?"

The whistles blew, the fireworks went off, the bells started ringing, and I had another epiphany. It was then I understood the statement in the Bible, "Except you become as a little child."

So what was the revelation that was so important as to interrupt my breakfast?

Being an adult is an act!

None of this is serious. This life is just an illusion, Earth is a playground, so enjoy it - as a child. Have fun, play with life and learn. Look at everything with eyes of wonder. Keep your curiosity working and always ask why.

What Do You Know, You Don't Know You Know?

If memory is stored in the atoms, then what are you learning from the water you drink, the air you breathe, and the food you eat? (And you thought this was going to be easy.)

"Lance, you just did a major leap in extrapolation," I heard you say.

Did I really, or is that the question we should be asking? Why, when you think up some new invention and fail to act on it, within a year you see it in the market place? If this is true, and it is, then all the "Wisdom of the Ages" is available by simply breathing, drinking, and eating.

Well, isn't it? "What do you know, you don't know you know?" As the most advanced critter on this planet (notice I didn't say galaxy), what information did you get when the wiggly smacked into the egg? How many generations, from both sides of your family tree, worth of knowledge and life experience did you get as a part of your basic programming?

On the North Slope of Alaska, a small bird is hatched by its parents, who raise it until it can forage for itself. Before it fledges out and can fly, the parents fly south. The fledgling finishes growing up, learns to fly and then flies to the Antarctic, returns to the North Slope, finds a mate, builds a nest, and repeats the reproduction process.

All this without going to school, no flying lessons, no compass, no topographical charts, no guide to follow, no construction classes and no sex education classes. And you don't think you came with a significant amount of "inherited" information?

I ask again, "What do you know, you don't know you know?" Isn't school about remembering what you already know? Who discovered what you're learning (remembering) first? And if you're a Soul operating a body, don't you (Soul) have access to all that has ever been, is, and is going to be?

Boy, if we just operated on those premises, wouldn't it change how we run educational institutions? Do you need a break, or can we just forge ahead? Good, I'm on a roll, and I've just about got your head opened up for the real brain mushing stuff (you can go sit in the corner later).

Let's just accept, in the overall scheme of things, the body is of no consequence. Did I hear you say, "Oh no, think of all the time and money I spent on clothes, hair care, food, baths, make-up, diets, and exercise."

Well just humor me a little bit. If the body's nothing but dirt, and it's going to be recycled back to dirt, and it wears out quickly, how important can it be? So what is important? Having experiences, cramming your cells full of information, and then getting the cells back out there so others can benefit from your experiences?

I'm absolutely against burials. Since we're using plastic and concrete to encase the bodies it'll take over 10,000 years for the information in the buried bodies' cells to get out there and do some good. Is that why humans are regressing? How are the "new ones" going to benefit from your life experiences? Your behavioral changes stored in your cells, need to be recycled.

Are you – the Soul – just trapped in a body, trapped in two dimensions, trapped in gravity having experiences and the cellular data really doesn't matter? Or maybe we've been given infinite choices (will) and the opportunity to find out whom we really are? Could it be through our own "free will" we've chosen to have these multiple life experiences to learn who we are? That the planning, coordinating, birth, life, death, transition, review, planning, coordinating, birth, life, etc. process we've been going through is not only for us but also for the "Big Computer in the Sky" to experience and therefore all other souls will gain from our lives. Or, maybe we're just playing the ball in the pinball game of life, and the Cosmic Joker is operating the plunger and paddles. And to think you were taking it serious. It's getting better!!!

Let's get something straight right now. When you look in a mirror, what you see is less than one percent of what you are. When the body, made out of dirt, is discarded, the soul will live on. When you cause the body to die, in whatever fashion you choose to make it happen (you are responsible – there are no accidents), there's no judgment or heaven or hell waiting for you. Heaven and hell are figments of our imagination. They're the carrot and the stick used by organized religion to keep you in line and line their pockets with your money.

You're making your time in this life, on this earth, heaven or hell – have it anyway you want it. And the spirits sitting in the bleachers eating hot dogs, drinking beer, and throwing peanut shells on the stadium floor are enjoying the show you're putting on in the "Football Stadium of Life" – sitcoms and soap operas, right?

Since the body doesn't matter and is going to be recycled, and since you get to do life over and over until you get it right or get tired of it, you might as well enjoy it. Reincarnation allows you infinite patience.

Did you notice I didn't try to convince you about reincarnation? I figured if you're reading this book, you either already believe or are ready to. If not, I guess I took you by surprise. I was educated "religiously" that there was no such thing as reincarnation. The Bible makes a whole lot more sense if you believe in reincarnation. Besides if you only get one try at it, you better be good or, of course, you could just buy your way into heaven.

You do realize I'll never be allowed in any church after writing this book? Oh well, I'd rather do my worshiping underwater anyway – less audio distractions. Besides if God talks to you under water, he/she/it is serious. But make sure it's God and not someone with an underwater communications unit or you could be headed to the Mission Field on false pretenses. If the preachers only knew how easy it would be to use an underwater speaker, they could "recruit" a lot of divers.

Imagine you're swimming along with the fish, enjoying life, the soul is getting its battery recharged because it has assumed its preferred body position and has three-dimensional mobility. Then, in Cousteau's

Silent World, a booming voice calls out your name, "_____, this is God, I want you." You'd sell everything, give the money to the church and be on the next plane to the Mission Field to save the world. I suggest you surface immediately and find out who the joker is. God is much subtler than a booming voice, but still a joker.

Modern Technology

So we're androids, a computerized machine made out of cosmic dust playing robot wars (you really can't take any of this serious).

Where's the CD reader? I want to be able to insert a CD and download, I don't have time to waste in school or reading books. I want a simple, quick, efficient way of reprogramming my computer and downloading data. We keep reading about and seeing on the Sci Fi Channel the hat with electrodes that's supposed to accomplish this.

One of the things Alien Abductees seem to agree about is there's some kind of "download, data gathering" or what's the point of the abduction?

Determining I needed to read faster, I studied "Speed Reading" but that would only get me up to about 800 words per minute at 50% retention rate. I discovered computers, and determined I wanted a plug-in and a CD read unit so I could just get the book on a CD and "download" it into my hard drive. The more data, the more experiences, the more wisdom, the faster I can learn my lessons and the quicker I can become who I want me to be. I was unable to find anyone who would install the plug into my brain's computer. Frustration and depression would rule – if I let them.

And then along came the book **PhotoReading** by Paul R. Scheele, M.A. and Learning Strategies Corporation www.learningstrategies.com. How would you like to "download" any and all reading materials with an 80+% retention rate at 25,000 words per minute? That's far short of a computer download, but significantly faster than anything we've had so far. Now whole books can be "photo read" in less than two hours and it's in your hard-drive (cells), retrievable and useable.

Think about PhotoReading dictionaries, encyclopedias, computer manuals, law books, procedures manuals, textbooks, etc. PhotoRead a language dictionary then do the language tapes – wouldn't that work about a thousand times better? No more "language barriers!" Would this help in the advancement of mankind?

This is the information age. Let's get the information into our computer-like storage system and crank up our brain use beyond the insignificant, less than 10% we're using now. Would it make a difference in the lives of those people who did it? Are you going to avail yourself of this technology and kick your total life into another gear?

One of my current projects is developing a "template" which can be put over any 4 unit – 40 hour course of study. The objective is to use current technology to speed up learning. This "new" way of learning would allow you to watch a two-hour DVD of the 4 unit course and retain 90+ percent of the information. I know it can and will be done, the only question is whether I'll be involved. Would you be interested in this new way of gathering data? How much would each two-hour DVD be worth to you? How about you using my template to produce the educational materials and I'll do the motivational speaking about it?

Star Trek showed us the way, Spock could just put his hand on a human's face/head a certain way and download what was in their mind – the "mind meld." I've had that kind of thing happen, and I haven't had to touch the person. So do we have the capability of "tuning into" someone? Yes, the phone rings and you know who it is, someone starts a sentence and you finish it for them, you're following someone in a vehicle and you know exactly what they're thinking.

We have these kinds of experiences all the time, however we have little time to develop them into manageable and directable skills. In fact, religions and governments would discourage you from becoming proficient in this skill, because you would then know who the lust-full ministers and the political liars are. That wouldn't do at all.

You better stop right now, get the **PhotoReading** book and get started, because here comes another significant read: *The 11the Element – The Key to Unlocking Your Master Blueprint for Wealth and Success* by Robert Scheinfeld. This will help you use your other senses and find your purposes in life – really what life is all about for you.

Given the gross amount of data available, we've got to develop a much better way of inputting information into our hard drives. You do know the problem this presents, the ability of those providing the disks to screw with our brains. Not to worry, that's already being done – screwing with our brains. The textbooks our children are using have many critical errors. Past History is being rewritten to include errors and exclude many salient facts and occurrences.

So is there a solution? Well, yes. And as always, it will be a lot more fun for me to take you on a journey rather than just provide you with an answer. Hang-on!

Why do some people migrate to certain areas? What do you think motivates archaeologists to work in certain specific areas? What causes people to choose certain professions? Could it be as simple as a carry-over from past lives? Have these people already been there and they're now trying to prove to themselves they really did exist in that time and place? Did they just drink some water, breathe some air or eat some food imbedded with information? Did they plan into their "Life's Script" the current experiences, careers and obsessions? Are those questions about you and your life?

So if we really want to know something, someone has already been there, done that. All we have to do is regress them to discover what happened and what went on. Oh, but then they wouldn't have to do all that digging, and all those diggers would have to get a different job.

There's actually another way to get this information. Just take a trip to the Master Library, the Computer-in-the-Sky, the Life-Experience records and look it up. You can do that, and you can find out how on your own.

When the student is ready, the information is made available – a universal truth.

I hope you don't think I'm just jaded. I'm presenting many things I've experienced and thought. I don't expect you to act on these things or think about them, unless you feel you must include them in your life adventures.

Einstein

Albert Einstein may have been one of the most brilliant men of all history. He estimated, as brilliant as he was, he was using less than 10% of his brainpower (his estimate was 6%). Based on the "i" before "e" thing, he got it wrong twice in just his last name.

Einstein is quoted as saying, "Imagination is more important than knowledge." The reason is; without imagination - imagining and dreaming – knowledge will do little good. Imagination is a **multiplier** of knowledge.

Were you ever told to, "Stop Daydreaming?" One of the biggest tools to help children expand their thinking processes and develop their brains is play. Kids play automatically via daydreaming. It's through play they learn about physics, physiology, geology, chemistry, and biology. Just maybe, none of us got to play enough, and we need to put more play into our lives if we want our brains to work better. And for sure, that means mommy has to go away and let us climb some trees.

I believe we're capable of doing anything we can think up – imagine (image?). I know we're not even beginning to utilize our total mental capabilities. Watch, **Rainman**, and then the TV Special about **Idiot Savants**. These people are capable of extraordinary mental and physical activities, but are incapable of functioning alone in society.

If one person has done something, then others can do the same thing. We all have a 3 pound brain (CPU) and the same basic human program/operating system. I believe we all have the mental capability of every other person that has lived, is living, and will live. What the Idiot Savants show us is just a glimpse of what we're capable.

Would it surprise you to find out in the "ability to learn" category, you are seriously under-achieving? Not all your fault, the Compulsory Schooling System has done an excellent job in curbing our imagination and learning capabilities in order to "educate" us. We've been categorize, labeled, graded and GPA-ed until we forgot, in order to learn, we must screw-up.

If after you took a test and then reviewed the test, do you think you would do better taking the same test again? **Yes!!!** Then the test is a part of the learning experience. The purpose of a test is to show the test taker/student what they were supposed to learn they didn't learn. The test should be a reflection of the educator's skill, not a means to "rate" the student.

The problem is taking a test then sometime later getting the grade. There's no review of the information to correct mis-takes. If this written test was on flying, it's a part of a program you're paying for to learn to fly, you got a solid 90%, an A, and you don't review the items you got wrong, does it mean out of 10 landings, you're going to crash on one? It certainly could indicate that. In this instance, I'd be real pissed. I paid to learn something, attended class, did my homework, did my best on the test, and didn't get 100%. I didn't get my money's worth. That's like paying for ten pounds of beans and going home with nine pounds.

You do know in every single educational program, pre-school, K-12, college, seminars, skill training sessions, etc. you or someone else is paying for you to gain knowledge and develop skills. So from now on, you're going to get 100% of what you pay for – right?

Would it change how you look at education if you found out the "trouble makers" are by far the brightest minds, and their antics are a result of boredom?

Summary

You add to existing knowledge and skills so broaden your life experience.

Avoid negatives in your speech, writing and test taking.

Go ahead, just try to follow the Ten Commandments which are imbedded with negatives.

Exercise your memory and use more of your brain.

Daydream, use your imagination, create!

Make learning fun, play at it and make sure you get your money's worth.

Chapter 16
Wellness

Intuitively, we know we should keep our body working well. The problem is we're into the game of life and we tend to act with little or no regard for life's affects on our body. When young, we believe we're invincible. Death and injury are at most a remote thought. Fun, excitement, intrigue, physical challenges and showing off are the primary focus. Even if we're injured, we heal and recover quickly.

At some point in time we begin to get stiff and experience aches and pains. Common sense (not all that common) allows us to relate these pains with previous injuries. And then the reality of our youthful transgressions hits us. We become more and more conscious of dangers, which could result in injuries and future pain.

As we age, we begin to face our mortality and this smacks right up against our survival instinct. We begin to intuitively realize we're here to learn, and haven't completed all our lessons. This leads to a desire to extend rather than terminate our life. We're heard saying, "If I could only go back, knowing what I know now."

Finally we reach the point where we have time, money, and a focus on enjoying life, but we're physically and emotionally unable – due to youthful transgression, injuries and fear – to pursue our dreams. Our bodies just won't function like they used to. Almost everyone says, "If I knew I was going to live this long, I'd have taken better care of my body."

Information in the Form of Cellular Vibration – Frequency

When driving from Key Largo, Florida to New Orleans, Louisiana with Rick Ford and Larry Heiskell, an idea struck me and we discussed it most of the drive. I'm going to present the summary of the idea and let you mull it over.

Every atom and therefore every cell is more space than substance. What's going on in all the space? Is this space where data, information is stored? If so, is this why transplant donors have memories and emotions of the donor? If every atom and cell stores data/information, were the natives of the past and the present right in believing that by eating a brave, strong or smart animal you were able to gather those attributes to you? Is this one reason for cannibalism and the eating of your ancestors when they die, so there's no loss of information or attributes? If information is stored in the atoms, then it can be gathered from what we eat, drink and breathe. What are we learning from feed-lot cattle and chickens raised in cages in barns? At least wild animals have some desirable attributes other than "someone will take care of me."

By eating meat from domesticated animals, are humans being programmed to think in terms of someone taking care of them – welfare?

If this is true, then when we breathe, drink, or eat a disease, isn't our body just "learning" from the disease cell how to be sick in a certain way – the specific germ's way? When we get an injection or take a pill to help fight a disease, are the drug molecules teaching us how to fight the disease?

If this is in fact what's going on, then learning to be diseased and learning to defeat the disease are possible. Well aren't they? Since placebos work about 30 to 80 percent of the time, are placebos just tricking our brain into learning to deal with a disease on its own? Isn't this just brain over matter? And if it works, maybe we can just use our brains to cure disease. Current medical and pharmaceutical research is doing this with drugs. Do the drug molecules have educational information imbedded in the atoms?

I don't have the answers, but I'm at least looking at the problem from a very different position. We know we can make people sick, by "teaching" them about a disease (commercials are very good at this). Then can't we just teach them about how to cure the disease, and they'll get well?

Wouldn't that be novel? You'd go to school instead of the hospital when sick. However, until we get the food, water, pollution, and population thing figured out, we need to keep thinning the herd. If we keep reducing the infant mortality rate and increasing longevity we're in for some real catastrophes in the near future.

Everything vibrates/cycles: sub-sonic, sonic, ultra-sonic, super-sonic, colors, light, radio frequencies and beyond. Vibration is in control and virtually operates everything – everything! Sounds and colors affect us in ways we still don't understand. Each letter of each language is a combination of vibrations. The combination of letters into words produce a word sound (tone). Vibrations contain power – words are powerful! Be impeccable with your words – what you say has a profound effect on others, the world around you and more specifically you! What you say you become – listen to the words you say regularly – is that what you want to become? Listen to what others are saying to you, is that what you want to become? The word(s) is/are mightier than the sword.

Placebos

If placebos work, and research shows they do, then how much of getting well is "brain over matter?" Why do some cancer victims recover and others die? Could it be as simple as learning your lessons and putting that phase of your life behind you – rewriting the script? You want to get healed, you write a script, create and voice a mantra and you heal.

Oops, if this catches on, there'll be a whole lot of people on unemployment.

What if you're a smoker? What if you do drugs? What if you're an alcoholic? What's your body "learning" to do from these drugs? Each drug has a specific message – program – vibration – tone. You continue to succumb to a substance which is programming your life negatively, become ill because you violate your body (won't learn your lesson), and someone is supposed to feel sorry for you? NOT!! Why would anyone want to give over control of any part of their life – to a substance or other people? "Drug Users" (all kinds) are just trying to get out of their conscious brains and into the super-conscious (spiritual) side of their being. There's better ways to reach the Spiritual side of your being.

Take control of your life – reprogram. The way you learn a habit is through repetition. Some information "sticks" quicker/easier than other information. Isn't the cure for any addiction just a matter of changing the habit? Wow, sounds like a sure cure for drug addiction.

The Cure for Cancer and Other Diseases

All terminal cancers were cured in 1932. The research was done by Rife at UCLA, it was published, and is on record – 50% rule – go check. The sonic device was fairly simple, it used the antithesis (opposite) of the vibration of the cancer, which killed the cancer cells. Like the singers voice that breaks the glass. Like the music made by steel drums that vibrates different organs in your body. Every atom has its own vibration – tone. Molecules (a combination of atoms) have their own specific combination of vibrations - tone. Everything we know about is made up of molecules. Therefore every organ, form, bacteria, virus, fungus, material, and even planets have their own sonic frequencies – tones.

With this 1930s device, you simply tune into the disease's frequency – any disease – set up the correct sonic frequencies, and walk through the tone, like the metal detectors in an airport, and walla, you're healed. No drugs, no cutting, no extended stay till you die, just well.

So why did the AMA put the inventor of this cure in jail where he died? Always follow the money. Remember if cancer is cured, billons of dollars will be lost to the medical profession, universities, other research institutions and pharmaceutical companies.

Oh, you didn't like that bit of information. That pissed you off, didn't it? Well, good! We got some emotion going, which means you'll learn and retain something of what you're reading. Keep in mind the biggest problem on earth – over population – maybe the AMA is actually trying to do the planet some good and not just line their pockets.

Part of the Doctor's uniform of the day includes a prescription pad. Consider this. Prescription drugs are "toxic chemicals," Poisons which will kill you, therefore, they **require** a Medicine Doctor's administration. The Doctor is supposed to Prescribe the right drug, for the right disease, for the right person at the right dosage – or you die!

The third leading cause of death in the US is Prescription Drugs – 180,000 people per year.

I'm going to suggest another book, "**Honey, The Gourmet Medicine**" by: Joe Traynor. Information from as far back as recorded history, not allowed to be used by the AMA? (Natural, cheap but doesn't support the drug companies.)

Years ago, before I found out about the "vibration" thing, I always wondered why the doctors "poisoned" the whole body (chemo-therapy) instead of just injecting the tumor or cancer. Why use radiation to "cook" the cells when a long needle, well placed would be much more effective. And just now on TV, I heard researchers in Europe are beginning tests on animals of the direct injection program.

If I had just gotten off my ass and acted on my idea, I could be making millions instead of the Medicine Doctors, but then I'd be the one in jail. I could have been a ND (Needle Doctor) instead of the MD (Medicine Doctors).

Do you get a funny vision every time I say "Medicine Doctor?" You know what I mean, feathers, rattles, drums, dancing, smoke, body paint, masks and bad tasting natural herb stuff – all the things the current crop of Medicine Doctors outlaw.

Why did _I_ have to tell you this, when My Doctorate is in Education?

30 Years Old – Full Maturity

It appears the human body was built to reach full maturity, then hold at between 28 to 32 years of age - forever. If the pituitary gland is working correctly, and the body is not destroyed by accident, we should be able to maintain our bodies in perfect working order at age 30.

In order to do this, we would have to completely repair any damage – no scars or residual damage. Imagine how "smart" you would be if you lived a mentally and physically active 30 year old life until 150 years old. Interested? So do you think the 3 score and 10 year thing in the Bible programmed humans to age and die at 70 years old? When the Bible was written, that was old.

We spend our whole lives trying to get the toys we wanted in our youth. Just about the time we get rich enough to afford those toys and time to play with them, we're too beat up to enjoy them. What we really want is to be 70 years old with the 30 year old body of our youth so we can play with the toys. We want the maximum entertainment every day, plenty of energy, wellness and fitness so we can *Live* (not just exist) till we decide to die.

The Healing Process

So how does the body repair itself?

When the body suffers any injury, the first thing is an increase in blood circulation to the damaged area. This is so the blood can bring the required re-building materials, and oxygen. An increase in blood flow causes swelling, which decreases blood circulation. This defeats the whole purpose of increasing the circulation. The next thing which happens is an infusion of calcium to stabilize the damaged area.

If there's a broken bone, all well and good, the bone heals.

If the damage is to muscle tissue, calcium builds up in the damaged muscle reducing its elasticity – *bursitis*.

If the damage is to tendon, ligament, or cartilage calcium hardens them and reduces their flexibility - *tendonitis*.

If the damage occurs to a joint, the calcium attaches to the tissues in and around the joint – *arthritis.*

So under current "body wisdom" the body fights itself when performing the healing process. As we all know, when a cut occurs, the result is a scar. The scar tissue is less flexible than the surrounding tissue (calcium?), which restricts motion.

Consider what happens when a cut occurs. Cutting of arteries and veins (which must be regenerated) restricts blood flow, causes swelling, tissue death, calcification, and scaring. All result in a restriction of motion. Immobilization of the damaged part is necessary to give the body time to heal the damage. Once the healing is complete, we need to increase the circulation to the damaged area and eat the right kinds of food to force our system acidic so the excess calcium will be carried away. We need to start flexing and stretching the area as soon as possible to keep the scar tissue flexible.

Vibratory massage, hydro massage (Jacuzzi jets) and massage therapists can all be used to speed healing. Heat and then cold applied alternately to the injury site will speed up circulation. Movement in water should be the choice, because water offers some resistance and you're not affected by gravity.

If you have access to a **hyperbaric oxygenation chamber**, the healing process can be speeded up by a factor of up to seven times. Hyperbaric oxygenation reduces swelling and infuses the tissues with oxygen. This reduces cellular death which means less cells need to be regenerated: including strokes and heart attacks. The AMA has all but "damned" the use of hyperbaric oxygenation chambers except for crush, burn, septic sores and gangrene victims, because, if people find out disabilities might have been prevented with its use, lawsuits will occur.

So if we use common sense about dealing with our injuries, kick our pituitary gland into action with a good mental picture of the repair needed, and get the circulation going in the injured area ASAP, there will be a lot less residual damage from any one injury.

Because of our basic program to survive, we need to look at longevity differently. We need to step back and get a better view – information – as to what is really going on. Given the state of the human animals on earth, we don't have it all figured out.

The Fountain of Youth

And then along came a step in the search for the "Fountain of Youth," organ transplants. Right now, another war is raging – cloning human beings for "spare" parts. Makes sense if the human body is a machine. I can see it now, the corner Napa Body Parts Store.

The question I have is when the cloned body takes a breath, does it right then take on a Soul as the operator, and if it does, then won't the clone be "different" than the original. No wonder there's a war raging – church, state, and those wanting to extend their stay in the same body instead of exiting and re-entering a new one, and the Napa company wanting to sell Body Parts.

Maybe there's a way for the Soul to kill the old body and take over the new body, its clone – would that satisfy the warring parties? Of course, we'd have to have a *legal* way to prove the correct transition occurred and not hold the Soul in the new body responsible for murdering the old body. We could weigh the bodies – the one that dies loses 6 ounces and the living one gains 6 ounces. However if the new body already has a soul, would the addition of the old body's soul mean the new body would be schizophrenic?

No, that wouldn't work, the doctors don't believe in souls. Besides, if the clone is going to gather all of the original body's experiences, wouldn't it have to eat the original body? Hang on, I'm not lost yet, and I'm leading you someplace – I hope.

Regeneration

Ever since I got rid of my arm, I knew I could have it back. So, in one of my "middle aged crazy" experiences, I asked some learned people about the possibility. I had heard about experiments with animals where amputations had grown back. I was ready – at least I thought I was – to grow my arm back. I knew the key was the "regenerative organ," the pituitary gland – the growth gland.

The younger the person, the more active the gland and the faster they heal - regenerate. At full maturity, the gland has almost stopped functioning. The trick would be to get it to work, but specifically on the problem. No one wants to be 20 feet tall. And no one with a broken nose wants to have two noses (like lizards with two tails).

Let's see, if we stimulate the regenerative organ and mentally focus on repairing or replacing the damaged part of the body – we wouldn't need doctors. Go ahead and try – what have you got to lose.

Ooops, now maybe I'll be put in jail to rot.

Just think about the possibilities. The body was actually meant to live forever at the age of around thirty – full maturity. 95+% of your cells are replaced every year. If you have a damaged or dysfunctional part of your body, focus on it as perfect and kick the pituitary gland into action (use a mantra: "Perfect DNA – age 30"). The part regenerates and you go on living with a perfect body. We don't have to worry about the clone. If you haven't yet, you need to watch the movie *Multiplicity*.

You're writing your own script – so if you want to live longer – go ahead and do it. And choose how healthy you wish to be. Me, I'm working on the arm thing, if my ego will let me.

I Hate it When That Happens

I've written about how humans love problem solving. I've also explained what happens when I'm told something is impossible. Apparently, I'm not alone. When the bible inferred that humans could not make themselves taller, someone took it as a challenge. I saw a TV program where doctors are able to break a leg, and over a period of time, make it "grow" longer. This of course makes the person taller. So obviously we know and can do a lot more now than our ancestors knew and could do 2,000 years ago.

How much more can we learn, and do? What do we know, we don't know we know? Does it take making it against the law, telling us we can't do something, or that it is impossible to get us motivated? Let your imagination run free, we've only just begun – 90+% of your brain's not working yet.

Genetic Selection

"In The Beginning" it was survival of the fittest/smartest. To survive, you had to defend yourself from the elements, beasts, and other humans. You had to be tough to even make it to an age you could "survive" through your genes – procreate. You built up an immune system to the local diseases or you died. As new germs were introduced, if you survived the invasion you built up immunity to the disease and passed it on in your genes. Bubonic Plague, Small Pocks, Measles, Tuberculosis, Polio, Asian Flu, and now AIDS have all tested our immune systems. Historical death data shows a consistent curve with or without drug/vaccination intervention – bodies learning to combat the recyclers.

Consider the current situation throughout the world. The trend is for more and more mothers to **_not_** breast feed their babies. By drinking mother's milk, the antibodies in her immune system teach the baby's cells to fight diseases.

What exactly is in the "formula" which in many instances has replaced Mother's Milk? Exactly who is making the stuff? The Tobacco Companies? Is formula being made from balanced "organic" materials or oil based chemicals? What is formula "teaching" the baby's cells?

Mothers everywhere are training their children to avoid germs which might make them sick. Don't eat that, don't touch that, wash your hands, drink only bottled water, etc. Contact with germs is unavoidable, and some people are going to die – oh well. As long as it isn't you or yours, right?

Well the best defense against bacteria, fungus and viruses is a strong immune system. A strong immune system is the result of the right cellular-building blocks and contact with germs. Inoculation is one way to contact and counteract germs. I'm for instituting the 30 second rule, if it falls on the floor and it is there for less than 30 seconds, pick it up – don't brush it off – and eat it. Keep your immune system guessing and alert.

The last thing you need, is to let yourself become complacent about survival. I'll testify, one of the most dangerous places to be in the world is a hospital. If you don't believe me, check the statistics. There are germs in the hospitals which have learned to survive our counter measures to them – our drugs. The doctors and staff make mis-takes – by accident or omission. 100,000+ people die yearly from medical mis-adventures.

Anyway, get your bones set and your cuts stitched and get out quick. I had seen the movie **Hospital** just three months BAL. Most of the bad things shown in the movie happened to me. Scary?

"What you fear, happens unto you." I don't know exactly where that comes from, but it's true and easy to explain, because whatever is in your brain and you put power and strong emotions to, will be created in your reality.

You program it into your experience – a Universal Law. The only thing you have to fear is fear it self, the only thing that ever holds you back from doing anything is fear. To overcome fear, move through it. Fear is **F**alse **E**vidence **A**ppearing **Real**.

You know the "redneck" joke. What are the last words of a redneck? "Hey guys, watch this."

You've heard about the Darwin awards – all given posthumously. In other words "genetic selection" at work – where if you're going to be dumb, you better be tough – watch the **X Games**.

That's very simplistic, but get outside your box, and do a little thinking about it. If you're smart and tough you have even a better chance for survival. If you're smart but weak – watch *Mad Maxx*.

It seems now days everyone is after "The Easy Life." Well OK, but when a catastrophe occurs, you better have lots of guns and bullets.

Boy, that got your attention, didn't it. I know a few tough, smart people with guns – it would be a good idea to avoid them – got it?

So am I advocating a "Human Breeding Program?"

NO!! Not me. That wouldn't be "politically correct." Besides, it would mean I get to chose who has sex with whom, I'd be in control, and responsible for the result.

I understand Hitler had a breeding program, but interestingly, he didn't fit the "Mold." Have religions, races, cultures, and societies advocated "Human Breeding Programs?" Yes!!! Is there any culture, race, or religion you've been "taught" not to marry? Enough said?

Medicine

Some of you aren't going to like this part, but to heck with you if you can't take a joke. Try to step way back and let's get through this without a fight. Come with me to the other side of the fence. Let's try a view of earth and humans from space and take a realistic approach. Let's look at the human species as if it were any other animal on earth.

I ask, "If right now, all the drugs in the world were cut off, what would happen?"

"Many people would die." You say.

"That's right. And who'd be left?"

"Only the fittest and strongest would survive." You say.

Then humans are the only animals on earth down breeding. We need a breeding program, and if we don't start paying attention, someone/something else is going to inflict one on us.

Because of drugs, humans are breeding who would, a few short years ago, have perished, and they're passing on their "defects" to their offspring through genetics.

We're eliminating: diseases through drugs, drought through irrigation, effects of food sources being destroyed through international commerce. However, all of the agricultural lands worldwide are being depleted of minerals.

Over population leads to famine, leads to lowered immune systems, leads to death and disease, leads to population control by nature in every species but man – so far.

Let's take a look at an insidious thing man has perpetrated on man.

We've gone into a balanced eco system without increasing the productivity, decreased infant mortality, increased longevity and caused an exponential increase in the population.

Then to make matters worse, when Mother Nature in her infinite wisdom tries to balance everything through famine and plague, man jumps in again and transports food and drugs to the starving and sick people so they can produce more offspring. The productivity of the area hasn't changed, the land can't produce more food, but still more people are produced.

Now who in the world would do such a thing? Missionaries! Mother Nature will not put up with what humans, regardless of their beliefs or motivation, are doing in any other animal in the world.

Do we think we're immune to Mother Nature?

Action – Reaction

We're using hormones to get chickens and cattle to mature faster, and now we're seeing eight year-old girls developing breasts. This isn't a coincidence, its cause and effect.

Blights on society are refined sugar, refined flour, and dairy products. Propaganda and convenience have made fast food the desired way to feed ourselves. Agribusiness has influenced the government to tell us to use their products.

The pharmaceutical and medical professions are in the business of injury and disease not wellness. And the FDA is in collusion with both agribusiness and the medical professions. The FDA and EPA know Chlorine and Fluoride are toxic poisons, but still those toxic chemicals are being put in our drinking water. Americans began to have heart attacks and strokes 20 years *after* Chlorine was added to their drinking water – DA! Human experiments occurred during the Korean and Vietnam wars with military personal. The affect of Chlorine on the good fat in your body is to cause it to change and "stick" to your blood vessels causing heart attacks and strokes the #1 killer in the US @ 700,000+ deaths per year. Collusion?

We eat the same food day after day, when our forefathers were subjected to seasonal changes. We're developing allergies to the food we eat because of a lack of seasonal variety. And we're passing on our allergies to our children, only in them, the allergies are worse.

We're becoming so soft as a species, that without change, we can't survive. Each generation is getting fatter and weaker. We have to use supplements to get the vitamins and minerals we used to get out of our food. Our immune systems are weakening and there are ever changing and more disastrous diseases being produced by Nature to attack us and put our bodies back into the big circle of life.

Our forefathers who populated this continent were tough, dealt with heat and cold, seasonal changes in food, lack of food, injury, and disease. They had their babies at home, and over 50 percent of the babies died before age two. The humans who were weak did not survive. People who were tough lived to reproduce, and initially we as a nation were up-breeding as a species.

We played God with animals, and through selective and cross breeding, we produced cattle which produced good meat and were healthy in our environment. Then we went after the plants and did the same thing. Through mechanization, we've been able to reduce the number of people it took to feed the masses.

In the process we made life "easier" on humans, and the result is the potential elimination of our species from this earth.

In a catastrophe, who's going to survive? If you don't think this is possible, think about how vulnerable we are. One meteor, volcano, tidal wave, or 100 foot rise in sea level (a possibility in as little as four years since every glacier in the world is receding) and civilization as we know it ceases to exist. Who will be left? I suggest you read **Spirit Walker** and **Medicineman** by Hank Wesselman.

Now a little bit of perspective, I really don't care what happens, because it will all work out in the end. In the big picture, my existence doesn't matter (neither does yours – sorry).

You're here in this illusion playing a part, and it's all just an act, a movie, a sit-com, a soap opera, and what will be will be. You can "go along," or you can create life the way you would like it to be. You can look at the other "poor souls" and feel sympathy for them or observe what they're doing, learn and feel empathy for what they're putting themselves through and admire their script writing ability. You can change, how you live and what you believe, and make something new happen in the right direction for balance and reason – as we know it. Or you can just continue on your course.

Believe me when I tell you it really doesn't matter either way. You're still going to survive as a spirit being – a part of God – and all that has, is, and will happen on this illusion we call earth will just be data we will play with in finding out who we are.

There is no Heaven or Hell. When you transition from this life the souls will "kill the fatted calf," turn the water into wine, throw a party and laugh with you as you eat, drink, and be merry during the review of your sit-com.

So does it matter if humans wipe out their own species, and/or destroy the earth in the process? NO!!! Enjoy!

Evolution

Do I believe that we evolved from monkeys?

NO!

Do I believe that other species including humans have and are evolving?

YES!

And I'll use just one example – balance.

I see youngsters doing things on skateboards, roller blades, bicycles, surfboards, windsurfers, and skis that circus performers couldn't do when I was young. Evolution is Change – for the better.

OK, so if you were technically advanced enough for interstellar travel and you wanted to create life – after your own image – how would you do that? Maybe just like our scientists are currently working to develop "cloning" and DNA duplication? Do you think these scientists have already done this in another time and place? What do you know, you don't know you know?

One space ship (called the Ark) with DNA from each species we decided to take with us, and we could populate any "similar to earth" planet where the ship landed.

The Earth and All it Contains – One Organism

Let's start over again with the cosmic dust thing. There may be some other "building materials" out there someplace, but let's just reference the "Periodic Chart" of atoms, and consider everything in the universe is made from these atoms.

Imagine one atom of carbon and see what happens over time. Whenever and however this one atom of carbon was originally formed, it was given carbon information – what it was. It gets pulled out of the air in the form of carbon-dioxide by grass, the carbon is converted to a part of a cell in a blade of grass and oxygen is released back into the air. Soon the grass is eaten by an herbivore, processed by this animal's digestive system and delegated to muscle tissue.

A predator kills and eats the herbivore and the carbon atom goes through another digestive process and becomes part of the bone marrow of the predator.

The predator dies and begins to biodegrade. Bacteria work on the bone marrow and the carbon atom becomes part of the bacteria. The bacteria flow out onto and oozes into the ground where the carbon atom is gathered up by tree roots and it becomes part of the tree body.

Eventually the tree is cut down and becomes a dwelling. The dwelling deteriorates and the carbon atom now becomes a part of the body of a termite.

The termite is eaten by a lizard and the carbon atom becomes part of the stomach lining. The lizard dies, and the carbon atom in the stomach is absorbed by fungus.

The fungus dies and returns the carbon atom back to the ground where it is again incorporated into grass via the root system.

The grass is eaten by a cow and the carbon atom becomes muscle.

The cow is eaten by another predator – man – and the carbon atom becomes a part of the human's body.

Around and around it goes. It never loses its singular identity. It never is destroyed. It is used in any number of "Phases," "Configurations," and "Entities" – all of which have life. The carbon atom has been an integral part of each of its incarnations of life. It has been "recycled" without losing its singular identity.

The human, now utilizing this carbon atom, is part and parcel to all of those incarnations of the past, because, the carbon atom has brought with it information from all that has gone before. Everything is one with everything else. We are and everything else is made up of the same stuff – cosmic dust – dirt – being recycled over and over again. Everything is connected. Everything is adding to the information available to everything else. We are advancing through our experiences and what makes up our body cells.

Humans are constantly inputting new information through not only their experiences, but also from the food they eat, water they drink, and the air they breathe. The body cells, as they are replaced, are being recycled with the information from the ages and the new information from the experiences had while a part of the living body.

Was that heavy or what?

Feed The World

A project I worked on for some time is called "Feed The World." The objective is to design a system using readily available, off-the-shelf items which will fit in an 8' X 8' X 40' shipping container. Deliver this system to a desert near the ocean or a desert island, hand a non-language, non-education specific picture booklet to a family of four (the parents must be neutered to participate) and go away. Come back a year later, and they, through their own efforts, should be producing more than they're consuming. Think of all of the deserts between the Tropic of

Cancer and Tropic of Capricorn and there's a lot of unused land available. Baja California is an example.

This is a "bio-dome" project that's "open" and capable of improving the quality of the land by bringing in "energy" from the ocean. It was originally designed as an interdisciplinary, integrated, project based educational program from preschool to grad school. These institutions we throw so much money at could give the students problem solving projects that would "Save the World."

It seemed like a good idea at the time. However, no one seemed interested in investing money to make it happen.

I stepped back, reevaluated the program, and realized people with the money it would take to make this project work, weren't interested, because they understood the real implications of the project – the increased survival of humans. Basically every problem we face on this planet of ours can be traced directly to over population and greed. To "Save The World" we should **not** increase the population of human inhabitants. Maybe the NAZI Ecologists have it right – "kill the humans (everyone but them), save the critters."

Summary

Are you outside of your box yet? Are you thinking thoughts you never thought before? Are you thinking about things you never even considered before? Are you getting emotional one way or the other? GOOD!!! I'm doing my job.

In order to have experiences in this plane, the body should be in reasonable shape – or not if you're collecting disease/injury data. To avoid bodily damage, we need a strong immune system. The body "learns" how to be sick, therefore it can "learn" to be well – go to school.

Humans are down breeding and passing on their "defects" to their children, not good for the survival of the human race. Mother Nature keeps trying to "thin the herd," but man is interfering.

The land we grow our food on is becoming depleted, which requires supplements to keep us healthy. How do we know which food supplements are natural/organic and really provide us with the critical minerals, vitamins and phytonutrients (plant produced products) we need?

Maybe Murphy's Golden Rule will take over and the men/women with the gold will refuse to fund an increasing population, if reason prevails.

Keep the churches out of it – they're just interested in increasing their flock for the money, regardless of what they say.

Read, ***What Your Doctor Doesn't Know About Nutritional Medicine May Be Killing You*** by Ray D, Strand, M.D.

Chapter 17
Rites of Passage

In almost all of the aboriginal tribes, there was a specific act a boy could perform to become a man. Some of these acts were: undergoing pain (circumcision, and body scarring), facing fears, performing an act (killing a lion, taking a scalp, stealing a horse, capturing a woman), or having a spiritual experience (induced by drugs, starvation, or steam baths). The point was to have a definite point in time when a boy made the transition to manhood. For modern boys, the world has left them dazed and confused.

For modern girls, the transition from girl to woman hasn't changed, it occurs when they have their first period.

Boys Growing Up

We learn by "parroting" – copying others. Our parents, teachers, relatives and community provided us the examples we parroted to become adults. Be a good example.

What determines when a boy becomes a man? For some boys, besting their fathers was their transition to manhood. But what happens if everything you try, your father is better than you are? You have to find something – anything – you can do better than your father.

So what happens if you're the offspring of a single mother? How can you best a father you never knew? Is there another way you can show your prowess? Could it be getting the highest score on a video game? Will getting the high score get you a mate or get you laid?

At last we have a means – tattoos and body piercing – pain and scaring. Or, the boy could approach a "Gang" and go through an initiation like stealing, doing drugs, or killing someone, to be allowed in. Proving yourself through sports is another way to become a man. But our society isn't set up anymore with a specific, uniform act to becoming a man – to prove your manhood.

I sure wish I had known this when raising my boys. I would watch them struggling with something and say, "Here, let me do it." What they were having trouble doing, I'd do with one hand. They sure didn't make it to manhood by besting their father, because to win against a cripple is not a win.

Proving My Manhood

I can remember as a teenager wondering if I was a man yet. I was never sure if or when the transition occurred. I hadn't killed a lion, stolen a horse, scalped an enemy, had my body scared, or completed any of the other "rites of passage" things to prove I was a man. Had I made the transition by producing white fluid, growing pubic and face hair, playing football or swimming competition?

Possibly it was doing something most others wouldn't even try – SCUBA Diving.

Would serving my country in the armed forces help me meet the criteria for manhood?

Did having offspring mean I was a man?

Was it getting a job and supporting a family that made a boy a man?

Maybe it was earning a college degree.

When I was maturing, in my culture there was no specific, defining moment that helped me make the transition from boyhood to manhood. So I was never really sure I was truly a man.

Losing an arm, destroying Ego, and wiping out Vanity, put my manhood in question. AAL, I had to find a way to prove to myself I was a real, manly man. Assuming I had actually made it to manhood before, with the loss of the arm, was I still viable as a man? Redoing my occupations was a step in that direction. Teaching diving again, helped.

Investing the malpractice lawsuit case money in real estate and attending real estate school was a start, but I didn't take the exam to become a realtor (I just needed to be able to speak their language). I went to Contractors school, and became a general contractor.

At one time, I owned five houses in Morro Bay, California. While remodeling, adding decks, building saunas and hot tubs, making major upgrades and modifications to several houses, I learned two major real estate laws.

- The three most important property rules are: location, location, location.
- Never over-build in a neighborhood.

This should have been more than enough to satisfy my ego, but not enough people were aware of what I had done.

One of the most helpful things in rebuilding my ego was being able to bring home tons of seafood. For some reason, that seemed like it met my need to be a provider. Re-designing existing and designing new tools, assisted me in harvesting the bounty of the sea. Bringing in more game on a dive boat than all the other divers combined did set me apart. Especially since I did it with only one arm and used a pole spear. I had always been good at hunting, but AAL, I became a Master at under water hunting and gathering.

My statement about this skill is, "I love the sound of steel penetrating flesh and bone. I want to hear them scream and fight them to a stand still. Cut the meat off of the bones while they're still kicking and cook it while it's quivering. Shove it in my mouth. **Yes**, it doesn't get any better than that!"

I joked, made fun of, and cajoled the other divers. My much used saying was, "Diving is a one handed sport, your problem is trying to do it with two hands." Initially, this was not so much a joke, as a put-down to build up my ego. I was a better hunter than they were and I was crippled! The problem with diving, it's not a "Spectator Sport." So I received recognition only from the immediate participants (who I had just insulted and put down). Once onshore, with the game put away, how could I bolster my broken ego?

Not having artistic talents, but loving to dance, I practiced and eventually became a good dancer. At least at dances "showing-off" for attention was a public event. Having a belly-dancer ask me to dance and try to learn my moves and then having a Caribbean band buy me a drink helped.

With the manhood issue, sex had to come into question. Vanity has a lot to do with how you deal with sexual issues, and my vanity had been shattered. I knew I couldn't compete in the sex arena of life from a physical standpoint (try doing multiple push-ups with one arm).

So I reasoned, *If I perfect sexual techniques, maybe I can compete.*

I studied, and experimented, and began to think about sex as an art form. Even though married, somehow I needed to know I was viable sexually and the sex with my wife was not just a "pity screw." And finally sex had to come from an outside source – preferable more than one.

Piece by piece (pun intended), my ego, based on sex, was assembled and remolded.

Two Years From Now

Dad had been a "Golden Gloves" boxer when in high school. He taught me to fight by the "Marcus of Queensbury Rules" – a Fair Fight. It didn't take long for me to realize if I ever got into a fight with only one arm, I wasn't going to fight fair. Since losing the fear of dying and not liking pain, if a fight were to happen, it would be to the death, no chance for retribution that way. This created a very dangerous person to get into a fight with. The thought process presented a plan and a procedure, however, there would have to be some kind of criteria if I was ever going to fight again.

The criteria, which has worked so far, is the "Two Year Rule." If angered enough to even think about fighting, I ask myself, "Is this going to matter two years from now?" If so, I'm prepared to kill, if not, I'll walk away.

Only twice have I had to call someone by saying, "You have three choices: you walk away, you kill me, or I kill you, and you have exactly three seconds to make up your mind, starting right now." In both instances, they've walked away.

What's better, is using this same two-year criteria whenever I get angry – for whatever reason. It certainly eliminates a lot of stress, because almost nothing is going to matter two years from now.

Anger

My wife and I had a tiff, and I was angry (read that really pissed) enough I thought it best to go for a walk and calm down. I walked down to the embarcadero in Morro Bay still stewing over our argument, and not the least bit calmed down after about a ½ mile hike. It was wintertime, dark with only a few locals on the street. Just as I was about to turn around to go home, someone shouted from the street, I turned to see who it was, and got hosed down from head to waist.

The cold water did nothing to cool me down, in fact, it did just the opposite. I started for the car with five young people in it, but they sped away laughing.

When I looked back at the event the next day, it was a good thing they left, because if I could have caught them, I would have torn the car and them apart – with only one hand. I've never been that pissed about anything. My reaction to the incident was totally out of proportion to being sprayed down with water on a public street by strangers. There's no doubt I would have reeked havoc on those kids, and could possibly have killed them all. Pissed, totally beyond reason, and jacked up on adrenaline, I was super strong.

What the experience taught me is you don't know the level of anger someone is already working on. Anger is fear in some form and it's **cumulative**. You may just be the catalyst to set them off, push them over the edge. Pushing someone's buttons, for any reason, could get you badly hurt or killed. The calls, cops fear the most, are domestic disturbances, because the built-up anger can turn on them.

If you're in a reactionary mode, you're not able to reason. I don't like to react, I like to act – to think my way through a given situation.

Putting People Down

In the BAL life, I used to put other people down, make fun of them, and point out their failings, but I hated it when people did it to me. In the AAL learning period, I was able to identify what this was all about. I watched and listened to teenagers, and it seemed putting people down was about all they did.

Here's a broad, bold statement which may shed light/truth to help you understand why you and others put people down.

The reason is quite simplistic, a lack of self-confidence and self-esteem. Everyone has a store of self-incriminating evidence of their failure to meet up to their own expectations. We wouldn't be here if there weren't things we needed to change. If you want to get weirded out, just start obsessing about the things you want to change about yourself. As soon as you start this introspection process, in your own self-defense, you try to find someone you can be "better than" – in any way.

We'll go to great lengths to make up something about another person so we can be better than them, and therefore not deal with our problem(s). This can be a dirty "chicken fight." We consider looks, weight, clothes, brains, possessions, personality, education, skin color, nationality, religion, language, athletic ability, and on and on.

I hear you say, "So Lance, how do we build our self-confidence and self-esteem?"

Learn and change your behavior. Realize you're perfect for this particular point in time, and you are and will be changing for the better. You can't be like someone else. You're unique and special. Nothing, absolutely nothing other people say about you matters. Your only job is to make you – over time – the person you want you to be. It's a process not a destination.

This is not the person your parents want you to be, not the person your peer group wants you to be, not the person your spouse wants you to be, not the person your employer wants you to be, but the person **you** want to be.

One change you need to start today is stop trying to build yourself up by putting other people down – do unto others. Just do it!

When you catch yourself putting others down, realize where it comes from, and refuse to do it. As you begin this process by refusing to tear others down, you'll begin to build yourself up. There's no trick to it, it's Universal Law – it works.

Eventually, you'll build enough self confidence to start building others up by catching them doing something right and telling them about it. You'll actually get more out of this than they will.

A quick story – I know you prefer stories to lectures.

There we were in Kona, Hawaii training SCUBA Instructors, eating out almost every meal and spreading the wealth around – varying where we ate. We went into Sizzler for lunch, ordered our meals, paid, and sat down at a table.

The waitress was there almost instantly, she did everything right, brought us our food and drinks, kept checking back to make sure we were satisfied, and I noticed we weren't unique in her attention.

I signaled for her to come to our table. She smiled and asked "How may I serve you?"

I said, "I want to talk to the manager."

She almost panicked, and asked, "What's wrong, can I get you anything else, did I do something wrong?"

I told her, "Everything is OK, but I want to talk to the manager."

She hurried off, but was interrupted by several other patrons. Eventually, I called her over again and said, "I still want to see the manager, and I want you here when I talk to him."

She was really flustered, she said, "I'm sorry for whatever I did, please don't get me into trouble, I just started last week and I need this job."

"Please," I said again, "I want to see the manager and you together,"

She took off for the back, and reappeared with a huge Hawaiian. When he reach the table, he said in a booming voice, "I'm Dave, the manager, what can I do for you?"

I said, "I want to complement you on your choice and training of this waitress. I've been eating out three meals a day for the last 18 days here in Kona, and she is by far the best waitress or waiter who has served me here. I think you should give her a raise."

Dave almost fainted, the waitress just stood there with her mouth open, face red – in shock.

After several seconds for review, Dave said, "I've been the manager here for over four years, and this is first time I've been called up front to receive a compliment. I want to thank you, very much. Also, I'll take the raise under advisement. If you want anything else, it's on the house – anything." He looked at the waitress, smiled, nodded, and left.

We didn't want anything else, left a good tip, and departed. That little compliment only cost me a few extra minutes, it screwed with the manager and possibly got the waitress a raise. I done good! I try to remember to give compliments often for good work. Now it's your turn to join in the fun.

Summary

Proving your manhood/womanhood appears to be critically important in your transition from child to adult. If something happens which affects your ability to work or produce (money, products or kids) it will have a definite effect on your self confidence.

Anger is cumulative and hurts you not others. Anger comes from fear – of some kind, Figure out where it comes from and why – then give it up.

Avoid putting others down. It comes from a lack of self confidence and self esteem. Compliment others for jobs well done, looks, clothes, any and everything. It does much more for you than for them. And, sincerely compliment your "enemy," it really messes them up.

Just remember nothing is impossible, proving that to yourself is invaluable, and it will build your self confidence. Building your self confidence is what the transition from child to adult is all about.

If you must figure out what real, manly men are all about read ***Wild at Heart – Discovering the Secret of a Man's Soul*** by John Eldredge – my life lessons were about the wisdom in this book.

Cooperation

Conflict always causes delays. Cooperation produces results. So how can we reduce conflict and increase cooperation?

It would appear, from the dichotomy between the body and soul agendas, that the Standard Operating Program (SOP) for humans is conflict. Conflict requires aggression and it is obvious that the humans worldwide are aggressive towards one another. Therefore aggression is a worldwide, programmed-in, basis of life for humans. Conflict is taught in the K-12 Government Legislated Compulsory Schooling System and higher education – through competition via GPA.

Mother Nature has used aggression as a tool in genetic selection to produce the strongest and toughest of each species. And through aggression, species have been eliminated.

After two million years of evolution on Planet Ocean, body and soul have yet to cooperate. Works – Doesn't Work.

If the soul informs the body of the Meaning of Life, Life Mission and Life Purpose could the body "agree" to cooperate with the soul to develop personality and character, provided the soul could agree with the body to avoid creating survival issues?

Understanding the dichotomy of the Soul/Body entities is a key step in the advancement of mankind and spiritual advancement of the soul.

Something has to change, because of the conflict, it appears humans and souls are regressing not progressing.

Chapter 18
My First Prosthesis

The day after the arm was amputated, while waking up from the anesthetics, the MRDF staff brought in a "Playboy" magazine.

The Playboy incident had me designing prosthesis from then on. Deciding a variety of special arms for different uses and occasions would be needed, I imagined making them made out of giant bamboo, mahogany, and fiberglass. Ready to begin the manufacturing process, I began gathering the raw materials: plastic bags, Plaster-of-Paris, giant bamboo, a mahogany log, resin, catalyst and fiberglass. But having to wait until the stump drained, the skin graft healed and the swelling went down, was frustrating.

The first arm I built was for diving. As soon as the swelling went down, I took a Plaster-of-Paris mold of my stump, made a plug, and laid up a fiberglass "paddle" for "swimming" with a stainless steel hook for help in climbing into the boat and habitat. The second prosthesis made, was a tubular fiberglass one which extend the stump to help push on things and steer the car. These were made before visiting the Prosthetist.

However, the bamboo and mahogany was way too heavy and too much work – I was still running the La Chalupa project.

The Prosthesis Prescription

I broke my arm on the job, so it was a Workman's Compensation Case. As such, "they" seemed to think it was important to get a person patched up, and, if necessary, retrained so they could go back to work (make more money, pay more taxes).

In their minds, before any retraining could begin, the prosthesis and physical therapy thing had to happen. About twelve weeks after the amputation, I was scheduled to see an orthopedic doctor on a Tuesday to get a "prosthesis prescription."

While looking at my medical record, the doctor said, "I know all about your case."

I said, "I don't recognize you. You weren't one of my doctors."

"No, but I should have been. Your injury was an orthopedic case from start to finish. Those doctors who attended you were general surgeons and interns. They put you on the surgery ward instead of the orthopedic ward. They didn't call even one of the three orthopedic surgeons who were on call when you got hurt. You were brought in on Sunday, and the first any of us heard about your case was Thursday, and they didn't do what the consultant wrote in your record." The doctor's voice raised in anger as he continued, "They put rush pins in your arm to stabilize the bones, closed up the wound, bandaged it, and put on a half cast. Then they wrapped your arm with stretch bandages, which cut off the circulation and caused the gas gangrene. You should sue them for five million dollars."

I asked, "What would you have done?"

"We would have put in the rush pins, hung the hand up, put in drain tubes, and left the wound open so it could have been watched to insure if infection started, it could have been treated right away."

"Thank you for the information. I'll consider what you said." I said, "May I get the prescription now?"

The orthopedic doctor examined the stump, made some suggestions and asked, "When would you like to make the trip to the San Juan Medical Center."

I said, "As soon as possible."

He had his secretary call for an appointment on the coming Thursday afternoon.

I went back to the Laboratorio Submarino site, told Ian what the doctor said and asked if he knew an attorney I could talk to. That afternoon, I met with an attorney.

After I explained what the orthopedic doctor had said, the attorney told me, "Without a copy of the medical record, there would be no case, because either it would be changed or it would just disappear."

I said, "If I can get you a certified copy of the medical record, will that help?"

The attorney said, "Well of course, but you can't get a certified copy of your own medical record."

I said, "That's my problem. Will you take the case if I can get the medical record."

The attorney said, "Yes!"

Panic

I've been through many life-threatening experiences, and I don't panic. As a diver, I trained myself and others to stop, think, and act.

Thursday morning, as I walked into the front lobby of the Mayeguez Hospital, the smell caused a kaleidoscope of images. It was like my life in the hospital flashed before my eyes: being left at X ray in extreme pain for several hours, being handled roughly by the technicians, throwing up with broken collar bone and ribs, the rotten smell of the gangrene, being helpless and not getting the attention I needed, and the sinking feeling when the doctor told me an amputation was going to be needed.

It was all I could do to not run away.

I had never felt such a strong fear emotion, and it was my first and only experience with a panic attack. I had to stop and get control of myself before I could go to the records section.

At the records section I showed the clerk the prescription and asked for a certified copy of my medical record and the X-rays.

The clerk said, "NO! We can't give patients a copy of their medical records."

Very calmly, I said, "Que es su hefe, su hefe numero uno?" (Where is your boss, your number one boss?)

I kept asking that question until I got to the head of the hospital, where I explained, "I have an appointment this afternoon in San Juan, here is the prescription and you know I'll need a copy of my medical record and the X rays or they won't work on me."

The head of the hospital agreed, and called the clerk. I got what I asked for.

In San Juan, I gave the prosthesis technician the prescription, showed him the medical records and X-Rays, and told him, "I need to take these back with me."

Friday I was back in my attorney's office with the certified copy of my medical records and the X-Rays (the hospital never got the X-Rays back). That afternoon, we began preparing the medical malpractice lawsuit.

The Prosthesis

The Prosthetic Technician was new to his profession. He had completed his schooling and the required apprenticeship. Watching as he made a mold of my stump I asked, "What kind of an arm are you going to make me?"

He said, "You'll have one with a hand that looks like the other hand so people won't stare and embarrass you."

My response was, "No, I want one I can use for working, I don't care what it looks like."

You know I got one with a hand on it.

When delivered, the prosthesis was three inches longer than my other arm, and hung down to my knee. It didn't look like the other hand, and drew even more attention than when it wasn't worn. It was so heavy I couldn't raise it up with the short stump – leverage. I had to use my other hand to put it where it was needed. The fingers on the prosthetic hand would open if I flexed my shoulders forward, but not enough to hold a beer. The grip was so weak as to render it useless. The only thing it was useful for was holding down paper so I could sign my name.

There was one function that made it fun and entertaining. By pushing a button on the wrist, the hand would come off. If I caught someone not paying attention to me and needing some assistance, I'd push the button, pass over the hand and say, "Here, let me lend you a hand."

The reactions of complete strangers were hilarious.

Then one day in a department store, a little, old, blue-haired lady was trying to get a bag of dog food from the shelf, I stepped up, pushed the button, reached out the hand and rattled off the line. "Let me lend you a Hand." She turned around, saw the hand, grabbed her heart, and started screaming and staggering around the isle.

I quit wearing the prosthesis. Damn, and it was such a good joke.

My Second Prosthesis

After a stump revision at the VA Hospital in Miami, Florida, I had another prosthesis made. A working one from my design, and all three of the prosthesis manufacturers in the greater Miami area tried to hire me. The prosthesis was useful, short as possible, had all the functions of a regular prosthesis, was light so I could lift it, and had a functional hook.

The real problems were not immediately evident. In order to work, a strap went around the shoulder of the good arm. After a short time, the good arm would go numb, and quit working, then nothing worked. There was also a ninety-degree arc the prosthesis would transverse on its own because the upper-arm muscle rotates around the bone. It was rather entertaining when the prosthesis would find its way into the steering wheel of the car and interfere with driving – at the most hazardous times.

Another thing soon became evident, the public reaction to the "hook." Damn Disney, Peter Pan and Captain Hook. Some kids looked at the hook and ran away screaming.

It is fun at Halloween or a costume party though.

One of the things I figured out with time is, "If you've got it flaunt it, if you don't have it flaunt it, but whatever you do flaunt it." So I've flaunted not having an arm since it took its leave of me. I'm not embarrassed by it. I wear it as a badge of honor.

Functioning as an Amputee

Since I couldn't wear a prosthesis, I had to figure out how to do common, ordinary tasks. The result of my inventiveness meant I used my feet, legs, teeth and stump a lot more than "normal" people.

What took the most abuse were my teeth. They substituted for the fingers on my missing hand. The problem became apparent 15 years AAL when I tried to bite a thread in two and found my front teeth didn't touch. Soon after that the fun began. A nerve became exposed and the tooth was extracted. The next two exposed nerves received root-canals.

Finally, after about 25 years, I had all but five of my teeth capped – at the same time, without Novocain! I offered to tell the dentist anything if she would just stop the torture. I'm being a little more careful with my teeth now – I'm learning.

Summary

I now have empathy for people who have "panic attacks." My advice is get help in moving through whatever you're afraid of – never let it control you. Just stop, think, and act.

As a thinking, experienced amputee I know what works for me. The ideal prosthesis for me would not be allowed on a commercial airliner since 9-11. The single most useful working prosthesis-hook combination for me would be fairly short, bend at the elbow, and have an extendable, rotatable, fireplace hook on it. With this prosthesis I could push, pull, carry and hold food down to cut it. That's the best I could expect since it wouldn't be very stable. So would you want to sit next to me on a plane if I was wearing a tool like that?

As a diver, this tool would allow me an unfair advantage over other divers, because they can't use hooks to catch lobsters.

Prosthetics

Almost everyone is using prosthetics of one kind or another. The creation of prosthetics has allowed people to function and be productive contributors to society. Prosthetics are any device that can replace or assist human performance.

So let's just list a few to get the idea: glasses, hearing aids, tooth fillings and caps. Humans who couldn't see or hear didn't last long in the caveman days. Humans who couldn't chew their food or who developed gum abscesses also didn't survive long.

If a joint became too painful to allow the full use of the limb (arm or leg), before joint replacement, a person didn't last long. If a person couldn't keep up with the group migration, they were left behind to be recycled. A simple broken bone could be fatal if it prevented hunting or gathering. Even a sprained ankle could result in death if it prevented defending from or outrunning a predator. So the lose of a limb was certainly a death sentence.

Just recently, in the two million year history of man, have limb prosthetics been created. From the crutches to attached prosthetic legs and from hooks to operational hands man has created devices to allow disabled people to function and be a productive part of society.

With the invention of wheels came wheel-chairs. With the invention of battery-powered motors, came motorized wheel chairs and mobility for paraplegics.

The creativity and problem solving ability of Soul operated humans has allowed many people to survive who a few generations ago would have perished.

Chapter 19
My Mental Ordeals

If I were to say I never experienced intense mental and emotional swings after the amputation, it would be a lie. But almost immediately after leaving the hospital, people began to ask me, "How long did it take to adjust to being an amputee?"

My reply was, "I was over it before leaving the hospital, it took less than eight days."

I didn't know enough to understand I'll never be "over it." My "over it" had to do with accepting it and getting on with my life. I was too "busy" running the under water habitat to cogitate about my emotions or mental state. The learning process of losing my arm has slowed down with time, but is still going on. The destruction of my ego was intense, but the mental effects were very entertaining – if not so much in the beginning, certainly now.

Phantom

Initially, the phantom arm and hand troubled my brain, especially the "Rubberman" thing. Eventually, it became entertaining and finally fun when I could make people move away or mess with women about feeling with it. I pretty much ignore it now, unless it begins to move around on its own. With some effort, I can move it on command.

Effect on Others

By getting rid of my arm, I put myself into a new category of humans – cripple. I became **dis-abled**. This condition solicits sideways looks and questions unvoiced.

Most people have been taught from a young age (4 to 5) to: not stare, not make fun of others, not ask what happened and not talk about people with a deformity. Up until that age, youngsters will walk-up and ask what happened to my arm. I'll thank them for noticing, kneel down, explain what happened and show them the stump.

The normal reaction of most adults is to feel sorry for me – sympathy. A typical statement from an adult pertaining to my missing arm is usually, "I'm sorry." And then they intuitively want to "help" the cripple.

My condition is good for them in one respect, because if they have two arms, I'm one person they can be "better than." I've even had women open doors for me. If the interface stops there, all well and good, but if they ask what I do, or watch me work, they're usually taken aback by my abilities.

I enjoy more, the people who stand around and watch how a one-armed cripple copes with a challenge, without offering assistance. My friends have a tendency to "set-up" projects just to watch me cope. Sometimes, they even learn something new.

Other cripples are interesting to interface with, because I'm never sure where they're coming from, and our interactions could be a real psychological study. Given exactly the same program as other humans, there's usually a "pissing contest." My injury is worse/better than yours, I can do more/less than you can, my accident story is better/worse than yours, etc. If you understand what's going on and not take it serious, it can be quite funny, especially when we start undressing to show our scars.

I'm always looking for someone with their right hand off so we can exchange. I have a lot of useless left hand gloves. We usually have a good laugh, then stand side by side and comment about how the two of us could now be a whole. Oh, and shaking hands is a trip.

At the yearly dive show, I spotted a guy with both hands missing – two hooks. I was pissed, stealing my thunder, the nerve. I couldn't resist, I jumped right in the middle of his stuff. Stepping in front of him, I said, "Boy and I thought I had it rough diving with one hand. I'll bet you punch a bunch of holes in your wet suit getting it on."

He laughed, and explained, "I dive in warm water, no wet suit, but you should see my swim suit."

We kibitzed in the middle of the aisle and entertained a large group of divers for about ten minutes. Several of them had to leave for the bathroom to pee from all the laughing. It was a sick joke fest.

He'd burned off both of his hands, at mid-forearms, by flying his hang glider into a high power line. And I thought diving was dangerous. He was the first PADI SCUBA Instructor as a double arm amputee – good going. I can't wait to see him again, we had fun. But I do wonder how the victim of an open water rescue feels about having their nose squeezed (sealed off) with a hook.

Beliefs

As a result of my education, training and life experiences, I developed a "Belief System" which goes like this.

What will be will be, so learn to go with the flow. There's a reason for everything, you may not understand it now, but pay attention and the reason or purpose will present itself. Regardless of how good or bad life is, this too will pass – change is inevitable. Everything, always works out for the best, have patience.

Armed with my belief system, I charged out of the hospital and went back to work. I kept on doing my best to do my duty, solving problems, and keeping people alive.

Depression

Before the skin graft was put on the stump, I was on one of the boats bringing the habitat back into the harbor when the wind shifted and the lab started moving toward the breakwater. We pulled up to the habitat and tossed the technician on deck a line to attach to a bollard so we could use the boat to keep the lab off the rocks.

One of the guys attempted to tie the line to the back of the boat, but when tension was put on it, the knot came undone. He tried again, and again the knot came apart. I jumped to the back of the boat, took the line, and started to tie a Boland.

With two middle fingers in the loop of the knot, the boat drifted, tightening the loop, I yelled, "Hold it!"

The operator thought I said, "Hit it!" and he gunned the engines.

With my two fingers in the knot, I was pulled almost out of the boat, and ended up suspended between my fingers in the rope and my knees on the stern of the boat. I was expecting the fingers to break, or be "squeezed" off.

I yelled, "an obscenity!"

The operator turned, saw the problem, and chopped the throttles. I was pulled back into the boat, fingers removed from the knot, then the operator gunned the engines and kept the habitat from beaching on the breakwater.

I didn't go to the hospital to have the fingers X rayed (don't trust guys in white), so I'm not sure if they were broken, cracked or just badly sprained. The MRDF staff nurse splinted them with a tongue depressor and taped them together. As I thought about how close I had come to loosing two fingers of my remaining hand, the first depression I'd ever had set-in. Although it only lasted for a couple hours, it was intense. This was also the first and only time my voice broke and tears came to my eyes, not because of pain, but because of frustration at my vulnerability.

Summary

Regardless of what happens to you, your Ego will use it to its advantage.

Everything you do has an effect on others.

Your belief systems are in a constant state of flux – change.

Depression happens, deal with it or it will not go away.

Head Trips

We speak at around 120 words per minute. Our internal dialog runs at around 1,800 words per minute. So we're "talking to ourselves" over 10 times faster than someone from the outside is talking to us. All data input is evaluated based on our box-of-reference and our filters. We compare, contrast, judge and make decisions about everything someone else says to us, what we read, what we see, what we smell, what we taste, what we feel, events and what we hear – without conscious effort. The analysis of the incoming data stimulates our emotions.

The internal dialog also compares and contrasts the input against our belief system. Our head trips are a result of incoming data being analyzed in comparison to our belief system resulting in internal conflicts. The greater the discrepancy/conflict between what we believe and what the incoming data shows us, the more intense the head trip.

Just because you're having a "Head trip" doesn't mean your belief system or the incoming data are wrong. However, a "Head trip" does, indicate you need to pay attention and discover what you are to learn.

"Head trips." are constantly running, pay attention!

Chapter 20
My Physical Ordeals

My life has been very stimulating, filled with lots of entertaining adventures. Putting myself out there and taking risks meant my body took the brunt of multiple mis-adventures.

Many times, I told people, "I doubt if I'll make it to age 40." I didn't, I died in the emergency room at age 32.

I broke ribs, right arm and left collar bone; damaged my right knee twice; dislocated my left and right shoulders multiple times; slight dislocations of both hips at different times requiring chiropractic adjustment and wearing women's girdles (which have no place to put my "stuff"); suffered a concussion; several third degree burns; cuts on my knee, thumb and bottom of my foot; puncture wounds in the thumb, thigh and butt; a hernia; bone bruises in several places; miscellaneous cuts and abrasions; and teeth problems. Being rear-ended ripped four ribs lose in my middle back, caused sciatica in both legs and damaged my spinal cord at the base of my neck (lose of grip in the right hand again). I've needed to sit by the fire and lick my wounds a lot.

I never considered myself accident-prone, but my body suffered a lot of abuse over time. However, the physical suffering and abuse as a result of the broken left forearm, infection, amputation and subsequent medical experiences made all of the other abuses pale by comparison.

Pain

When you're asked, "How much does that hurt?" What do you say? Is there a pain meter? How do you measure pain?

Whenever I was asked how much pain I was in, I was confused. The amount of pain I endured on a daily basis would have put most people in the hospital on a morphine drip. I just turned off the pain mentally and got on with my life.

The answer I finally started giving the questioning doctors was, "Pain is relative. It just depends on what level of pain you live with and then you can measure the *increase* in pain you feel." That usually confused the doctors. They never thought about "relative pain" except in relationship to mother-in-laws.

The only way I could relate to pain was how it affected my "moods." If I began to feel "grumpy," I knew my pain level had increased. The more mental activity it took to offset the pain, the less mental process available to learn and solve problems. There were times when the pain was so intense, I was basically an unthinking zombie.

Door Blowing Closed

Feeling the wind gust, I held out my stump to catch the van door, but the door brushed the end of the stump and closed. It felt like someone had cut the arm off with a machete. The pain was intense, and lasted for several hours. If you can imagine a knife slicing through your arm in slow motion, a part of the arm at a time, that's what I was feeling, over and over. I'm still not sure if the van door just stimulated the nerves or brought back the cellular memory of the original amputation with the cutting and sawing.

In either case, the pain was very entertaining.

The Shoulder Injury

The left shoulder was ripped out of the socket (dislocated) far enough that the skin of my armpit was torn. The collarbone broke at an angle and when the shoulder snapped back, the pointed bone speared into the tendon at the shoulder end of the trapezious muscle. This resulted in a lot of trauma to the shoulder joint, collar bone, tendons, ligaments and muscles. The result is a barometer. I can tell weather via my left shoulder.

My Damaged Right Wrist

Four years after the amputation, I reached into the refrigerator to take out a carton of milk, and the milk fell out of my hand. I was loosing my grip. I had "sprained" my right wrist two years after the amputation but never thought about the long term results of the sprain.

Brother John the Chiropractic, X-Rayed and examined the hand and explained what I could expect from Orthopedic Doctors.

The Orthopedic hand specialist's X-Rays showed two each of my carpal and metacarpal bones in the right wrist were misaligned – slightly dislocated, and the joints were calcifying (arthritis). This calcium buildup was around several nerves and resulted in a reduction of the nerve energy to the hand – loss of grip in my one good hand.

The Doctor examined the hand, tested for range of motion, grip strength, and stuck needles in the right arm in several different locations then sent electrical pulses through the muscles (another very interesting torture) which indicated nerve damage. Then he explained, "What I need to do is operate on your hand. I'll open it up, chip and grind away the calcification, wire the bones into proper alignment, and apply a cast."

I asked, "How long do I have to wear the cast?"

The Orthopedic Doctor replied, "Six months."

I asked, "Since were talking about bones that move, the cast is going to have to enclose the fingers and go above the elbow, right?"

The Orthopedic Doctor replied, "Right."

I asked, "Assuming you correct the problem, how long will it take before you have to operate again?"

The Doctor looked bewildered but answered, "Well it should last for four years."

"Four years? Or maybe two, at the most?" I Questioned.

The Doctor corrected his statement, "OK, it might last two years before needing to be operated on again."

I asked, "What are the odds you'll make the hand worse during the operation?"

The Doctor looked shocked but answered, "There's about a 50/50 chance of making the hand worse during the operation."

"50/50 or 60/40 you make it worse?" I Questioned again.

The Doctor again corrected his statement, "Well, the statistics show this type of a hand operation has a 60% chance of making the hand worse. There are a lot of nerves and tendons concentrated in the area."

"So," I said, "if I allow you to operate, there's a best case 50/50 chance you're going to make my hand worse, and the operation is going to have to occur again in two years with the same odds, right?"

The Doctor nodded.

I continued, "I'll have my hand in the cast for six months?"

The Doctor nodded again.

I asked, "And who am I supposed to get to wipe my ass for six months?"

This learned, hand-specialist, Orthopedic Doctor in the room with and examining me for almost an hour answered, "Oh, that's right, you only have one arm."

Do I need to say the operation didn't occur. I went to my brother and other Chiropractors who applied ultra-sound to the damaged area, I kicked my system acidic, and the calcium buildup receded enough for my grip to come back.

Back Injury

The original accident jerked me sideways to the left, ripping and tearing muscles all over my body. Individual ropes of muscles were ripped loose pulling bone fragments through the muscles leaving visible "bruise" like indicators. Due to the extent of the trauma of almost being quartered, the low back injury was not immediately apparent. Over time, compounded by only being able to carry weight on the right side and the constant five-pound weight differential between the left and right arms, the low back began to deteriorate.

The back pain was now added to the Phantom and nerve pain. Add in the "weather sensitive" left shoulder area, with calcium build-up in my damaged right wrist, and I was experiencing an increasing pain level, which at times I was unable to mask with my brain.

At one particularly painful time, I succumbed to taking a couple aspirin. Since I had never taken drugs of any kind, except immediately after trauma, the aspirin did wonders. As the pain increased, I increased the aspirin dose.

Then one fairly painful day, I happened to take two "arthritis strength" aspirin with a glass of wine, wow, what a relief. From then on, it was aspirin taken with wine.

It finally dawned on me I was taking two arthritis strength aspirin with wine four times a day and drinking at least a full bottle of wine. I knew I was hooked on drugs, and something had to be done. The "Betty Ford Clinic" was too far away for treatment and the house projects needed finishing, so I just quit using aspirin and wine to help deaden the pain.

By this time it was taking over ½ hour of kicking the waterbed to send a wave through the body to loosen up the damaged back so I could roll over onto the floor and crawl to the door jam to pull myself to my feet. Then I'd take a hot shower to loosen up some more so I could go to work and carry more lumber and hurt my back some more.

Don't even say it. I said it enough to myself. I could project into the future, and see myself in a wheel chair. Knowing quality of life was much more important than just life, I began to get angry at my deteriorating physical condition. Something had to change, but I could see no immediate solution.

The Collar Bone

The original X-Rays, at the hospital in Mayaguez, the ones received with the certified copy of the medical record, showed the left collarbone speared into the end of the trapezious muscle and all the left side ribs separated from the sternum.

The 11 foot high deck we had just completed on one of my rental houses, came up to the master bedroom. The hot tub was installed in the deck, and the last thing we were doing was removing a window and replacing it with a sliding glass door. In this way, the hot tub could be accessed from the master bedroom.

The last board of the deck, next to the house, was left off to allow us to replace the siding and trim after the sliding glass door was installed. To provide stability, we were installing a 4"X 8"X8' header beam above the door. We had framed the opening correctly, and all we had left to do was lift the beam up onto the frame, nail it in place, install the sliding glass door, and replace the siding and decking.

We'd planned out exactly how we would accomplish this task, and since Mike (one of the technicians from PR) was not tall enough to set the beam in place, I would place my end, and then set his end in place. We picked up the beam, and moved into position and just as I set my end of the beam on the frame, I stepped in the hole left by the missing board, and landed on the end of my stump.

Now that was "entertaining" enough, but above my head was a beam weighing about a hundred pounds. If it fell, it would probably kill me. Mike was about to fall down laughing, and he couldn't set his end on the frame to help me.

While Mike laughed, I was trying to control the nausea, not pass-out, and wait for the pain in my stump and shoulder to subside enough for me to crawl out of the hole.

Eventually I managed to put Mike's end of the beam in the frame. What I wouldn't give for a video of this event. It would be certain to win the Worlds Funniest Video contest.

The fall had ripped the collarbone out of the tendon at the end of the shoulder. I went home to ice down the shoulder and recover, while Mike finished the job. The next day, I went to a doctor and got a referral to an orthopedic doctor at the UCLA Medical Center, specializing in sports injuries to shoulders. The resultant operation spliced my collarbone back together, and I had another out-of-body experience while under the anesthetic.

After recovering from being Over Dosed on morphine (the fourth medical mis-adventure), getting an infection where the pin extended out of the skin, and almost passing out from pain when the doctor tried to remove the pin and screw with a pair of pliers instead of the proper tool, I decided to "Cut a Deal with God."

Have you ever cut a deal with God?

Reaching the point where I'd had enough pain, I knew something had to be done! The more I experienced pain, the angrier I got, and now I wasn't masking the pain with drugs and wine.

So I got up close and personal with God. The conversation was a little one-sided and I said, "OK God, you've got enough pain data from me. I'll do whatever is presented to me to deal with this pain, but if doesn't get better within six months, I'm leaving this planet for a real face to face confrontation, and one of us is going to get a real ass kicking."

I shut down my construction, went to a pain clinic, started doing exercises, and began getting better. The quality of my life continues to improve.

Summary

Whatever the physical injury: broken bones, muscle damage, cuts, sprains, strains, whiplash and joint damage are going to get worse with age. The damaged areas are also more susceptible to further damage. If something hurts, it's your body's way of saying you need to pay attention to, deal with and **fix** the problem. Masking pain with drugs allows you to do more damage.

Common sense (I know it's not common) will stand you in good stead when dealing with your body, *if* you pay attention. Look not only to the pain but also what caused it. Eliminate the cause. Get at least two different opinions and don't let the doctors talk to each other, they wont oppose each other's opinions. Realize they're just opinions and educated guesses. There's a reason why doctors call what they do "practice." Is their "money" in keeping you well or sick? Ask your heart what to do.

I have personally experienced the "hypocrites" oath.

Have fun cutting deals with God/yourself.

Acupuncture, alternative medicine from the far-east, has resulted in several miracles in healing my hip, shoulder and back injuries. Non-force Chiropractic and Naturopathic medicine should be the preferred choice in most of your injuries and illnesses.

Chapter 21
Religion

My parents read the exact same "version" of the Bible – "The Word of God" – and got into knock-down, drag-out battles (yelling, screaming and physical reprisals) over their individual perception and interpretations of its meaning

Mother and her family, raised me to believe in the "One God," and taught me that anyone else who believed in the "One God" different than they did was going to Hell to burn in everlasting fire!

Then my Dad had a different way of believing in the "One God," and if I didn't believe his way, I was going to hell fire and damnation.

Even though they used the same "version" of the same Bible, Mom believed my Dad was going to Hell and Dad believed my Mom was going to Hell.

I was told by both of them – separately, "If you believe in the One God my way and give the preacher 10 percent of what you earn you'll go to heaven – if not, you'll go to Hell!"

At nine years old, I was supposed to choose between their beliefs?

One day John – about five years old – took a handful of coins he had saved back from his meager allowance and refunds on soda bottles to give to God. He went out into the field behind our house, and beseeched God, "God, here is my offering so I won't go to Hell. Please take this offering." He threw those coins high into the air, and God just sent them right back to him. It seemed God didn't want or need his money. (Or maybe it wasn't enough or it was already too late.)

The Religion Vision

Early on in my religious training, I asked, "Is what I'm being taught true? Are all of the other religions wrong and their believers going to hell and only those, who believe as we do, going to heaven?"

"That's a good question." The Counselor said. "All religions are crowd control. All religious books have been written and rewritten by men with hidden agendas. What you're about to see will help you to understand. Observe."

The vision displayed a huge mountain reaching into the sky with a "castle" at the top. This castle was shining with a glorious light. Starting at the plane extending out from all sides of the mountain were multiple roads, which spiraled round and round the mountain leading to the top. It was obvious from the dress of the people moving toward the mountain from all around the plane, they represented different cultures and religious organizations. Each respective religious group had their own path/road. Every path/road led to the top.

The closer one got to the top, the more "enlightenment," the brighter the light/truth radiating from the top. However, along all the routes, there were "campsites" where good meaning people had stopped, forming congregations of "believers" who had found "The Way." If you wanted to reach whatever was at the top, you had to believe their way, or you were lost. As people would leave a given congregation to move further up the mountain toward enlightenment, they would be awarded some more information, change their behavior, find a new campsite further up the hill, and gather up "believers."

I could see campers from each group busy trying to "steal" campers from other groups to believe their way so they could bring them into their campsite. They went from camp to camp and tent to tent trying to sell their ideas and myths (some came in pairs and rode bicycles). Campers (missionaries) were being sent to camps (other religions) not on their path to recruit. No one allowed any quarter or gave credence to other groups (religious beliefs) because *they* knew the "Truth."

As I glided around the mountain, there were masses of people of every description, every age, every color, every culture, and every religious belief. All were being drawn to the top. Even though everyone was headed to the same objective, groups on different paths were at war, and even people on the same path but at different elevations were fighting. Death, massacre, genocide, rape, fire, pillage, torture, suicide bombers, destruction and all justified in the name of the same objective – making it to heaven/nirvana.

Cries could be heard reverberating from the mountain – "Our way is right, and only our way. Follow the straight and narrow way, or you're doomed. Beware of false prophets. If you don't believe our way, we're obligated to rid this mountain of your kind." Prejudice was rampant, the result of limited religious beliefs and the inability to see the whole picture.

My peripheral vision narrowed to a slit and from whatever side of the mountain I looked, I saw the many spiral roads created a staircase leading straight to the top. If you just focused on the light at the top, and headed towards it, the fastest, and shortest way to the top was straight up. The whole mountain was a staircase straight to the top. Anyone, at any time could simply turn straight up the mountain and use the different paths/roads as a staircase to the light/truth. Of course, this meant you crossed *all* of the religious beliefs on your way to the top. Of interesting note, all who died or were killed went directly to the top, regardless of belief or religion.

"What did you get from the vision?" The Counselor asked.

"As a result of this insight," I answered, "you could never get me to believe in any one religion – not if the objective is the top. Also, you couldn't get me to say any religion or belief is wrong – everyone has truth and all have the same objective."

"Good. You got that what you believe in works." The Counselor said. "Now let's clear up one more misconception. There is no such thing as heaven or hell. They're the carrot and stick used by organized religions to coerce and control the believers."

"Wow! That belief would mess up most of the people I know." I said. "Their whole lives are based on avoiding hell and making it to heaven."

"Yes, some of that 50% you keep referring to." The Counselor said. "What did you learn/remember from you death experience?"

"There's nothing to fear about death."

"Good, but it goes beyond fearing death." The Counselor said. "Souls incarnate are creating their own heaven and hell right here on this plane of existence through their sitcoms and soap operas. When the body dies, the soul, a spirit, becomes an integral part of UI again. Nothing you can imagine is better than that experience."

"OK, I get the body is not important, but if avoiding hell and seeking heaven is not the objective, what is?" I asked.

"The objective is to have body experiences so you can change your behavior to create a positive personality and character. Willpower choices allow humans to make decisions about how they want to be. The extremes provide the options. In most instances, the nature of your birth determines what you're taught to believe. What you believe is not right, wrong or indifferent. Neither is it good or bad. It is just what you believe. What you believe, UI and Mother Nature will reinforce as being correct, regardless of the situations or circumstances. What you can conceive you can achieve – what you believe you will receive – Universal Laws."

OK, it must be time to take up a collection after that "sermon."

Being Right

How many people, believing what you believe does it take to make what you believe "Right?" Of course what you believe is "Right" for you, but how many "converts" do you need to make your beliefs – doctrine – another legitimate religion? Would it take 100, 1,000, 10,000, 100,000, 1,000,000 or more followers of your faith to make your beliefs legitimate? Now, consider there were 9,000,000 people in the Nazi party – did that make it a legitimate religion? You realize, based on the above, Hitler's soul is now a part of UI (you and I).

There is **only one criteria** I've found to legitimizes any belief system – "Do unto others as you would have them do unto you."

It works for everyone and in every instance. Now, just for fun, let's throw in "an eye for an eye" and "forgive those that transgress against you," then "Love your enemy." Are you confused yet? You know if our legal system was doing the job we're paying them for, they could "pluck out the eye" for you.

If you "being right" is at the expense of someone else, then you need to rethink your "right." Other people/souls have rights too. Always try to work towards win, win situations.

Getting to go to Heaven

In the Bible, there's talk about the 140,000 righteous souls who are going to heaven. When you converted to your faith, did you get a number less than that number? In other words, "What's your number?" Who gets to determine who goes to heaven if only a finite number get to go? How do you "qualify" to go to heaven? Is it the percentage of your income you tithe to the church (purchase your way in). Perhaps, "good deeds" will get you into heaven (you do know, no good deed goes unpunished). Does one religion or another get a certain percentage of the "chosen few" (many are chosen, few qualify). If we're competing with all who have gone before and all who will follow, what kind of a chance do we have? Is heaven "limited" in size? How many souls will your heaven hold? You're better off playing the lottery.

What if, in your best judgment and nature of your birth, you select the **wrong** religion, or all of their numbers are already taken (I know, you're absolutely sure your religion is **The One** – someone told you so – right)? Is there any way for you to "hedge your bet" to insure yourself a mansion in the sky?

What if you've been a saint for your whole life, and just before you die, you commit one little sin – do you miss out? Oh, yea, your relatives can "buy" you into heaven.

I told you what I got as a result of my experiences was more questions than answers. The next time someone tries to "recruit" you into their church, tell them you want a guaranteed number – less than 140,000 – with proof of its authenticity. That's only fair, they want 10% of your hard-earned money, you ought to get something tangible for it. The definition of "Tithe" is the 10% you hold back from your crop to have seeds to plant next season – DA! Your tithe is meant to be a Financial Freedom Account!

What if . . . there's a good definition of God and what we're all really working towards, would you want to know what it is? OK, here we go – Life, Truth, Love, Mind, Soul, Spirit, and Principles – *From Science and Health* by Mary Baker Eddy.

Infinite Possibilities

Somehow I managed to take Physics three times: high school, the Naval Academy Preparatory School and Santa Barbara City College. But I missed Quantum Physics – as far as I know, it hadn't been presented yet. Having no knowledge of Quantum Physics concepts when I wrote this book, I simply presented my interpretation of personal experiences.

As a SCUBA Instructor and SCUBA Instructor trainer I had to teach Physics at the basic and Instructor levels as to how it applied to diving. I applied Physics concepts and laws in everything I did. Physics makes sense to me, because it explains how things work – the Natural Laws.

If you're ready to expand your understanding of what's happening on the Planet Ocean, I would highly recommend buying and watching, *What The Bleep Do We Know?* multiple times. This movie will help you begin to understand what God and the Universe are all about and why our "Definitions of God" don't work.

Planet Ocean is a hologram. Atoms and molecules are energy. We Gods were given the framework within which to create. Our only limitations are our limited ·perceptions based on our teaching and life experiences. Sci-Fi has and is showing us the future. We have simply to "imagine" it into existence.

Any attempt to define God, done by mere mortals, is going to be skewed. I have my definitions – from my perspectives. My definition of God is Universal Intelligence (you and I) which is benevolent, loves its creations (remember the definition of love – learn, change) and needs nothing from us. You must come up with your own definitions of God.

Seeking Knowledge

Loosing an arm and my multiple OBEs sat up an insatiable desire to gain knowledge. I admire how man has problem solved to improve the world and his living conditions.

Having the opportunity to observe different technical levels of society – Norway, Holland, Germany, France, Spain, Morocco, Mexico, Puerto Rico, Haiti, and the US, I tried to be an observer without imposing my beliefs, life experience and viewpoint. I realize everyone's society works for them. I discovered new ideas, new skills, and many challenges from watching other people.

Although I haven't "studied" them, I have read some about most of the major religions of the world in a quest for understanding.

My observation is, regardless of whether you believe in Voodoo, Mohammed, Jesus, Buddha, Krishna, Moses, etc. what you believe in works – a universal truth. I wish I could believe it all. I believe if you could take all of the religions and belief systems and sift them together, you would have a pretty good guide, but it would still be incomplete and biased due to man's agendas and skewed definitions of God.

If we glean the conscience truth and redefine God, maybe the spiritual aspects of what organized religions *say* they're trying to do through men might have a chance to develop. Of course, we must redefine God if we're to change and not keep repeating what doesn't work.

We haven't and aren't operating spiritually. Until we change our belief in God and develop spiritual skills, we'll continue to have and create problems.

Organized Religion

I'm really going to piss some people off with this little bit, so if you're not ready, avoid reading this. If it starts to sound like your religion, you better pay close attention.

Believe me, I thought about starting my own church. In my evangelistic training days, a group asked me to start a church, which I was led to close after only a few services. I wouldn't take up a collection, and I couldn't afford to support the church and my family.

After many years, I got the papers delivered to start The Mother Ocean Church and here is what I came up with.

First, just like the donkey, which I want to control, I would need a carrot (reward-heaven) and a stick (punishment-hell) to get you to do what I want.

I'd have to establish that my way was the only way to get to Heaven, otherwise, I might loose you (my flock of lambs) to another church. My rules must be followed to the letter, any deviation would be grounds for expulsion (ostracism) from my church – therefore you don't go to my heaven – you have to go to hell – the stick.

Your *fee* for getting the privilege of going to my heaven is ten percent of your gross income – the Bible says so. And you must work and pay from the time you join my church until you drop – dead.

You must produce a lot of little "yous," and indoctrinate them into my church so I can continue to live the good life after you wear out. You can't marry outside my belief (I get to choose or council you in the choice of a mate), so there's no confusion about what to believe.

You have to tell me everything you've ever done, which goes against our rules – confession – so I have even a greater "hold" on you – blackmail. Of course I won't tell anyone what you've done unless you're kicked out of my church or quit.

Be good to yourself and others of my belief – outside of our belief – oh well.

You must go out and try to bring in others to my belief (be a missionary) to expand the congregation and thereby my income.

You must support a "mission" program to bring in the less worthy to our group of believers. This of course increases the bottom line, and I get a bigger/better place to live and a bigger/better church.

NOTE: I'm a mercenary.

Now I hope you understand why, if someone says church to me, I get ready to run – fast. If the preachers were really doing their job, getting you in touch with God so you could communicate directly, then they would have preached themselves out of business a long time ago. Read the **Conversations With God** series by Neale Donald Walsch.

If religion really worked, don't you think we'd be a lot better off, after the thousands of years it's been being fostered on the general public, than we are now?

With all the different interpretations of all the different religious books, don't you think someone should have gotten *"IT"* right by now?

Could it be as humans, we totally missed the God concept? Did humans, in an attempt to define God, overlay the negative aspects of being human in their descriptions, and thereby screw everything up? Isn't the basis of a really good religion – "Do Unto Others?" Of course, some of the religions believe you should "Do It To Them First" before they get a chance at you.

Some of this is being written after September 11, 2001. However, the events of that day have not in the least changed what I believe. Just don't stand up on a plane and make any loud noises when I'm aboard or you may get recycled early.

You Are A God

As a soul, which is a part of the universal soul you call God, you're also a God. The Bible says, "Ye are Gods!" A God's job is to create. Look around you and realize everything you have, live in, wear, drive, fly, sail, furnish your house with, the tools you use at work and at home, were all creations. If you can dream it, it can be created. If you can conceive it you can achieve it. So, dream the big dream. Use your imagination, make life the way you want it to be. You can have whatever you want – you just can't have it all at once. If you don't create it, someone else will.

Entrepreneurs rule! They dream, gather knowledge, change their behaviors, take risks, and change society. Dream the big dreams! Imagine your dreams into existence! Fulfill your destiny, create a better world than we inherited.

Think about what we as humans are embarking on now – genetic engineering. Do you think we had a choice? NO!! We're creators, and if we see something we think we can do better, we're going to do it, legal or not, moral or not, right or not. Besides, who's defining legal, moral or right?

We Gods will not be denied. As for cloning – of course we'll do it, are doing it. How do you think everything got down here on earth – "after my own image." All it took was DNA, dirt and water. And if a catastrophe occurred which wiped out all life, one small ship with DNA on board and the same technology we're currently working on, could arrive and recreate everything. Isn't this what we're planning for Mars?

Or we could play with the DNA and come up with dinosaurs again. Using DNA we've already created an extinct wooly mammoth and an extinct antelope. Watch *Jurassic Park*.

Satan

What is this thing Christians call Satan? Isn't it just the negative side of the yin and yang? Isn't Satan just fear? Aren't you supposed to face up to and move through fear/Satan? Aren't you supposed to "put thee behind me fear/Satan?"

Are you giving to much credence to Satan? How big is your God? Who created your Satan? God? Then the attributes and powers given to Satan, were given by God.

So who's screwing with whom? How about a new definition of Satan? Satan is God doing Crack! Does that change your perception of God/Satan? How about we rethink why we're here – sitcoms and soap operas – life is a stage and we're just putting on a show?

If you believe you're a living soul, you're a part of the universal soul which is God, then you're a part of God. If you're a part of God, created by God, then you have powers also. If God created Satan, then it was for a reason and Satan is a part of God just like you are, and that means you're connected to God/Satan.

Remember whatever you believe in works. Most of the time, I hear "professed Christians" talking more about Satan than about God. Who are they "worshiping?" What are they fearing, and why? Does what you fear most happen unto you? What are they "programming" into their reality by all this fear about Satan? Isn't their God concept wrong?

If you take responsibility for your life and your decisions, then you/your soul/UI is in control of what happens to you. If your life on this planet is just for learning who you are, then pay attention. Your "Satan Experiences" and "God Experiences" are just a part of the overall script you wrote to find out who you are.

By the way, Satan is fear. The only thing you have to fear, is fear itself. The only thing which keeps you from doing anything is fear/Satan. The only thing you have to do to overcome fear/Satan is to face up to it and move through it – never let it control you. If you believe you – Soul – are going to live beyond the body, then the basis of fear goes away – fear of not surviving. Believe in the survival of your Soul, give up fear/Satan and enjoy life.

Other's Belief's

Because of the Universal Laws, whatever you believe in, works. So whatever religious beliefs you hold, work for you. That's good, because it means if you change your beliefs the new beliefs will work. Realize other people's beliefs work for them, so it may be difficult to convince anyone to give up their tried and proven belief system.

Works – Doesn't Work.

Immaculate Conception – By "Faith" we are to believe.

Given our current technology, we human/Gods could create an "Immaculate Conception." Assuming we could find a virgin old enough to conceive.

All we would need is an "egg" plus sperm. We select the donors of course (that is the ultimate control) so we can cause this creation to be "after our own image." We start the embryo, select the sex then "inject" the embryo into the surrogate's womb. The small injection hole heals, and walla – we done it.

Now let's consider Mary of the Bible, God "himself" impregnated her, so it is written by man in God's book. Is this why we conceive of God as male? That must have been the ultimate Big "O" (orgasm). After that, would any mere mortal man have ever been able to satisfy her?

Mohamed

The Moslems believe, "By Faith" that Mohamed came from a man. He couldn't have come from a woman, because women are "unclean" (they bleed every 28 days), it says so in the Koran – the Moslems Holy Book from Allah (The One God) written by man.

Assuming a man could conceive, in the "good ole days" they didn't do "C" sections, so where did Mohamed come out? The delivery of Mohamed must have been very interesting for the deliverer and the deliveree. And did Mohamed's birth parent, his father, nurse him?

Before toilet paper, the Moslems established the left hand was for wiping and the right hand was for eating. There's no way I could become a Moslem, I'm missing my left hand. Besides, in some Moslem countries, they still chop off your left hand as a major insult and punishment for stealing.

Buddha

Given the above two examples, I'm going to have find out how Buddha came to be – the result of a lotus flower?

Being Saved

In the multiple Christian religious programs I've experienced, the most important thing (next to giving the preacher money, they take up the collection **before** the alter call) was being "Saved." The importance of being saved from sin was you got to go to "their" heaven – as long as you don't sin again.

What I never figured out was why once you were saved, the preacher didn't have you killed or advocate suicide before you sinned again, so you could go directly to heaven.

Why go through all of that religious stuff, and then take any more risk you might go to hell. Oh, I guess some of the cults did that, Jones Town and the San Diego thing.

False Prophets

You've been told, "Beware of false prophets." I have a question for you, "Just how big is your God?" Don't you think if you're seeking "truth" with an open heart and the toilet tube and filters recycled, your God will provide you with "proof" of any new "revelation?" Well I do!

Do me one big favor, don't consider me a prophet, and avoid, at all cost trying to incorporate anything in this book into an existing or new religion. After all, I used four letter words. This is not about religion. It's about my "perspective" of the lessons associated with me getting rid of an arm and my death experiences. However, I will take a percentage of the tithe if you do start a church using my book.

Summary

Determine what you believe. Make sure it makes some kind of sense. Always check against the "Golden Rule" and Works – Doesn't Work.

If you're going to give them money, get a verifiable number.

Well wasn't that special? I hope that did or didn't shake up your "belief" system. After all that's my job. If you've just been accepting what other people told you and their "interpretation" of some "version" of a book written by man, then just maybe **_you_** need to go "up to the mountain" yourself and get in touch with whatever it is that's screwing with us.

Get rid of your box and screens and **_you_** bring back the "word." Try not to camp out.

Chapter 22
Politics

There's one thing I'll never have to worry about – ever being elected to a political post of any kind. I've hired illegal aliens to do work for me. I've had sex before marriage and extra marital sex. I believe women should have the right to make their own abortion decisions, including as soon as they're old enough to become pregnant. I believe death sentences should be carried out within two days of conviction – guilty or not. I believe you should have to earn your position not be "appointed" to it. I believe **ALL** drugs (tobacco, alcohol, recreational drugs, and marijuana) should be legalized and made available to anyone who is willing to sign-up, be neutered and pay a reasonable amount for them. I believe in a "flat tax" where everyone is obliged to pay the same percentage – equality. I believe everyone should take responsibility for and be held accountable for their actions.

I believe if you really want to stop criminals, train and arm everyone. In communities where this is done, there's no crime. If you want to take my guns away, you'll have to pry them from my dead hand while they're still smoking. I believe the following classes should be the major emphasis starting in Junior High School: sex, integrity, interpersonal relationships, emotional control, responsibility and financial intelligence. Given just those beliefs, I don't have to worry about any "political" party ever soliciting my support or supporting me.

I Had To Do It

We could use a good World War III, but this time, let's send all of the prisoners and 4Fs (men and women) to do the fighting.

Oh, that got your attention. I'm on a breeding program kick, remember? Look at what this would do to everyone trying to avoid the draft. If you don't want to go to war, you have to be 1A and not a criminal, and that means the 1As are left behind to breed. The 4Fs run away, die, or are in another country.

That's what livestock breeders do to improve their stock. They keep the best to breed and get rid of the rest (in fast food hamburgers?).

Fidel Castro, of Cuba fame, is smart. Think about what he did to the US. In 1982 Cuba emptied its prisons and insane asylums and sent those people to the US. We're still trying to recover over 20 years later.

Maybe the next time we need to go to war, we just take all of our prisoners, load them into huge planes, fly over the enemy and parachute the prisoners with weapons and food for 30 days into the offending country. If the prisoners survive, they can live over there, and we don't have to support them.

We free up a lot of money and personnel (prison personnel) who can become producers in our society. Now if all of those prisoners get killed, oh well. We didn't want them anyway or we wouldn't have put them in prison in the first place.

What country would want to take the risk that every other nation would drop armed criminals into their country. We could eliminate most of our military. The prisoners wouldn't need training, they would be motivated as every human is to survive, and we've solved a lot of our internal problems. Someone else, who was "bad," now has to deal with armed criminals, kill and dispose of them or capture them, put them in prison and guard and feed them.

The offending country would be so busy with the criminals sent by all nations, they couldn't do war. What a great idea. But then the CLU would get involved. Well maybe we could send the CLU attorneys along with the prisoners and if the prisoners were caught, the CLU could defend them in the foreign country.

If you have any question as to the validity of this idea, think about how America, Australia, and New Zealand were populated, prisoners and indentured servants (slaves) from Europe. And look at what the US did to England and where the US is today.

Oops, maybe that wouldn't be such a good idea. What if our prisoners, after a few generations took over the country they were dropped into and it became the major force amongst nations?

In a few more years, maybe we could just use the prisoners to populate other planets in our solar system and beyond. Oh, now you don't think just maybe that's how life on earth started, do you? The CLU of another planet won't let them execute those people who don't fit into their society, so they just ostracized them to earth.

Just an idea, to get your head out of the box.

Some Brain Mushing

I wasn't going to do politics, but I already did the organized religions, so what the heck, let's see where this goes. As I'm writing this section, it is mid December 2000, and we still don't know who the next president of the US is going to be.

Less than 50 percent of the eligible voters actually voted. The problem is, regardless of whom wins, at least 55 percent of the actual voters are going to be pissed. Regardless of the winner, they did not get a majority of the popular votes – over 50 percent – they actually got less than 25%. Therefore our "democratic process" in which the winning politician is supposed to represent the majority – over 50 percent of the voting population – will have received less than 25 percent.

Besides, the new President is going to take the fall for the next crash of our financial institutions and it won't have had anything to do with him, is party or his administration – a no win situation. (This actually is happening – I'm editing this January 2004.)

What really bothers me is when tax money is spent on things I wouldn't put money into and isn't spent on things I would put money into. And it doesn't matter whom I vote for.

I figure I've missed many great opportunities to make a billion dollars on bumper stickers, so I might as well let another one go. "Bureaucrats/Politicians – Fire them all!" I think one term is enough, any more, and there's too much corruption. If you weren't worried about getting re-elected, you could do what was **_right_** for the future of our country and not just the vested interests for your state or district.

I also think anyone who's been to Law School should be eliminated from any possibility of running for or being appointed to a position in any government entity. Attorneys make their money looking for problems not solutions.

How can a country which has proof of the addictiveness and health hazards of tobacco still use my tax money to subsidize the growing of the stuff, especially when we have people in our country who are going hungry? Politics? Why is the first thing the politicians do when starting a new session is vote themselves a raise? They did it again in 2005.

How can the "Law of the Land" change just because one of nine Supreme Court Justices changes?

How did an "illegal" entity in our government ever become so powerful as to intimidate, coerce, persecute, seize property, and imprison? The IRS.

Right now, we're in danger of toppling our governmental system through two very simple methods which have happened multiple times in past and recent history to other nations.

- When there are more non-producers than producers, the system fails.
- When the taxation reaches the point where over 50 percent of the earned wage is paid out in taxes, the system fails.

Don't believe me, check for yourself. Find out what the ratio of producers to non-producers is in our country. Find out how many months a year you work to pay taxes before you start making any money. Then check past and recent history to see what happens when either of these ratios goes the wrong way. Check out what happened to Argentina.

OK, so let's just have a flood, and start over again.

Oh, but what would happen to e-commerce and cell phones, electricity and all it supports, vehicles and the fuel they use and pollutants they give off? Those "bad" enough to survive will have to go back to hunter gathers and primitive tools. The more sophisticated you are, the more vulnerable. Those unable to defend themselves will be eaten – by animals, bugs, or humans (long pig). Only the strong would survive.

Einstein said, "I'm not sure what weapons will be used in WWIII, but WWIV will be fought with clubs, rocks and spears." Someone was paying attention, our national pastime is baseball (rocks and clubs?).

Summary

And you want the church mixed with politics? Either one is bad enough, but together they can really screw things up. Our constitution was based on the Bible, and every time we turn around, some politician is using "A" church doctrine to support an agenda. And then there's the church always trying to impose, through their local politician, their hidden agendas. And every choice is based on a misconception of what God is.

I know I'm jaded. So what are you? Which political party are you being a slave for?

Chapter 23
Ego/Vanity Lesson

On one instance, being missing an arm almost put me into a depressive state. About two years after the amputation, I was cogitating "what if?"

What if I had not put myself in that place to get hurt?

What if I had caused more trouble in the hospital and the doctors had taken better care of me?

What if I had lost it below the elbow so I could wear a prosthesis?

What if I could grow it back?

What if I could just have it back?

Then I realized I wasn't sure I'd take it back because it was such an ego trip to do everything I did with one arm.

Even though I never studied psychology, the insight made me aware of how big and powerful my ego was. It took some time in the corner thinking and looking back down my life's track, to realize every time I got into trouble of any kind, it had been ego based. I've learned to feed my ego and never let it get hungry. Because of the missing arm, I stand out in a crowd, which gets me recognition, and I needed it.

Hearing about a new disease, Attention Deficit Disorder (ADD), I realized we all have it. No one I know has ever or will ever get enough attention. But I have a much better shot at attention than "normal" people. I also realize everyone is handicapped in one manner or another. Some afflictions are not obviously apparent, it was nice to know what my handicap was, ADD. Ha, and you thought I as going to say a missing arm.

Ego/Vanity Facades

If Ego/Vanity control is my Life Mission, *Façade* recognition is critical for my advancement.

After the "Castle Vision" it took many years of life events to cause me to recognize the need for and formulate the request for help.

"Help me recognize and deal with the facades I use to bolster my ego/vanity." I asked.

"In what form do you want this help?" My Counselor asked.

"I have no idea what form," I said, "just make sure you get my attention. Oh, wait - no more lopping limbs off."

"OK, but it was such a good lesson, and it *almost* got you attention."

"Destroying my ego/vanity and then demonstrating how it was built on a façade via the Castle Vision was interesting." I said. "But can we move this forward?"

"Sure," the Counselor said, "we'll provide the feedback, your job is to pay attention, learn and change. If you ignore the signals, we **will** get your attention. Remember, you asked for it."

Retirement

As the SCUBA Instructor, I was always the first one in the water and last one out. My job was to protect and respond to my students. After surfacing from the deep, wreck dive, I had been holding position just behind the dive boat, swimming against the current. With the last diver on board, I struggled to the stern, gasping for air and experiencing pain in my chest. Rick grabbed my extended hand, pulled me up onto the dive platform, and asked, "Are you OK?"

"No," I gasped, "give me a few seconds to catch up."

Rick removed my rebreather, sat it up on the deck, then helped me sit up. Forcing myself to take long deep breaths, my breathing returned to normal. Rick was watching and before he could say anything more, I signaled for him to be quiet. Rick assisted me up, I climbed onto the deck and moved to my place. Rick brought over the rebreather and shut it off, gave me a questing look and received an OK hand-signal back.

The SCUBA Instructor Trainers I was working with were excited about the dive and rebreather performance and had no idea of my situation. As the boat moved to a sallow water dive site, I briefed them on the location and final dive performance requirements.

While making the second dive, I remained under the boat, just in case.

After wrapping up the course, and alone in my room at last, I sought counseling about the near heart attack.

"I know the problem today was major ego/vanity feedback." I said. "I don't remember when this lesson started. I know if I don't get it figured out, the next **prompt** will be a real heart attack. Can we avoid that? You have my attention."

"It's about time." the Counselor replied. "You prefer not paying attention. Let's review the major ego/vanity lesson feedback you've received. You slipped on the rocks while entering the water causing a hernia at Catalina Island in 1988. In 1998, you tore the hernia open moving the pillar in the lagoon by Jules Undersea Lodge and had it repaired. The hernia patch was torn loose handing dive gear and the under water video equipment forcing a five month rest during which you gained 35 pounds and then today the near heart attack. Is there a common thread in this?"

"Yes." I said. "Diving."

"And why is this about diving?" The Counselor asked.

Considering the question, I ran the movie several times before answering, "Diving is my super ego/vanity façade."

"What do you need to do?" The Counselor asked.

"OK, I get it." I said. "It's time to retire from diving."

The Lesson

Looking back, the feedback given was obvious. However, when involved in the situations and circumstances of life, the feedback was but faint whispers in a whirlwind.

As situations and circumstances continued, I asked "It feels as if I'm peeling layers off an onion. As I identify and begin to deal with ego/vanity issues, it seems as soon as I gain a measure of control over ego, another, more intense, example is presented. Is this what's happening?"

"There are no finished products." The Counselor said, "The onion example is good, but, in effect you're working on the onion from the inside out. You must deal with the smaller issues before taking on the next layer."

"Is there an end to the layers?" I asked.

"Yes and no." The Counselor answered. "The legacy you leave behind, your Life Mission, is a result of the lessons learned and behavioral changes you make, demonstrated through personality and character development. You chose Ego/Vanity as your Life Mission. Life Missions are a process not a destination."

"Remind me again," I requested, "what's the end objective; where am I headed; why me, here, now?"

"It's obvious from our perspective," The Counselor said, "once the soul is involved with a human body, the distractions make staying focused on the bigger/higher purpose difficult. With each soul incarnate writing their own script and being allowed to change their script as they proceed, they tend to forget their individual role. It's easy to lose your way. Remember, you're in training to fulfill your Life Purpose. The objective you've chosen is writing and speaking to help humans make better use of their brain potential."

"A light at the end of the tunnel, a light house to navigate by, some way points and sign posts could help," I suggested, "and how about a map to follow and a personal guide."

"We can and do provide those on your journey." the Counselor said. "Most souls won't accept counseling or advice, let alone look at a map or follow a guide. They get involved in the game without even learning the rules. Even if they know the rules, few will follow them."

"Ouch, that hurt." I said. "It sounds like you've been following me around taking notes."

"Yes, and you've been quite entertaining." The Counselor said. "You fought the process for a long time. We observed and choreographed the events of your life to help you stay within your scripted play. Although it may not seem so, everyone is on the path they scripted, in spite of their efforts to the contrary. Due to will based choices, some souls advance faster than others."

"OK, but what's the big picture, the overall objective for us incarnated souls?"

"The overall objective is the expansion and improvement in all things, working towards positive evolution." The Counselor said. "As you've learned, everything exists as a result of Universal Intelligence. UI is Spiritual, therefore everything in the universe is spiritual in nature. Humans are backing up instead of advancing spiritually. As a species they're seriously underachieving because they tend to deny their potential and the duality of their being. They are into the game and not really using their brain potential. Your job is to remind those willing to listen, how to do this."

"You mean the Body/Brain - Soul/Mind connection?" I asked.

"Yes." The Counselor said. "You've begun to ask the right questions to gain understanding of how the two entities must learn to cooperate in order to fulfill their Life Purpose."

"I ask you provide me the material from which to learn what I need to know to fulfill my Life Purpose." I said. "And let's do this without anymore physical dings."

"That's up to you." The Counselor said. "You wrote the script."

Shutting down a twenty year career, which had seen me at the top in my field, was an emotional struggle. Realizing it was just a façade and another way to stroke my ego/vanity was frustrating. But getting my attention took more physical pain and a serious survival threat. Just when I started to think about starting to dive again, hip and shoulder dislocations quelled the idea and helped in re-finding and focusing on my Life Purpose – writing and speaking. Peeling the onion is a process, involving tears (pain).

Summary

Physical injury and survival threats have been the prompts used to get my attention when I became too involved in the situations and circumstances of life and refused to address my ego/vanity issue.

Care in formulating the right questions is necessary if you want to advance spiritually. Spiritual advancement is the overall reason we souls incarnated. We become so involved in the game of life, we tend to forget our purpose and forget evolving is a process.

Chapter 24
Just to Prove a Point

As I bounced down through life AAL, "opportunities" showed up to challenge my "resolve." If people said or inferred certain things I might need/want to do were impossible it was a challenge to my ingenuity and I charged right into the activity. Some of the activities were obvious a person with one hand "couldn't" perform. Other "opportunities" were fairly subtle. So let's have some fun looking at just some of the "opportunities" I've had on this playing field of life.

There were many things edited out of this book which were layers of the ego/vanity onion. But in order to use my life experiences as an example to others of just some of the human potentials, I'm cutting my ego loose in this chapter, so hang-on. (The fact I'm recognizing this as and ego/vanity façade, represents positive advancement. I've mostly kept the onion under water to reduce the tears.)

Kayaking

There were eight of us at the Kayak Diving Instructor program in Monterey, CA. While we were signing the waivers and releases, I noticed the staff standing at a distance, talking in low tones and it was obvious they were discussing me.

Finally they walked over and asked, "Lance, how do you plan to paddle a kayak?"

My reply, "I don't know, but I'll work it out as we go along."

As I was launching my kayak into the bay, a bystander asked, "Excuse me, I noticed you only have one arm, how do you paddle the kayak?"

It was a legitimate and obvious question needing to be answered, so I said, "I use one paddle, on the right side, it works fine. The only problem is I have to see the same thing over and over as I go in circles."

Having the double-bladed paddle handle "strapped" to my forearm, I was able to paddle the kayak forward, backward, and sideways. I passed the course, even if I couldn't go as fast or last as long as the others. I could do all of the maneuvers and run the obstacle course forward and backward. The real tricky thing about kayaks is the "retraining" of the swivel at the base of your spine allowing you to wobble your butt to stay upright.

The art of kayaking is not going in circles, so I had to learn how to paddle a kayak with one hand. I later devised several adaptation paddles allowing me to move and maneuver the kayak.

First Paddle – my forearm slipped into a piece of plastic tubing attached to the double bladed paddle, and a bicycle type handgrip was attached at 90 degrees – like a crutch.

Duckbill –(used by duck hunters for walking in mud), with two stiff dive fins attached, it opened up when you pushed back and closed when pulled forward.

Skull – a long dive fin attached to an aluminum oar, just sweep it back and forth in the water like kicking a fin.

I bought a double kayak, and it all became much easier. I'd just sit in back and let my wife paddle. I'd pretend to paddle and issue orders like the Captain of a ship. What I was never able to get was a small, wind-surfing, training sail to use with the kayak.

Swimming

I have a hard time remembering when I didn't swim. I swam competition, was a Red Cross Water Safety Instructor and a YMCA Lifeguard and Swimming Instructor. After I lost my arm, I had to figure out how to keep from swimming in circles. It didn't take long before I had re-mastered one of the great loves of my life.

Before I could become a PADI Course Director (SCUBA Instructor Trainer), I had to be a current Red Cross Water Safety Instructor. This meant going through all of the timed distance swims with the different strokes and the stroke demonstrations (breaking down the component parts of each stroke and kick) to qualify to teach swimming. Of course I could do everything perfect with my right arm, the Water Safety Instructor Trainer (WSIT) just had to "fill in the blanks" on the stump side.

The WSIT was not happy with me being able to do everything, and was confident she could fail me on the Life-Saving test.

The Life-Saving test almost cost her Senior Life Guard/WSI his life. In the Real-World of Life Guarding as a profession, there's one thing you can depend on: if a person is in trouble in the water, the last place they want to be is "under" the water. Hold that thought.

With multiple opportunities, when life guarding professionally, to "rescue" swimmers in trouble, I found, swimmers in distress wanted to climb on my head to keep their head above water. In a pool, as long as I could touch bottom even with my head under water, I'd just swim up to the person, they'd climb onto my head, and I'd walk over to the side of the pool, where they'd scamper onto the deck and disappear. If I couldn't make it all the way back to the pool side on one-breath, I'd go under water, and the swimmer in distress would have to make do until I got a breath, then they could remount.

In the WSI Life-Saving test, you have a whole series of "ritualized" maneuvers to release someone who grabs you from the front or from the rear. The first thing you do is get a breath, tuck you chin, and submerge – then perform the maneuver.

The Water Safety Instructor Trainer (WSIT) called the WSI/Life Guard over and told him, "You hold on so Lance can't perform the releases, and break every one of his carries and tows."

I warned the Life Guard who was going to grab me, "I don't fight fair." I saw the twinkle in his eye, as he smiled and accepted the challenge.

Right here is a good place to put one of my axioms – I stole it from someone, and when teaching at SBCC I put a sticker in my window that said "Old age and treachery will overcome youth and skill every time."

When I swam competition, my stroke was the Breast Stroke, and we swam it "under water." The fewer breaths you took during the race, the faster you could swim. This meant you not only had to swim fast, but you had to be able to hold your breath for a long time. It was common to have the competitors "pass-out" during the swim or when they finished.

The current version of the breaststroke requires the top of the head to stay out of the water, making it slower, but safer.

The breaststroke uses the "Frog" kick, and I trained to use my muscular legs to provide the most propulsion possible. I can do several version of the frog kick including the "egg-beater" which gives continuous propulsion (used by water polo players).

Let's see, strong kick, can hold breath for a long time. Doom on the Life Guard trying to test me.

The Life Guard, much younger, bigger, in better shape and stronger, attacked me from behind. I kicked up, got a BIG breath, tucked my chin, pulled us underwater, and swam down to the bottom of the twelve foot deep pool, put his back on the bottom and used the egg beater kick to hold him there.

Now he should have turned loose when I took him under water, not twelve feet down.

When he finally ran out of breath, I held him on the bottom until he was panicking and fighting to go up. Finally I let him loose, he started up, and I grabbed his swim trunks, spread out to offer as much resistance as possible – slowing him down. When he reached the surface needing to breathe real bad, I put him into a cross-chest carry grabbing his pectoral muscle.

I talked real nice to him while towing him towards the WSIT. After catching his breath, he did as he had been directed and tried to break my hold. I'm sure it was frustrating and painful, because I squeezed his pectoral muscle with a death grip, grabbed his hips with my knees, rolled him over, and held his face underwater as I explained, "I'll let you up when you stop struggling."

Finally he quit fighting, and I rolled him over to breathe. His succeeding small struggles were half-hearted.

Then the front grab try to drown me "test." The Life Guard grabbed me around the neck – hard – from the front. I kicked up, got a BIG breath, tucked my chin, took us under water and headed for the bottom. About half way down, I felt him start to loosen up, but I used another trick, I jabbed him just below the ribs burying my thumb in his side. The automatic reaction is to drop your elbows and exhale – not a good thing when holding your breath under water. He took off for the surface, me towing him to the bottom, trying to pull his swimsuit off.

When I figured he was about to start breathing water, I let him drag us to the surface, and applied my pectoral torture, cross-chest carry again. He huffed and puffed for awhile and then, in spite of my calm rhetoric, he started fighting. I grabbed him by the hips with my knees, squeezed his pectoral muscle, rolled him over, and held his head under water again as I explained, "If you want to survive, it might be a good idea to calm down."

I towed him to the WSIT, who asked him, "Why couldn't you get loose from Lance, I've never seen anyone who could hold you on the surface?"

The Life Guard was wasted, and between gasping breaths explained, "He held me with his knees and look at my pectoral muscle, I thought he was going to rip it out. Also, he can hold his breath a lot longer than I can, I thought he was going to drown me down there."

I piped in, "You both know no swimmer in distress is going to hang on underwater, so you weren't playing fair. Besides, neither one of you has ever used any of these releases – you never have to – in the real world."

I kind of defied her to "pick on the handicapped" by getting in the water with me herself. I got no respect for plumbing. I passed.

First Aid and CPR

Another "prerequisite" to becoming a PADI Course Director in 1983, was being a First Aid and CPR Instructor. The "powers that be" knew I could never pass the Red Cross CPR test with one hand. You had to pull a "perfect strip" on a Resus-A-Anne.

The Red Cross First Aid and CPR Instructor Trainer said, "I'll bet you a Dos XX (Mexican beer), no make that a case of Dos XX, you can't pull a perfect strip on an Anne with one arm."

I don't care for beer, but you know not only did I do it, but I did it multiple times to become a CPR Instructor. I did it every time I ran a CPR course. That was a bad thing to do, because there were so many people who couldn't even come close to getting the fifteen chest compressions with two breaths done four times a minute for two minutes.

Flying

Six months BAL, I had completed an almost life long dream. Completing the commercial pilot's license course was one of the highlights of my life. When the FAA Examiner signed me off, I felt the same high as when I completed my SCUBA Instructor course. AAL, I was told I'd never be a pilot again.

That was a serious blow.

Six years AAL, I decided it was time to try to re-qualify for at least my private pilot's license. I was able to find a flight instructor who knew several people who flew planes with one arm. Before we'd go out for practice, he'd fly the plane with one arm, and at least have some suggestions.

But it was up to me to figure out how to do all the commercial pilot maneuvers, take-offs and landings. When he felt I was ready, he scheduled an FAA Flight Examiner to give me a flight test.

The examiner arrived a little late in the day, and it was obvious, if we didn't hurry, I'd be making qualifying landings in the dark. I wasn't sure if this was on purpose or not.

While performing the pre-flight check, the examiner explained what he expected, then we took off.

Was I nervous? You bet!

We went through the required commercial maneuvers, and I was sure I'd completed them well enough to at least get a private pilot license.

As we came back to the airfield to do the required landing, he said, "I won't pull any tricks on you, so just relax and do a standard power off landing. I'll wait till you're on final and chop the throttle."

As I turned onto final, the sun was just about down. At mid field, he chopped the throttle. I hedged my bets, slipped and maneuvered the plane, and was just about to land on the numbers when he said, "Go Around."

I pushed in the throttle and carburetor heat and the plane started gaining altitude.

At about 50 feet above the runway, the FAA Examiner chopped the throttle and said, "Land it."

I said a bad word, bobbled the plane a little, settled down on the runway nice and smooth, and taxied to the parking ramp where my flight instructor was waiting. While I tied the plane down and did the post-flight check, the Examiner and my instructor just stood on the tarmac and jawed. The more they talked, the more nervous I became.

Finally, I could take it no longer, walked up to them and interrupted, "Excuse me, but I've got to know, did I at least do well enough to get my private pilot license back?"

The Flight Examiner smiled and said, "Anyone who can do a landing like that deserves a commercial license, here, let me sign off your flight log."

I let out a hoop and a holler, and did a little dance. It may have been one of the highest times of my whole life. I was so excited I felt like I was still flying.

As I was flying (driving) home, feeling real good, an awareness began to take shape. It had been over six years since I'd lost the arm, and the pilot's license was the last of my occupations I needed to prove I could still do. Then the past six years of life played before my eyes showing all I had done to prove I could still do the things I thought, and was told I couldn't do.

Realizing all those things were done in the pretense of doing them to prove to others I could do them, but in reality, I had done them to prove to myself I could still do them, I got madder and madderer. Screaming and cussing, I became too emotional to drive, and had to pull off the road to calm down before continuing home.

It was 15 years before I flew again, and re-qualified as a commercial pilot.

I actually became a better pilot AAL, because I had to trim – set-up – the plane correctly and plan out every maneuver farther in advance. Anyway, the plane won't fall out of the sky when trimmed properly.

Other AAL Adjustments

Hot Oil Massages – I'm sorry it takes me twice as long – I'm the one the song was written about, the one she wants – "I want a man with a slow hand."

Teaching Skills – I can teach you how to perform skills with one hand, but not with two.

Sailing – Having one-hand adds a whole new dimension to "single-handing" a sailboat (sailing the boat by yourself). Stump, feet, knees, teeth and planning out what you're going to do help a lot. Qualifying with American Sailing Association as a Bare Boat Skipper, I can charter up to 50 foot sail boats.

Starting Nails – I never smash a thumb – at least not mine, but my teeth (to hold the nails) and back of my head (had to hit the back of my head to start the nail) took a beating (that was a joke – pay better attention).

Since I'm not all that fond of pain, I eventually figured out how to hold the nails between my fingers with the hammer head in the palm of my hand and start the nail easily and painlessly. Now, you can buy a hammer that will hold the nails and nail-guns are great equalizers.

Mechanical – Using vise-grip pliers to back up nuts allowed me to be fairly efficient at most mechanical jobs.

Electrical – Using magnetic and other screw-holding drivers, I was able to do electrical work. I learned to use the right tools, for the right job, for one-handed operations. And it's hard to get shocked if you only use one hand.

Buttoning My Shirt Sleeve – I get a woman to help. Men can only do it with one hand. Think about it, they only ever use one hand. Otherwise the sleeve gets wet from using my teeth and slobbering. Yes, I could design a buttoning device – in-fact one exists – but then I would get less female attention.

SCUBA Diving – is a "one-handed job" but most people keep trying to do it with two. Divers never have two hands to operate their gear, because they always have something in at least one hand – camera, spear, knife, reel, slate, game-bag, computer, etc

Of course, I have to be able to do something useful **and** operate my equipment. However, video taping myself pole-spearing fish was a bit too challenging.

When SCUBA Diving, it's important to master:
- Basic knowledge and diving skills
- Setting-up the equipment
- Suiting-up
- Entries & exits
- Using a pole spear (for the killers)
- Catching lobsters and crabs (for hunter/gatherers)
- Taking photos and shooting video (for the documentarians)
- Searching & Recovering (for the treasure divers)
- Doing research (for the curious)

Diving is the love of my life, and the only time I'm even close to pain free is when gravity is offset by immersion in water. Besides, my Soul really likes three-dimensional mobility.

Typing – (I'm a writer) – problematic with one hand, but do-able. Doing with one finger, what used to take ten fingers to do. I took typing in high school and learned to type without letters on the keyboard.

Two months after losing my arm, I had to type the La Chalupa Operations Manual. When I sat down to type the first time, I was absolutely amazed I could type with one finger. The super brain had taken the training (10 finger typing) and converted it to one finger typing. I use my eyes to locate, I still can't tell you where the letters are on the keyboard. I take no credit – the brain is real special.

Recent technology has provided us with "voice recognition." I now have to teach the computer instead of the other way around. I'm concerned, because now the computer will know the words when I cuss it. I'm a little concerned it's going to start talking back to me.

Summary

OK, I know that was some serious ego manifestation, but after all I was an egotistical maniac and my Life Mission is working on ego/vanity.

The point is you can overcome your situation or you can let it bury you – your choice/will.

Whatever your problem, pick up your cross and run with it.

You're capable of a lot more than you can even imagine. Take time to dream and imagine your ideal future. Keep your brain active by solving real and imaginary problems. Get and keep your body in good physical conditions for the fun, adventures and challenges to come.

Hurry and finish this book and get out there – adventures await.

Chapter 24
My Life Lessons

First a reminder, the book's objective was to get you to think out-side-your-box-of-reference. Did it do that? What should you have gotten out of this brain dump?

This book is about the life lessons I've learned from losing an arm and dying, OBEs, Visions and varied experiences.

All right, let's go through the key points to help you remember them – repetition and review are key elements in learning/remembering.

Some of the major lessons I'm learning (notice I didn't say I have learned them) are:

Choices

I chose my parents, sibling, friends, enemies, bosses, jobs, homes, locations, race, creed, and basically everything that happens to me to find out who I really want to be. I am responsible – I must take charge.

DNA, the result of a war, plus dirt and water made my body what it is – but I **chose** to be and do. Realize life is a result of choices. When making decisions, try to gather all of the information available, correct any incorrect information, and take the risk of making the decision knowing more information will be forth coming. Control my emotions so rational decisions can be made.

Try never to beat myself up or allow anyone else to do so because of a mis-take as a result of my decisions and actions.

Question Everything

50+% of what I have seen, heard, read or been taught is not correct. Question everything, including "authority" – maybe especially "authority."

My database is lacking – I must get out there and gather more data and be open to new truths.

Patience

Learning to be patient can take a long time and be very entertaining, if you can avoid frustration.

Pay Attention

Listen to the "wee small voice" which actually knows about everything. I wish there were a megaphone for the quiet, little bugger. When driving, if "Highway Patrol" pops into the brain, avoid exceeding the speed limit. (I'm getting better, and in some instances, I even agree with the voices.) Whenever possible, defer decisions to a woman – they actually are more sensitive.

You Never Make a Mistake

Accept always making 100% correct decisions. The data the decision is based on may be incorrect or incomplete or biased by negative emotions. Mis-takes in my life movie are do-overs, pay attention and learn to avoid repeats as much as possible.

Sin is refusing to learn – repeating mis-takes with no change in behavior.

Crazy is doing the same thing over and over, expecting a different result.

Avoid Doing Guilt

Learn from the past, it can't be changed. I must avoid doing guilt or others will control me.

Behavioral Change

Review reactions to people and events in an effort to change and control how I act and react. If I get angry, I know I have some more work to do. Identify the real problem and expect to get more chances to demonstrate a different behavior. Life is about learning, learning is fun, and the only way I know if I've learned something is if my behavior changes.

What I think or feel is one thing, but what really counts is what I do. My behavioral changes are my legacy to the Universe.

To quote my mentor, Chuck Goetschel, "Align your actions with your goals – not your emotions."

Fear/Satan

I must face up to fear, move through it, and never let fear control me. Fear is "survival based" emotion – what am I afraid of? Satan does not exist!

God

My soul is a part of the God Spirit – I am a God. Gods create, so I'll be creative in whatever way I deem necessary and comfortable.

God is the "glue" that holds every atom in the universe together. God is not vengeful. God is not separated from anything or anyone. God will meet me on the other side of right and wrong. God needs nothing from me (but a good show?).

Whatever Will Be, Will Be

What a great song, and a great way to run a life. Take my best shot at life, continue to improve who I want to be, and bend with the changes – evolve. I know whatever happens is for the best in the big scheme of things – after all I wrote the script.

However, my mantra is: ***"If it's going to be, It's up to me!"***

The Body Doesn't Matter, it's Just a Vehicle

I realize my body's not important. It's useful because it allows the soul to have experiences. It should be in as good a working order as possible, given whatever the circumstances.

Taking Responsibility

When I accept I've chosen the life I'm living, I'm scripting the life experiences and have allowed myself freewill choices along the way, then I can take full responsibility for what I have and am experiencing.

By taking responsibility for my life, I can make wise choices about what I wish to experience and learn. This is much better than being a ball in a pinball machine.

Death

Birth is a Death sentence. There is an "after death" life of the soul that is operating the body. When I transition from this "life" there will be no guilt or condemnation – only a party to attend in my honor. I'm putting on a good show now!

There is no such thing as heaven or hell in the after life. I'm creating my own "heaven and hell" right here, right now. I can have it anyway I want – I'm writing the script. I can have fun or not – my choice.

The body came from cosmic dust and when it dies, it will go back to it - dirt.

The Soul weighs 6 ounces/21 grams and, as a part of God is going to live forever. I have no worries.

Conclusion

With these basic concepts, I can bounce along through life making decisions, and enjoying the process from a fairly detached viewpoint.

Remember I wrote about what I experienced as a result of losing an arm and dying. This was my opinion based on my view through my box-of-reference when I wrote it and it may/will change with time – or not.

It's my opinion, I have a right to my opinion and I accept no arguments with an opinion! You have an opinion also – right? Analyze where it comes from.

You've made it this far, so thank you for sharing a portion of my life. I hope you were entertained. If you gagged, laughed, gasped, were offended, agreed or disagreed with anything in this book, I/you done good.

The objective of this book is to take you outside-the-box of references your life has created. What was created by your life experiences is not all correct, not complete and is biased by emotions.

Have a great life, have fun experiences, seek adventures, play a lot, make some behavioral changes and put on a good/bad show for yourself and others.

Just remember we're all watching.

Dr. Lance "The One Armed Bandit" Rennka

Additional Books by Lance Rennka

"Body/Brain – Soul/Mind – Two Entities, With Different Agendas, Equals War." A "How to" manual on recognizing and programming your mind to create the lifestyle you want. This book is about how to reduce the internal wars and gain cooperation between the entities with the end objective of mutual, positive evolution.

"21st Century Learning –Simpler, Easier, Faster, Better." A Sci-Fi book and "brain use" enhancer, which provides hope for life on the Planet Ocean (Science Fiction predicts the future.). How to make learning fun, easy, simple, fast and be able to retrieve everything you learn.

"Back In O2 – When There Were Wooden Tanks and Steel Men" A hilarious autobiographical book about how Lance and his Dad learned to SCUBA dive in the late 50s from the "school of Hard Knocks" where you get the test before the text.

Lance Rennka's Life Purpose is to help humans utilize their brains better. He is available for book signings, speaking engagements, interviews and training seminars. Lance can be contacted through www.Lance-Rennka.com

ISBN 1412070140-7